REGISTER OF
FREE BLACKS

Rockingham County, Virginia

1807-1859

Dorothy A. Boyd-Rush

HERITAGE BOOKS
2019

HERITAGE BOOKS

AN IMPRINT OF HERITAGE BOOKS, INC.

Books, Cds, and more—Worldwide

For our listing of thousands of titles see our website
at
www.HeritageBooks.com

Published 2019 by
HERITAGE BOOKS, INC.
Publishing Division
5810 Ruatan Street
Berwyn Heights, Md. 20740

Heritage Books by the author:

Marriage Notices from Extant Issues of The Rockingham Register
Harrisonburg, Virginia, 1822–1870

Register of Free Blacks, Rockingham County, Virginia, 1807–1859

International Standard Book Numbers
Paperbound: 978-1-55613-658-0
Clothbound: 978-0-7884-8207-6

DEDICATION

This book would not have become a reality without the unfailing encouragement of my husband, my mother, and my uncle.

CONTENTS

INTRODUCTION

In 1793, the Virginia General Assembly enacted legislation "to restrain the practice of Negroes going at large." To correct this "problem," the statute went on to require that "free Negroes or Mulattoes ... be registered and numbered in a book" which was to be maintained by the clerk of the court in the city or county where the free blacks resided.[1] Reregistration was required yearly in the cities, and every three years in the counties.

Some Virginia clerks of the court subsequently began to maintain a Register of Free Negroes. Other clerks preferred not to keep a separate register. They frequently listed free blacks elsewhere, e.g., in the county order books. Regardless of where the "registers" were maintained, the entries recorded the "age, name, colour and status" of the freeman. Additionally, "by whom and in what court" emancipation had been granted was duly noted. However, if the free black being registered was a freeborn individual that fact was noted instead. The law further provided that a copy of the registration was to be given annually to all free blacks for the sum of twenty-five cents, to serve as proof that he or she was free and could, therefore, remain within the jurisdiction and accept work. The 1793 law actually fixed a penalty "for employing a Negro without a certificate; the Negro may be committed to jail."

In the case of free black women, custom

---

[1]The Statutes at Large of Virginia, From October Session 1806, Inclusive, vol. 1, printed by Samuel Shepherd, Richmond: 1835, pp. 238-239.

determined that they were registered under
their maiden name, with their married name
being given as an alias. Occasionally,
however, the reverse was true. Care must be
taken, accordingly, by the researcher. A
great deal of cross-checking may be necessary
to ascertain the correct situation, i.e.,
siblings may, indeed, bear different surnames
within the same register depending on how
their mother's name was recorded. It is,
moreover, wise to keep several other
interrelated facts in mind: 1) the status of
blacks at birth was determined by the status
of the mother, not the father, 2) freed slaves
did not always or even generally assume the
surname of their former owners, and 3) most of
those who were registered after 1793 had never
been slaves. On the contrary, the majority of
the free blacks who were registered to comply
with the 1793 law claimed freedom by birth
from free black or white mothers.

The next largest group who registered
was, however, made up of emancipated slaves.
Usually they were freed by the last will and
testament of their owner. Throughout the
first half of the nineteenth century, the
number of such emancipations gradually
increased. It should, however, be stressed
that individuals freed in this manner were not
free during the lifetime of the owner, but
only after his or her death and the probation
of the will.

A small but nevertheless significant
number of blacks achieved freedom by acquiring
deeds of emancipation from their owners, which
they subsequently filed in the county court.
Such deeds were on occasion purchased for an
extremely small sum of money. On other
occasions, however, what amounted to the
current rate or market value of the slave was
demanded. In essence, a deed of emancipation

conveyed to the former slave the ownership of his own person. As such deeds were recorded customarily in the land books of the county, the property status of slaves is further underscored.

It should be kept in mind that the presence or absence of an individual's name in a register of free blacks is not conclusive proof of anything. The laws regarding the registration and re-registration of free blacks were not uniformly or even consistently enforced, even within the same locality. Moreover, some laws, such as the 1806 law which required all slaves emancipated after that date to leave Virginia, were ignored almost totally by all local authorities within the Commonwealth of Virginia. The intent of the 1806 law was to restrict the growth of free blacks as a group. Apparently, their very existence was viewed with fear by those in Richmond. The fact that the 1806 law was so generally ignored across the state suggests, however, that the state legislators clearly misjudged the concerns of their constituents. Initially, slaves freed after 1806 simply continued to register or not to register as before. Only later, by the 1850's, did the county courts, at least on occasion, begin ruling on individual cases. It can be viewed as an indication that the times and the concerns of the day had altered to some degree.

The fact that many free blacks felt no compulsion to either register or re-register their freedom is significant. It suggests that in many regions of Virginia during the antebellum years free blacks were not harassed by local slave patrols, interrogated as they travelled about the community, or questioned routinely about their status. The laxity regarding registration suggests that all those

ix

within at least the more rural communities of
Virginia were not only known to each other but
coexisted with relative harmony. It is,
accordingly, very likely that Rockingham
County follows the pattern already detected
elsewhere in the Commonwealth of Virginia:
that the majority of free blacks never
bothered to register at all. To count the
number of entries in a register is, therefore,
of limited worth.

The carelessness indicated by some of the
entries in a register further suggests the
general lack of compliance with the law, e.g.,
spelling is erratic, blanks are common, and
dates are often missing. Such carelessness
may, however, also suggest the general lack of
concern for the well-being of free blacks
within the community by those "in charge."
In general, however, the separate register
maintained by the clerks of Rockingham County
is better than most of the registers that
remain from elsewhere in the commonwealth.
One can only speculate as to the reason.
Perhaps, the individuals who served as clerks
of the court in Rockingham County and their
deputies were just conscientious men by
nature. Perhaps, because as late as 1850 the
census for Rockingham indicates only 467 free
blacks within the county, it was just
relatively easy to comply with the law, and
the clerks did so with care when asked.

Although the front cover of the leather
bound volume transcribed in this volume is
loose, the entire register maintained in
Rockingham County is essentially intact. Only
a very few of the unnumbered pages of the
index at the front of the volume are missing.

Those interested in both Rockingham
County in particular and Virginia in general
are fortunate. The Rockingham register of

free blacks provides: 1) some much needed, additional information on the free blacks who lived in the western portion of Virginia, 2) invaluable, supplemental data on the burnt wills of Rockingham County,[2] and 3) valuable raw material on which further research can be based. The original register remains at the Rockingham County Court House. It is with the kind permission of Wayne L. Harper, the present clerk of the court for Rockingham County, that I have been able to do the transcription which constitutes the bulk of this volume. His cooperation and that of his staff is much appreciated.

To a degree, transcription and editing represent an art, rather than an exact science. To an extent, the transcription varies with the text, the handwriting, and the purpose of the editor. A word of explanation is, therefore, in order. As much as possible throughout the following transcription, the original spelling and punctuation have been retained -- to convey more readily the somewhat individualistic spirit of antebellum Virginia. Where confusion might, however, result, brackets have been added in which missing letters, sic, or corrections have been indicated. Occasionally, the misspelled portion of a significant word has been underlined -- to assure the reader that no typographical error has crept into the transcription. However, very obvious and persistent misspellings such as "direts" for "directs," "perticular" for "particular," "rist" for "wrist," "scare" for "scar," "ocationed" for "occasioned" and "verry" for "very" have not been noted.

---

[2]See the appendix for additional information on the burnt wills of Rockingham County.

The following conventions have been followed: a solid line indicates a missing word or words in the passage, i.e., a blank; the use of an ellipse (...) indicates that a repeated word or phrase has been deleted from the transcription; and all editorial comment and/or elaboration appears within brackets. On occasion, the pages have been numbered incorrectly. When that occurs, it has been indicated, e.g., p. 130 [sic, 131].

An every name index appears at the end. Not only do the names of all registered free blacks appear in this index, but also the names of those whose affidavits helped secure recognition of freedom, and those whose wills granted emancipation. Since the wills of Rockingham County, which was created in 1778 from Augusta, were largely destroyed during the Civil War the latter references are unusually significant.

In using this or any index for the period, it is important to check variant and/or phonetic spellings of a name. For example, Hackly and Hackley; Colly and Colley; and Gordon and Gorden are merely variant spellings of the same family names. Conversely, phonetic spelling is probably the reason for Hewes and Hughes.

The names and/or initials of long-time Rockingham County officials, i.e., the early clerks of the county court, such as Samuel McWilliams (1792-1817), Henry Jewett Gambill (1817-1847),[3] Littleton W. Gambill (pro

---

[3]In addition to serving as clerk of the county court, Henry Jewett Gambill served as clerk of the superior or circuit court (24 April 1809-11 May 1847).

tempore 1848; 1852-1869),[4] and Erasmus Coffman (1848-1852) have been omitted from the index, as their names recur with such frequency. In a similar vein, although he was never a clerk of the court, David Holmes Gambill's initials also appear with some frequency, e.g., D.H.G. His name too has been omitted from the index. The names of county officials from elsewhere in the commonwealth, however, have been included in the index.

Dorothy A. Boyd-Rush, Ph.D.

---

[4]Littleton W. Gambill was also clerk of the circuit court (11 May 1847-1 July 1852; 1872-1875). In 1852, however, he began serving as the first elected clerk of the county court in accordance with the constitution of 1851.

REGISTER OF FREE NEGROES

Joshua Peters, No. 1, p. 1:
Culpeper County to witt
The bearer hereof a dark Mulatto about 5 feet
4 7/8 Inches high 21 years old about the 30th
March last this day produced and filed in my
office his certificate in the words following
"Culpeper County to witt Margaret Lindsey came
before me William Broadus one of the Justices
of the peace for the county aforesaid and made
oath that Joshua Peters who was bound to her
husband Thomas Lindsey by the overseers of the
poor for the said county, to serve untill he
arrived at the age of 21 years, became free
about the 30 day of March last and that the
said Indenture has been misplaced so that at
this time she cannot find it, and that she is
willing and does hereby relinquish all further
claims to the Services of the said Joshua.
Given under my hand this 26 July 1804.   Will.
Broadus" and applied to me John Jamison Clerk
of the Court of the said County to Register
the same according to Law, I have therefore in
pursuance to the act of assembly in such case
made   and   provided   Registered   the   said
Certificate and Granted him the said Joshua
Peters this copy Given under my hand this 29th
day of August 1804 and in the 29 year of the
Common-wealth.
                    John Jamison   C.C.C.

The above produced and filed in my office the
_____ day of August 1807 and duly Registered.
                    Teste S. McWilliams C.R.C.
(cop'd Del'd 4 August 1814)

Andrew Virid, No. 2, p. 2:
Culpeper County to witt
A free black man named Andrew Virid about 5
feet 8 Inches high 21 years old 10th day of

March last and who was bound by the over-seers of the poor in this county to William Barbour, by Indenture bearing the date the 26th day of July 1789, which Indenture he produced and filed in my office this day applied to me, John Jamison, Clerk of the Court of the said County to Register his freedom, I have therefore in persuance of the act of assembly in such case made and provided Registered the said Andrew Virid and Granted him this copy. Given under my hand this 22nd August 1803.

John Jamison C.C.C.

Registered in my office the 31st December 1808.

S. McWilliams C.R.C.

James Boswell, No. 3, p. 2:

Rockingham County to witt

The bearer hereof James Boswell a Mulatto man about 26 years of age, about 5 feet 9 3/4 Inches high, with a large scare on his right cheak bone, thick bushy head, who was set free by the last will of John Boswell dec'ed of Louisa County, which will is of Record in the said County, an extract from the said will he produced and filed in my office, and this day applied to me Samuel McWillliams Clerk of the Court ... of the said County to Register his freedom, I have therefore in pursuance of the act of assembly in such case made and provided, Registered the said James Boswell, and Granted him this copy Given under my hand this 1st day of April 1809.

S. McWilliams C.R.C.

James Hywarden, No. 4, p. 3:

At a Court continued and held for Stafford County the 14th of January 1806

It appearing to the satisfaction of the Court that James Hywarden, a dark Mulatto man, about 32 years of age, about 5 feet 6 or 7 inches high with two Scars in his forehead & short curly hair was born free, ordered that the

2

same be certified.

V. Peyton C.S.C.

Registered and filed in my office the 10 day August 1809 and copy Granted.

Teste S. McWilliams

Billy Hackley, No. 5, p. 3:

Culpeper County to witt

The bearer hereof Billy, who is emancipated by the last will of John Hackley dec'd, (a copy of which will he has produced) the said Billy is about 25 years old 5 feet 9 1/4 Inches high of a dark complexion, this day applied to me John Jamison, Clerk of the Court of the said County, to Register his freedom. I have therefore in pursuance to an act of assembly in such cases made and provided, as also in pursuance of the above order, Given and amended Copies. Given under my hand this 16th day of August 1804.

John Jamison C.C.C.

The above certificate, and copy of the will, produced and Registered in my office the 30th September 1809

S. McWilliams C.R.C.

The above named William Hackley produced the copy of the former register and was reregistered the 11 October 1825 as No. 81 (see page 32.)

Isaac Hackley, No. 6, p. 4:

Rockingham County to witt

The Bearer hereof Isaac Hackley about 5 feet 3 Inches high a small scar on his left cheek 21 years old 4th June last, was emmancipated by the will of John Hackley dec'd and was bound by the overseers of the Poor untill he was 21 years of age to Jacob Stout, the said Indenture he has produced and filed in my office, and has applied to me Samuel McWilliams Clerk of the Court of the said County to Register his freedom. I have therefore In pursuance of the act of assembly

3

in that case made and provided, I have registered the said Isaac Hackly [sic] and Granted him this certificate Given under my hand this 5 day May 1810.
                              S. McWilliams C.R.C.

Peter Mayo, No. 7, p. 4:
Rockingham County to witt
The bearer hereof Peter Mayo, a black man, about 6 feet high, several small scars on each cheek bone a large scare on his left breast 30 years old the 25 day of December 1810. Produced to me Samuel McWilliams Clerk of the Court of the said County a certificate of the clerk of Cumberland County shewing that he was emmancipated by the last will of Joseph Mayo, deceased, and has applied to me to Register his freedom. I have in pursuance of the act of assembly, Registered the said Peter Mayo, and Granted him a certificate Given under my hand this 1st day of March 1811.
                              Teste
                              S. McWilliams C.R.C.
Renewed the 4th July 1815 and old one filed in the office.

Hannah McCoy, No. 8, p. 5:
Rockingham County to witt
The bearer hereof Hannah McCoy about 5 feet 8 Inches high a large scare on her right hand about 21 years of age [deleted: "about 7th June"] a Dark Mulatto, was born free as appears by the certificate of William Parrott, and which is filed in my office, and has applied to me Samuel McWilliams Clerk of the said County to Register her freedom. I have therefore in pursuance of the act of assembly in that case made and provided, registered the said Hannah Given under my hand this 11 July 1811 [the date is actually written as 18011]. [In the margin] Copy Granted by order of the court at Dec'r 1811.

John Higgans, No. 9, p. 5:
Rockingham County to witt
The Bearer hereof John Higgans about 5 feet 8
inches high, a large scare on in his forehead
and one on the back or side of his head, about
26 years old the 18th day of this Month
November, a Mulatto Man, was set free at the
age of 25 years by Peter Higgans deceased as
appears by his last will and Testament of
Record in the County of Rockingham, a
certificate of his age has been filed in my
office, and has applied to me Samuel
McWilliams Clerk of the said County to
Register his freedom. I have therefore In
pursuance of the act of assembly in that case
made and provided, Registered the said John
Higgans and Granted this copy the 13 November
1811.
[In the margin] Copy given.

Samuel Viney, No. 10, p. 5:
Rockingham County to witt
The bearer here of a black man named Samuel
Viny [sic] about five feet 7 1/4 Inches high
36 years old in December last who was bound by
the overseers of the Poor of Culpeper County
and duly Registered by John Jamison Clerk of
the said County as appears by a certificate
this day filed in my office bear'g date the
9th of April 1801 and whom I have duly
Registered and Granted him this certificate
Given under my hand this 22 February 1812.
                    Teste
                    S. McWilliams C.R.C.
[In the margin] copy given. The original
register Delivered to Samu'l the 28th of
September 1842. L.W.G.

Peachey Barrell, No. 11, p. 6:
Peachey Barrell, a woman of a Dark complection
aged 23 years five feet four inches high, has
no remarkable scars on her face, hands or arms
except that her for finger on her right hand

5

appears to be shorter than it Naturally was
which is said to have proceeded from arising
on the end thereof was born free in the County
of Albemarle. At a Court held for the county
of Albemarle the 1st day of October 1804.
It is ordered that the above Register be
certified as truly taken.

A Copy Teste
William D. Merewether
John Nicholas C.A.C.

Rockingham County to witt
On the 26th day of August 1812 the above named
Peachy [sic] Barrett [sic] produced the above
Register, which is duly Recorded and filed in
my office, and I have granted her a copy
thereof.

Teste
S. McWilliams C.R.C.

Jack Swingher, No. 12, p. 6:
Jack Swingher a Mulatto man, by trade a black
Smith aged Twenty four years five feet 9
inches high was born free in the county of
Albemarle has a small scare over his left eye
and a scare upon each of his wrists.
At a Court held for Albemarle county the first
day of October 1804. It is ordered that the
forgoing Register be certified as truly taken.

William D. Merewether
A Copy Teste
John Nicholas C.A.C.

Rockingham County to witt
This day the above named Jack Swingher
produced to me the above Register, which is
duly Recorded & filed in my office and I have
granted him this Copy.

Teste
S. McWilliams C.R.C.

Aron Mullins, No. 13, p. 6:
The bearer hereof Aron Mullins, a Mullatto man
about 5 feet 6 1/2 Inches high says he is
about 70 years of age, head bald no particular

6

scars on his face, hands or arms, except that
the thumb on the right hand is crooked and the
little finger on the same hand is crooked, and
the third finger on the same hand is shorter
then it naturally was said to be occasioned by
a felloun, was set free by County Mullins and
other heirs of Henry Mullins of Goochland
County Virginia, as appears by a copy of the
bill of emancipation produced and filed in my
office, the said Aaron [sic] having applyed to
me to Register his said freedom, which I have
done, pursuant to Law--the 27 August 1812.

Daniel, No. 14, p. 7:
The bearer hereof Daniel a Black man about 5
feet 10 1/2 Inches high, a scare in the corner
of his left eye, a small scare on his right
rist Just above the Joint a Very Dark Negroe
about 25 years of age the 26 of August last
was set free by the Will of Peter Higgans
deceased as appears by the said Will of Record
in the County Court of Rockingham has this day
applied to me Sam'l McWilliams Clerk of the
said County to Register him, which I have done
pursuant to Law this 10 day of October 1812.

Leve Lewis, No. 15, p. 7:
Rockingham County to witt
The Bearer hereof Leve Lewis a Dark Mulatto
Man about 5 feet 10 1/2 Inches high, 23 years
old the 14th day of February Next (1814), no
perticular mark or scare about him, (except
that his right arm appears to be stiff
occasioned by its having been broke) the said
Man was born free, a black smith by trade and
was bound as an apprentice by the Overseer of
the Poor of Rockingham County to Samuel Glyn,
as appears by his indenture this day filed in
my office--and the said Leve Lewis has applyed
to be Registered according to Law which I have
according done and Granted him this
Certificate Given under my hand this 18 August
1813.

[In the margin] Copy Granted by order of the
Court August 1813.
Duplicate Granted the 24 August 1814.
Reregisted the 2nd Dec. 1826. See page 47.

<u>Buck alias James</u>, No. 16, p. 8:
Rockingham County to witt
The bearer hereof Buck otherwise call'd James
a Bright Mulatto Man about 6 feet 2 1/2 Inches
high with a scare on his right Cheek, his
forefinger on his right hand crooked at the
first Joint, Dark Eyes, about 23 years old in
September 1814, was born free in the County of
Rockingham and was bound an apprentice by the
Overseer of the poor of the said county to
Dennis Lanahan to learn the trade of a Stone
Mason, as appears by an Indenture filed in my
office. The said Buck alias James has this
day applyed to be Registered, which I have
accordingly done and Granted him a copy
thereof this 21st day of December 1813. At
Court held for Rockingham county the 18
January 1814 the above Register was duly
examined and ordered to be certified as duly
taken.
                    Signed by E. Harrison.
                    Teste
                    S. McWilliams C.R.C.
[In the margin] Copy Granted.
[See entry No. 29]

<u>Shadrick Hill</u>, No. 17, p. 8:
Rockingham County to witt
The bearer hereof Shadrick Hill a Dark Mulatto
man, about twenty Eight years of age, five
feet ten inches, who has lost his right eye,
was born free in the county of Orange as
appears by a Certificate from the county court
of said county bearing date at November Court
1811 has this day applyed to be Registered
according to Law, which Certificate is filed
in my said office. Given under my hand this
18 day January 1814. At a Court held for the

8

county of Rockingham the 18 January 1814 the above Register was duly examined and ordered to be certified.

Signed: E. Harrison
A Copy Teste, S. McWilliams
[In the margin] Copy Granted.

Austin, No. 18, p. 8:
Rockingham County to witt
The bearer hereof Austin, a Dark Mulatto about 25 years of age the 1st January 1814, about 6 feet one half Inch high, with a scare on the left Rist, occasioned by a burn, with two scars over the right eye, was emancipated by William Ball of the County of Culpeper, by Deed dated the 16th December 1793 and duly Recorded in the county court of Culpeper, a copy of which is filed in my office, the said Austin has this 5th August 1814 applyed to me Clerk of Rockingham to be Registered according to Law, which I have done accordingly. Rockingham August Court 1814.
The above named Negroe Austin was this day examined by the said Register which was found to be duly made, the Court doth order a copy to be furnished according to Law.

Teste
S. McWilliams
[In the margin] Cop'd & delv'd to Austin the 4 August 1836.

Philip, No. 19, p. 9:
The bearer hereof Philip a Dark Mulatto about 23 years of age, Near five feet 9 inches high, no perticular mark or scare, except two small scars, one overer his left eye, and the other in the corner of the left eye,--was set free by William Ball of Culpeper county Virginia, by Deed dated the 16 Decem 1793 and is of Record in the said Court, a copy of said Deed is filed in my office, and the said Philip is hereby Registered according to Law. Given under my hand this 5 August 1814.

Rockingham County August Court 1814.
The above named Negroe Philip was this day examined by the said Register which was found to be duly made, the court ordered that he should be furnished with a copy thereof according to Law.

Teste
S. McWilliams C.R.C.

Sophia, No. 20, p. 9:
Rockingham County to witt
The bearer hereof Sophia, a Dark Mulatto about 19 years of age Near 5 feet 3 1/2 Inches high no perticular mark or scare, was set free by Catharine Williamson of Culpeper County Virginia by Deed Dated the 4th May 1802 which is recorded in said County Court a copy of which Deed has been this day filed in my office, the said Sophia is hereby Registered according to Law the 8th October 1814.

Teste
S. McWilliams

Judith, No. 21, p. 9:
Rockingham County to wit
The bearer hereof Judith (a black Girl) about 18 years of age about five feet 8 Inches high, with a scare on her right rist was set free by Catharine Williamson of Culpeper county Virginia by Deed dated the 4th May 1802 and recorded in said county court a copy of which is this day filed in my office, and the said Judith is hereby Registered according to Law, this 8 day of October 1814.

Teste
S. McWilliams C.R.C.

George McCoy, No. 22, p. 10:
Rockingham County to witt
The Bearer hereof George McCoy (a free boy) about 21 years of [age] the 1st of this Month; appears was born free, and was bound as an apprentice by order of the County Court of

10

Rockingham to Joshua Peters also a free man of
Colour to learn the trade of a Sadler, about 5
feet 7 inches high a dark Mulatto, his right
arm is crooked, has a scare on the four finger
of the left hand, the said George has this day
applyed to be Registered as the Law Direts,
June 20th 1815.
Copy Delv'd by order of the Court at June
Court 1815.

John, No. 23, p. 10:
Rockingham County to witt
The Bearer hereof John a Mulatto Man about ...
48 years of age was set free by the Will of
William Hedrick deceased of Record in the
court of said county has a cut in the right
ear, has no other perceavable mark, about 5
feet 7 Inches high, has this day applyed to
the subscriber to be Registered as the Law
direts 1st July 1815.
A Copy ordered to be given the said John by
the Court at July Court 1815 which was Deliv'd
July 19 1815.
                              Teste
                              H.J. Gambill

John McCoy, No. 24, p. 10:
Rockingham County to witt:
The Bearer hereof John McCoy a black man aged
28 years the 24th day of January next about
six feet three & three fourths inches high, a
scar on his under lip, also a scar in the palm
of his hand, also a scar on the wright side of
his head, and also two small scars on the left
side of his forehead; streight and well made;
& was born free--a copy ordered to be
delivered him at October Court 1815.
                              H.J. Tapp
Copy Del'd the said John the 7th Sept. 1816.

Joseph, No. 25, p. 11:
Rockingham County to witt: May 21st 1816
The Bearer hereof Joseph a free black of

11

Colour 21st year of age the 10th day of March 1816 about 5 feet 7 1/2 Inches high (of a light colour) the little fingers of both hands crooked from the Middle Joint to the end was born free, and bound by the overseer of the poor of said County, to Colo. George Huston, as appeared by his Certificate filed in my office,--the said Joseph was this day Registered according to Law--a copy ordered to be delv'd to the said Joseph at May Court 1816.

                         Teste
                         S. McWilliams
Copy delv'd the said Joe the ____ day of June 1816 by H.J. Gambill.

    Isaac Greenwood, No. 26, p. 11:
The Bearer hereof Isaac Greenwood a free man of Colour of the county of Rockingham about 25 years of age ... about five feet 7 Inches high, a small lump on the inside of his right Knee, which appears to have been occasioned by a cut, also a scar on the big toe of his right foot, a bright Mulatto, was emancipated by John Moore be Deed dated the 13th September 1815 which is Recorded in my office, has this day been Registered in my office according to Law.
Copy Delv'd him by order of the Court the June 1816.

    Abraham Greenwood, No. 27, p. 11:
The Bearer hereof Abraham Greenwood a free man of Colour of the county of Rockingham, about 21 years of age last March, 6 feet and one half inch high, with a scar a cross the upper Knuckles of his left hand occasioned by a cut, a dark Mulatto, was emancipated by John Moore by Deed dated the 18th March 1816 which is duly Recorded in my Office, and has this day been Registered as the Law direts.
Copy Del'd him.

Edward alias Ned, No. 28, p. 12:
The Bearer hereof Edward (commonly Call'd) Ned
a Very black man, about 26 years of age, 5
feet 6 1/2 Inches high, well made, has a scar
near the right Temple, a scar near his left
breast, and also one in the instep of the left
foot, all of which appears to have been
occasioned by cuts, remarcable hairy on his
breasts, was set free by William Cravens by
Deed dated the 10 July 1815 and duly Recorded
in the county court of Rockingham, and has
this day been Registered in my office as the
Law direts.
A copy ordered to be given said Ned by the
Court at August Court 1816 and Delv'd him the
23 August 1816 by H.J.G.

Buck alias James Ayles, No. 29, p. 12:
Rockingham County to witt
The Bearer hereof Buck alias James Ayles of
Harrisonburg a Bright Mulatto Man about 6 feet
2 1/2 Inches high with a scare on his right
Cheek his fore finger on his right hand
crooked at the first Joint, Dark eyes, about
23 years of age the ____ of September 1814 was
born free in the County of Rockingham, and was
bound an apprentice by the overseer of the
poor of the said County to Dennis Lanahan to
learn the trade of a Stone Mason, as appears
by his indenture filed in my office, the said
James alias Buck has this day applyed to me
for a new Register and Certificate agreeable
to the act of assembly which I have
accordingly done, he having deposited in my
office his former Register which is No. 16 and
is dated the 24th November 1813.
July Court 1816
Copy ordered to be Delivered to said Buck.
[See entry No. 16]

John Peterson, No. 30, p. 13:
On the 7th March 1817 John Peterson filed in
my office a Certificate of his Register,

13

Granted him by the county court of Goochland, which is in the words and figures following, "Registered in my office this 18th day of December 1816 as No. 182 John Peterson a free man of colour of dark yellow complexion, 22 years old in May last, short curled hair, about 6 feet high, a very small scar above the thumb on the left hand, and was free born. W. Miller C.G.C."
In pursuance of the act of assembly I have duly examined the said Register and Recorded the same--as No. 30 & a copy ordered to be given said John 17 March 1817.

H.J. Gambill C.R.C.
Attest
Joseph Baxter

Copy Del'd to said Peterson--with the county seal the 22 June 1822.

<u>Burket Bird</u>, No. 31, p. 13:
Registered in my office the 7th March 1817 as No. 31 Burket Bird, a free man of color, a Dark Mulatto, Twenty one years of age in October last (1816) about 6 feet high, his mouth a little prominant, a scar Just within in the hair, above the forehead, no other scars [are] perceavable, and was born free.

H.J. Gambill C.R.C.

The above Register was by Rockingham County Court this 19 day March 1817 certified to be truly made.

Attest
Joseph Baxter

[In the margin] Copy Delv'd the 5th October 1842. L.W.G.

<u>Nancy</u>, No. 32, p. 13:
Registered in my office the 5th May 1817 as No. 32 Nancy a free Woman of Color, a Light colored Mulatto about 28 years of age, about 5 feet 3 1/2 Inches she has no perticular mark perceavable, except a mole on the right side of her Jaw bone, and scar on her right arm

Just above her rist occasioned by a burn, she
was born free but bound to serve a certain
Number of years which she has duly served as
appears by her papers filed in my office.
The above Register was by Rockingham County
Court this 21 May 1817 certified to be truly
made.
                    Attest
                    S. Rutherford
[In the margin] A copy Del'd to Dennis Hollay
her Husband 5 June 1823. H.J.G.

   Andrew Alexander, No. 33, p. 14:
Registered in my Office as No. 33 the 15th
July 1817 Andrew Alexander (a free man of
colour) said to be twenty one years of age the
22d of Februay 1817, about 5 feet 4 Inches
high, a Dark Mulatto, rather a handsome face,
with tolarable full eyes, has a scar on his
left hand between the four [sic] finger, well
made, he was born free, and was bound by the
Overseer of the Poor of Rockingham to learn
the trade of a black Smith, which trade he
follows--which appears by a certificate filed
in my office.
                    H.J. Gambill C.R.C.
The above Register was by the county court of
Rockingham the 15 July 1817 ordered to be
certified as truly made.
                    Attest Peachy Harrison
[In the margin] Copy Delv'd the 16 July 1817.
Ret'd & a new one furnished the 25 Jan'y 1825.

   Polly McCoy, No. 34, p. 14:
Registered in my office as No. 34 the 22nd
October 1817 Polly McCoy (a free Woman of
Colour) twenty five years of age the 6th day
of March 1818 five feet Seven Inches high a
Bright Mullattoe with dark Brown Eyes has
three Moles on her face one at the left side
of her mouth one between her Eyes and one
below the right Eye she is the Daughter of
Betty McCoy who was a free woman at the time

15

of her Birth as appears by the certificate of William Parrott filed in my office.

H.J. Gambill C.R.C.

The above register was by the county court of Rockingham the 22nd October ordered to [be] certified as truly made.

Attest Joseph Baxter

Haney Hubbard, No. 35, p. 15:
Registered in my office as No. 35 the 19th day of January 1818 Haney Hubbard (a free woman of Colour) twenty four years of age in October Last past, five feet one Inch high a very dark Mullatto almost Black a Broad full face black Eyes has a Small scar on her right Eyebrow. Said Haney was born free as appears from the certificate of Benjamin Dawson of Faquire County Virginia filed in my office.

H.J. Gambill C.R.C.

The above register was by the county court of Rockingham the 21th day of January 1818 ordered to be certified as truly made.

Attest W. Davies

[In the margin] Copy Del'd 22nd Jan'y 1818.

David Newman, No. 36, p. 15:
Registered in my office as No. 36 the 19th day of January 1818 David Newman (a free Man of Colour) twenty Eight years old in December Last past, five feet five Inches high a little cross eyed a very dark Mulletto has a small scar on his forehead. Said David was Emancipated by Robert Carter on the 1st day of August 1791 as appears by the certificate of Benjamin Dawson Trustee for said Robert Carter Dec'd.

H.J. Gambill C.R.C.

The above register was by the county court of Rockingham the 21th day of January 1818 ordered to be certified as truly made.

Attest W. Davies

[In the margin] Copy Del'd 22nd Jan'y 1818.

<u>Bob</u>, No. 37, p. 15:
Registered in my office as No. 37 the 17th day
of March 1818 Bob (a free man of Colour) about
thirty two years of age five feet Eleven
Inches high a Bright Mulletto has a Black Mole
on his right Eye Brow is a S[t]out able Bodied
Man. Said Bob was Emancipated by John Baker
on the 16th day of October 1817 as appears by
his Emancipation bill filed & Recorded in my
office.

                    H.J. Gambill C.R.C.
The above register was by the court of
Rockingham County the 17th day of March 1818
ordered to be certified as truly Made.
                    Attest Jos. Baxter
[In the margin] Copy Del'd to self 18 March
1818.

<u>Mary Redman</u>, No. 38, p. 16:
Registered in my office as No. 38 the 18th day
of May 1818 Mary Redman (a free Woman of
Colour) appears to be about thirty five years
of age five feet four Inches and a half high a
Mulletto has been innoculated for the Small
pox on the left arm on which there is a scar.
She was born free as appears by the
certificate of Anthony Hughes and Ezekiel
Brandam of Culp[e]per County Virginia filed in
my office.

                    H.J. Gambill C.R.C.
The above Register was by the County Court of
Rockingham the 21 day of October 1818 ordered
to be certified as truly made.
                    Attest Geo. Huston
[In the margin] Copy Del'd.

<u>Elias Bird</u>, No. 39, p. 16:
Registered in my office as No. 39 the 20th day
of May 1818 Elias Bird (a free man of Colour)
twenty one years of age the 15th day of March
last past five feet Seven Inches and a half
high has the mark of a Cut above his right Eye
Brow and a large Scar on the back of his right

17

hand is a Dark Mulletto and was born free as
appears by the certificate of Nathaniel Hord
of this county filed in my office.
                    H.J. Gambill C.R.C.
The above Register was by the county court of
Rockingham the 20th day of May 1818 ordered to
be certified as truly made.
                    Attest W. Davies
[In the margin] Del'd to Byrd [sic] 25 Sept'er
1822 by H.J.G. [See No. 212, p. 155]

     Nathaniel Farman, No. 40, p. 17:
Registered in my office as No. 40 the 17th day
of August 1818 Nathaniel Farman (a free Man of
Colour) Twenty five years of age Six feet four
and a half Inches high a Bright Muletto has a
Scar on each Eye Brow he was Emancipated by
John Mackall in the year 1794 as appears by
his Emancipation bill of Record in the Clerk's
office of said county of Rockingham.
The above register was by the county court of
Rockingham the 18th day of August 1818 ordered
to be certified as truly made.
                    Attest Joseph Baxter
[In the margin] Copy Del'd Sept. 3rd 1818.

     Samuel Black, No. 41, p. 17:
Registered in my office as No. 41 the 18th day
of August 1818 Samuel Black (a free Man of
Colour) twenty one years of age on the first
day of May last five feet Nine Inches & half
high Slender Made has no scar or Mark Smooth
pleasant countinance was free born and served
his apprentiseship with Col. George Huston as
appears by said Huston's certificate filed in
my office.
The above register was by the county court of
Rockingham the 18th day of August 1818 ordered
to be certified as truly made.
                    Attest Joseph Baxter
[In the margin] Copy Del'd March 1st 1819.

     William Farman, No. 42, p. 17:

Registered in my office as No. 42 the 18th day of August 1818 William Farman a free man of Colour twenty four years of age Six feet and one half Inch high Slender made has a scar occasioned by a cut on his right leg from the Knee half way down the inside of his leg also a Scar on his ancle on the same leg was free born and served with Mary Ann Huston untill he was 21 years of age as appears by the certificate of Mary Ann Huston filed in my office.

The above register was by the county court of Rockingham the 18th day of August ordered to be certified as truly made.

Attest Joseph Baxter

[In the margin] Copy Del'd Sept. 3rd 1818.

Peter Armstrong, No. 43, p. 18:

Registered in my office as No. 43 this 20th day of August 1818 Peter Armstrong (a free Man of Colour) aged 37 years the 22nd of July 1813 five feet Six Inches and a quarter high has a remarkable scar on his right Elbow on the inside of his arm occasioned by a Burn he is a Dark Mulletto and served with William Clasby until he was twenty one years of age as appears by his Indenture which is filed in my office with an Endorsement thereon by said William Clasby that he served out his time with him.

H.J. Gambill C.R.C.

The above register was by the County Court of Rockingham this 20th day of August 1818 ordered to be certified as truly made.

Attest Joseph Baxter

Nicholas [Richison] alias Dave, No. 44, p. 18:

Registered in my office as No. 44 this 15th day of December 1818 Nicholas Richison (alias Dave) a free Man of Colour aged 21 years in May last five feet seven and three quarter Inches high has a scar occasioned by a burn

under his Jaw on the right side a Small scar
on his right cheek bone and a Small scar under
his left Eye he is [a] Black Man and served
with Valentine Miller of Rockingham County
until he was twenty one years of age as
appears by his Indenture filed in my office
his Trade is a Black Smith.
                    H.J. Gambill C.R.C.
The above register was by the County Court of
Rockingham this 15th day of December 1818
ordered to be certified as truly made.
                    Attest Joseph Baxter
[In the margin] Copy Del'd Dave Dec'r 18th
1818 by W. Herron.

<u>James Chambers</u>, No. 45, p. 19:
Registered in my office as No. 45 this 17th
day of August 1819 James Chambers (a free Man
of Colour) about 25 years of age in February
1819 five feet Eight Inches high has some
small scars on both Eyebrows and forehead and
a small scar on his right Rist is a Bright
Mullettoe Stout made Hazle coloured Eyes was
free born as appears by the affidavit of Mary
Chambers of Fredericksburg filed in my office.
                    H.J. Gambill C.R.C.
The above register was by the county court of
Rockingham this 17th day of August 1819
ordered to be certified as truly made.
                    Attest Joseph Baxter

<u>Martin Colley</u>, No. 46, p. 19:
Registered in my office as No. 46 this 20th
day of October 1819 Martin Colley (a free man
of Colour) about 45 years of age five feet
seven and a half Inches high has a small scar
on his left cheek bone is a Bright Mullettoe a
Man of Genteel size and appearance with Black
Eyes was free born as appears by the affidavit
of Abner Yates of this county filed in my
office.
                    H.J. Gambill C.R.C.
The above register was by the county court of

20

Rockingham this 20th day of October 1819 ordered to be certified as truly made.
Attest Giles Turley

Frank Morris, No. 47, p. 20:
Registered in my office as No. 47 this 21st day of December 1819 Frank Morris (a free Man of Colour) aged 18 years the 20th day of November 1813 five feet six Inches high has a Mark on his breast which he says was occasioned by his being snagged with a nail when small also a Mark on the rist of his left arm occasioned by a cut both of which marks are considerably above the whole skin the end of the second finger on his right hand has been cut off he is a pleasant looking black man and was Emancipated by Pink Eaton by his Last Will and Testament now of Record in the County Court of Rockingham dated the 17th day of January 1814.
H.J. Gambill C.R.C.
The above Register was by the County Court of Rockingham this 21st day of December 1819 ordered to be certified as truly made.
Attest John Bostin
[In the margin] Copy Del'd Dec'r 21st 1819. Deliver'd the 8 December 1825.

Wickham alias Isaac Morris, No. 48, p. 20:
Registered in my office as No. 48 this 21st day of December 1819 Wickham (alias Isaac Morris) a free Man of Colour aged 16 years the 2nd day of November 1813 five feet four Inches and three quarters high has no percieveable Mark is very round full faced well set for his height and was Emancipated by Pink Eaton by his Last Will and Testament dated the 17th day of January 1814 now of Record in the County Court of Rockingham.
H.J. Gambill C.R.C.
The above register was by the county court of Rockingham this 21st day of December 1819

ordered to be certified as truly made.

Attest John Bostin

1823 December 22 the above register returned to my office & destroyed and a New copy furnished by H.J.G.

Dennis Newman, No. 49, p. 21:

Registered in my office as No. 49 this 21st day of March 1820 Dennis Newman (a free man of Colour[)] about Twenty five years old some time in 1819 five feet eight inches high has a scar on his left Eyebrow also two small scars on his chin which are visible has rather a Down look has a very Black complexion is a Black Smith by Trade was Emancipated by Robert Carter Dec'd of Frederick County Virginia as appears by the certificate of Benjamin Dawson Trustee for said Robert Carter Dec'd filed in my office.

H.J. Gambill C.R.C.

The above Register was by the County Court of Rockingham this 21st day of March 1820 duly compared with the said Dennis and ordered to be certified as being truly made and that a copy be furnished said Dennis.

Attest Joseph Baxter

[In the margin] Delv'd to Dennis 28 October 1820. H.J.G.

Polly Colley, No. 50, p. 21:

Registered in my office as No. 50 this 18th day of April 1820 Polly Colley [(]a free Woman of Colour) about Twenty years of age some time in the present year five feet three and a half Inches high the little finger of her left hand is crooked at the two first Joints is a Very Bright Mullettoe has Clear Black Eyes and Curly Black hair which is long, said Polly was free Born as appears by the certificate of Joseph Baxter Esqr of this county filed in my office.

H.J. Gambill

The above register was by the county court of

Rockingham this 18th day of April 1820 ordered
to be certified as being truly made.
                        Attest Peachy Harrison
[In the margin] Copy Delivered to self on the
20th of October 1835 by D.H.G.

[Nos. 51, 52, and 53 are missing.]

     George Myner, No. 54, p. 24: [This entry
was apparently withdrawn or rejected. It was
deleted and bears no signatures.]
Rockingham County to wit
Registered in my office as No. 54 George Myner
a free negroe aged twenty two years five feet
nine and a half inches high tolerably well
made. The said George was emancipated by
Isaac Mynes dec'd as will appear by his
certain deed of emancipation bearing date on
the 21st day of May 1814 and recorded in the
clerks office of this county.
The above register was by the Court of the
county of Rockingham this 8th day of May 1822
ordered to be certified as truly made and a
copy to be furnished the said George.
                        Teste

     Lewis Rasow alias Zane, No. 54, p. 24:
Rockingham County to wit
Registered in my office the 1st June 1822
Lewis Rasow otherwise call'd Lewis Zane a
Mulatto Man about 46 years old at Chrismas
Next (1822), about 5 feet, 8 inches high, he
has a scare on the inside of his left leg Just
above the ankle bone, which appears to have
been occasioned by a cut, also a small scare
on his breasts, was emancipated by Sarah Zane,
as appears by a certificate of the Clerk of
Shanandoah County, filed in my office.
The above Register was by the County Court of
Rockingham duly compared with the said Lewis,
and a copy ordered to be delivird him, the
same having been truly made at June Court
1822.

                        23

Joseph Baxter
[In the margin] Copy Del'd 29 Sept 1824.]

Daniel alias Daniel Hopkins, No. 55, p. 25:
State of Virginia, Rockingham County to wit
Registered in my Office (as No. 55) the 31st
August 1822 Daniel call'd Daniel Hopkins, a
very black man about 28 or 29 years of age was
born free (but bound to serve untill he was 21
years of age) has large thick lips, no marks
or scars about him except a small scare near
the rist on the inside of his right hand,
about 5 feet 6 or 7 inches high.
The above Register was by the County Court of
Rockingham compared with the s'd Daniel and
found duly made and a copy ordered to be
deliverd to said Daniel, done at September
Court 1822.
[In the margin] Copy del'd.

Jack, No. 56, p. 25:
Rockingham County to wit
Registered in my office as No. 56 the 14th
September 1822 Jack a Dark Mulatto man said to
be 26 years of age in April last, was left
free at the age of 25 years by the last will
of William Smith deceased, whose executors in
pursuance of said will emancipated the said
Jack by Deed dated the _____ day of August
1822, which deed & will are of Record in my
office, he is about 5 feet 7 inches high, a
small scar near the corner of the left eye,
and one above the outer angle of the right
eye, has also a small scare on the thick part
of the inside of his right hand, and a scare
on the Middle Joint of the fore finger of the
right hand appears to have been occasioned by
a cut.
The foregoing Register was compared with the
s'd Jack by the county court and found duly
made and a copy thereof ordered to be
furnished him according to Law, done at Jan'y

24

court 1824.

Joseph Baxter

[In the margin] Copy of Del'd to Jack 20 Sept'er 1824.

Easter alias Easter Hopkins, No. 57, p. 25:

Rockingham County to wit
Registered in my office as No. 57 the 30th day of September 1822 Easter commonly call'd Easter Hopkins, a black Negroe Woman, said to be 31 years of age in March last, was born free (but bound to serve untill 18 years of age) about 5 feet 3 Inches high, the end of the Little finger of the left hand appears to have been split, she says with a sickel, no other remarkble scars or ma[r]ke about her, she is rather a handsom[e] woman.

The foregoing Register was compared with the said Easter by the Court and found duly made a copy thereof was ordered to be furnished her, done at October Court 1822.

[In the margin] ReRegistered on page 64 as No. 160.

James alias James Hopkins, No. 58, p. 26:

Rockingham County to wit
Registered in my office as No. 58 the 30th day of September 1822, James commonly James Hopkins, a [deleted: "handsome"] black man said to be about 22 years of age in January last, was born free, about 5 feet 7 inches high, has two scars on the fore finger of the left hand, & also a scare above the second Joint of the Thumb on the same hand, all which appears to have been cuts, he has also a Mole on the right cheek bone in his face. No other remarkable scare or mark perceavable.

The foregoing Register was by the court compared with the s'd James and found duly made, a copy thereof was ordered to be furnished him according to law, done at October Court 1822. Memo: another copy of the

25

above furnished said James 22nd March 1832 by order of March Court 1832.
[In the margin] Copy Delv'd to s'd James the 18 Nov'r 1823.

Washington Lucas, No. 59, p. 26:
Registered in my office as No. 59 the 2nd day of October 1822, Washington Lucas a free man of Colour of a dark complexion, aged about 22 years and 7 months, about five feet nine Inches high; the said Washington Lucas has a scar on the left side of his head occasioned by a cut; a scar on his breast near the right side; also a scar on the back part of his left shoulder; was born free as appears by an Indenture of Apprenticeship binding him to George Clarke, by the Overseer of poor for the corporation of Fredericksburg which is filed in my office.
The forgoing Register was by the court compared with the said Washington and found duly made; a copy thereof was ordered to be furnished him according to law, done at October court 1822.
[In the margin] Copy Del'd the 8 October H.J.G.

Theodrick Lewis, No. 60, p. 27:
Rockingham County to wit
Registered in my office as No. 60 the 3rd day of February 1823 Theodrick Lewis a very handsome dark Mulatto, says he was 23 years of age in January last, was born free, by trade a Joiner, about 5 feet 10 1/2 inches high, has no perticular mark or scar except a small scare on the Little finger of the left hand, the foregoing Register was by the court of the said county compared with the said Theodrick and found duly made, a copy thereof was ordered to be furnished to him according to law, done at February court 1823.
[In the margin] Cop'd & deli'd to him 20 Dec'r 1824.   H.J.G.   Received the 28 Dec'r 1829.

The former one delv'd up. H.J.G.

Phebe Hopkins, No. 61, p. 27:
Rockingham County to wit
Registered in my office as No. 61 the 4th day
of February 1823 Phebe Hopkins a Very Dark
Mulatto Woman above 29 years of age, who was
born free, about 5 feet 7 1/2 inches high has
a scare on the back of the left hand, and also
a lump on the left cheak bone, has no other
marke or scare perceavable,--the above
Register was by the Court compared with the
said Phebe and found duly made, a copy thereof
is ordered to be furnished the said Phebe by
the Court, at February Court 1823.
[In the margin] Copy Delv'd to Phebe the 23
June 1823. H.J.G.

Milton Bryant, No. _____, p. 27:
Rockingham County Court Clerks Office. This
day the following register was presented to me
and registered, to wit:
"Virginia, to wit:
No. 395
In pursuance of an act of assembly, entitled
an Act for regulating the police of Towns in
this commonwealth and to restrain the practice
of negroes going at Large, "I Robert Smith
Chew, clerk of the court of Hustings for the
Town & Corporation of Fredericksburg, do
hereby certify that Milton Bryant a black man
with a small scar on lower front of left ear,
& two on the right side of his neck & left
eye, aged 22 years, 5 feet 8 1/2 inches high
who was born free, is registered in my office
agreeable to the direction of the above
recited act. Certified this 28th day of
February 1823 under my hand & date of the said
Corporation.
R.S. Chew C.C.F.
Atteste Robt. Lewis Mayor one of the
Magistrates for the town of Fredericksburg.
[In the margin] Copy given.

27

<u>Dennis Holly</u>, No. 62, p. 28:
Rockingham County, to wit:
Registered in my office as No. 62 the 2nd day
of April 1823 Dennis Holly a dark mulatto man
said to be about 36 years of age the 5th of
August next about five feet eight Inches high
with a scar immediately above the left eye,
the said Dennis Holly was found to be entitled
to his freedom as appears by the Judgment of
the Court in a suit brought by him in the
court of this county against Clement Ervine
for that purpose which was tried at the
February term of the present year.
The above register was by the court duly
compared with the said Dennis and a copy
thereof ordered to be furnished him at April
Court 1823.
[In the margin] Copy deli'd Dennis 5 June 1823
by H.J.G.

<u>Edmond</u>, No. 63, p. 28:
Registered in my office as No. 63 the 5th day
of July 1823 Edmond a black Man about 25 years
of age in March last, five feet 9 1/2 inches
high, has a scare or Natural mark on his left
cheak bone near the corner of his eye, also a
small scare on the right cheak and a cut on
the Little finger of the left hand, the said
Edmond was emancipated by James Smith with
others in the year 1803 and at that time was
about 5 years of age, and to be free from and
after the 1st day of March 1823--all which
appears by the said emancipation of Record in
my office. The foregoing register was this
day compared with the said Edmond and found
duly made, a copy thereof was ordered to be
furnished him, done at August Court 1823.
[In the margin] Copy Delv'd the 7 August 1823.

<u>Lucy alias Lucy Freeman</u>, No. 64, pp.
28-29:
Rockingham County (to wit)
On the 30th day of September 1823 Lucy alias

28

Lucy Freeman filed in my office a certificate of Register Granted her by the County Court of Goochland, which is in the words and figures following:
"Registered in my office this 17th day of May 1817 as No. 184 Lucy alias Lucy Freeman a black Girl about 18 years old, about four feet Eleven inches high and was free born. Signed W. Miller C.G.C.
The above register was by the county court of Goochland this 9th day of May 1817 certified to be truly made.
Attest W. Bolling, Justice Peace of said county."
In pursuance of the act of assembly I have Registered the said Lucy as No. 64 & this day Granted her this Certificate,--Copy the seal of my s'd county thereto annexed.
[In the margin] Delv'd to Lucy the 7 March 1832 by H.J.G.

Jonathan alias Jonathan Hopkins, No. 65, p. 29:
Rockingham County (to wit)
Registered in my Office the 8th October 1823 as No. 65 Jonathan alias Jonathan Hopkins, a free Negroe, about 23 years of old, Near five feet Eleven inches high, has a scare on the back of his right hand, and a small scare near the Middle of his forehead, he is a Very dark Mulatto almost a black, a handsome straight man, and was born free,--The foregoing Register was by the County Court this day compared with the said Jonathan & found duly made, a copy ordered to be furnished him, done at October Court 1823.
[In the margin] Copy delv'd to Jonathan by clerk.

Moses Myers, No. 66, p. 29:
Rockingham County to wit
Registered in my Office the 1st March 1824 as No. 66 Moses Myers, a free Negroe about 22 or

29

23 years of age, five feet 5 1/2 Inches high, has a small scare on his forehead, and also a small scare at the lower end of the breast bone, he is a s[t]out well made man, Very Dark, and has remarkable small ears, the said boy was Emancipated by the last will of Isaac Mires deceased of Record in said office and to be free on 1st January 1824.

The foregoing Register was by the county court of said county compared with the said Moses and found duly made & a copy ordered to be furnished him, done at March Court 1824.
[In the margin] Cop'd.
[In the margin] Rem'd Dec'r 28 1829. The former Copy Surrender'd and destroyed.
J. Clark

Sandy Byrd, No. 67, p. 30:
Rockingham County to wit
Registered in my office as No. 67 the 14th day of August 1824 Sandy Byrd a dark mulatto man Said to be 23 Years of Age in September next about Five Feet 11 1/2 Inches high with a Small Scar about 1 1/2 Inches above the left Eye and a scare on the right rist, the Said Sandy Byrd was Born Free as proved by the oath of Nathaniel Hord filed in my Office.
The foregoing register compared & etc. by the County Court of Rockingham at September Court 1824.

H.J. Gambill C.R.C.
[In the margin] Copy Delivered the 18th of February 1825 by L.W.G.

Joseph Harrison, No. 68, p. 30:
Rockingham County To Wit
Registered in my office as No. 68 the 6th day of Sept. 1824 Joseph Harrison a Mulatto Man about 22 Years of Age Five Feet 7 1/2 Inches high with a Scar a cross the Right hand above the upper Joint of the little finger, two Small Scars on the left arm near together about 2/3 of an Inch in length and a Small

30

lump above the Right Breast. The Said Joseph
Harrison was Free Born as appears by the
Records of my office. The foregoing register
compared with Joseph as the Law direts, at
September Court 1824.

H.J. Gambill C.R.C.
[In the margin] Copy delivered to your Brother
Peter [Harrison] the 15th November 1826 p'r
your order. J. Clark

Milly alias Milly Lewis, No. 69, p. 30:
Rockingham County To Wit
Registered in my office as No. 69 the 4th day
of October 1824 Milly (otherwise Called Milly
Lewis) Supposed to be about 60 Years of Age,
Five Feet 2 1/2 Inches high with a Scar a
Cross her Right arm about one and a half
Inches long, Said Milly was emancipated by
John Ellison of New Kent County on the 7th day
of the first month 1783 as appears by the
Certificate of Will Clayton C.N.C. dated 13th
Feb'y 1783. Compared with the said Milly by
the Court and found right at October Court
1824.
[In the margin] Delv'd self the 20 Sept'er
1834 by H.J. Gambill C.R.C.

Nancy alias Nancy Hopkins, No. 70, p. 31:
Rockingham County, October 5, 1824
Registered in my Office as No. 70 on this day
Nancy commonly call'd Nancy Hopkins a Dark
Woman about 40 Years of age about 5 feet 3 1/2
inches high, a scare over her right eye, was
born free, but bound to serve a Certain Number
of years, as appears by the Records of my said
county. The foregoing was compared with the
said Nancy and found duly made by the County
Court, and a copy ordered to be furnish'd her,
done at October Court 1824.

Hannah alias Hannah Hopkins, No. 71, p.
31:
Rockingham County, October 5th 1824

31

Registered in my Office as No. 71 on this day
Hannah commonly call'd Hannah Hopkins, a Dark
Mulatto Woman about 27 or 28 years of age,
about five feet 4 1/2 inches high, two large
scars on the right arm, one Joint of the fore
finger of the left hand, which makes it
smaller than the others, said to have been
occasioned by a felloun, was born free but
bound to serve a certain Number of Years, as
appears by the Records of my said County. The
foregoing Register was compared with the said
Hannah and found duly made by the county
court, and a copy ordered to be furnish'd her,
done at October Court 1824.
[In the margin] Reentered the 11 Feb'y 1832 in
page 65, No. 164.

Jessee, No. 72, p. 31:
Rockingham County to wit
Registered in my office as No. 72 on the 2nd
February 1825 Jessee a black man about 25
years old the 20th of April 1824 about 6 feet
high, has a large scare on his right arm above
the elbow, and also a scare on the left arm,
and one on the left side of his face, and a
small lump, below the left ear, he was set
free by the Will of Peter Higgans deceased,
which will is of Record in my said office.
The foregoing Register was compared with the
said Jessee and found duly made by the Court,
and a Copy thereof ordered to be furnished
him. Done at February Court 1825 (Copy Delv'd
to s'd Jessee 2nd February 1825.)

Peter alias Peter Harrison, No. 73, p.
32:
Rockingham County To Wit
Registered in my Office as No. 73 the 3rd day
of May 1825 Peter (Commonly Called Peter
Harrison[)] a Mulatto Man Said to be 21 Years
of Age the 12th day of April 1825 about 5 Feet
8 Inches high Peter has a large Scar on his
left Leg Commenceing about Four Inches above

32

the ankle the Said Peter was Free born as
proved by the oath of Elizabeth Lang filed in
my Office. The foregoing Register was by the
Court Compared with the said Peter and copy
ordered to be furnished him done at May Court
1825.
[In the margin] Copied.

Dennis alias Dennis Hews, No. 74, p. 32:
Rockingham County To Wit
Registered in my office as No. 74 the 16th day
of July 1825 Dennis (otherwise Ca[l]led Dennis
Hews) A Black Man Forty Four Years old Five
Feet Six Inches & Three quarter High pretty
well Set for his hight he has a Small Scar
over the left Eye and an other over the Right
Corner of the Right Eye and a Scar on the back
part of the left Wrist immeadiately on the
Joint and was emancipated by William Hughes
[corrected from Hews] in the Year 1804 which
is of Record in the County Court of
Rockingham. The foregoing Register was by the
Court Compared with the said Dennis and a copy
thereof ordered to be furnished him, done at
August Court 1825.
[In the margin] Copy Delv'd 9 August 1825.
[See No. 286, p. 107.]

William alias William Lee, No. 75, pp.
32-33:
Rockingham County To Wit
Registered in my office as No. 75 the 5th day
of September 1825 William (Otherwise Called
William Lee) A Mulatto Man Twenty One Years
old in the Month of April 1825 the Said
William is 5 Feet Seven and a half Inches high
pretty well Set for his hight he has a Scar on
his Chin and an other Under his chin & near
his Throat and also one Small Scar on his
Forehead Just below the hair the said boy was
born free and bound as an apprentice to John
Effinger Jr. as appears by the indenture filed
in my office. The foregoing Register was by

the Court compared with the said William Lee, and a copy thereof ordered to be furnished him, Done at September Court 1825.
[In the margin] Copied & del. 7th Oct'r 1825 by J. Clark.

William alias William Strawther, No. 76, p. 33:
Rockingham County To Wit
Registered in my office as No. 76 the 4th day of October 1825 William (otherwise Called William Strawther) A Mulatto Man Thirty Years of Age the 26th day of August 1825 (on which day it appears he was free). The Said William Strawther is 5 Feet 6 1/4 Inches high and well Set for his hight he has Two Small Scars above the wrist on the left arm inclining a Cross and one other len[g]thwise and near one of the other Scars and is rather dim Sighted in the left Eye. The Said William was Set free by the Will of George Carpenter Deceas'd as proved by the Oath of John Carpenter . . . which is filed in my Office. The foregoing Register was by the Court Compared with the Said William and a copy thereof ordered to be furnished him done at October Court 1825.
[In the margin] Copied.

Richard Jackson, No. 77, p. 33:
Rockingham County (to wit)
Registered in my office as No. 77 [on the] 11th October 1825 Richard Jackson a free Negroe, a Dark Mulatto, about 5 feet 8 1/4 inches high has a small scare on the instep of the right foot, also a scare on the Nose and one on the forehead, Just where the hair Joins it, also one on the left rist on the inside--was born free as appears by a certificate filed in my office. The foregoing Register was compared with the said Richard by the court and found duly made and a copy ordered to be furnished him Done at _____ Court 1825.

Molly Jackson, No. 78, p. 34:
Rockingham County (to wit)
Registered in my office as No. 78 11th October
1825 Molly Jackson wife of Richard Jackson a
bright Mulatto, about five feet 4 1/4 Inches
high, has a large scare on the right leg on
the shin bone, and the third finger on the
left hand crooked, was born free as appears by
a certificate filed in my office.
The foregoing Register was by the Court
Compared with the said Molly and found duly
made and a copy ordered to be furnished her
according to Law, done at November Court 1825.
[In the margin] Copied & del'd 16th Nov'r 1825
by J. Clark.

Malinda Jackson, No. 79, p. 34:
Rockingham County (to wit)
Registered in my office as No. 79 11th October
1825 Malinda Jackson Daughter of Richard
Jackson, a Mulatto Girl about 21 years of age
in March last, five feet 6 1/4 inches high,
has a large scare on the right side of her
Neck occasioned by a burn, was born free.
The foregoing Register was by the County Court
compared with the said Malinda and found duly
made, a copy thereof is ordered to be
furnished her according to Law, done at
November Court 1825.
[In the margin] Copied & delv'd by J. Clark
16th Nov. 1825.

Nancy Greenwood, No. 80, p. 34:
Rockingham County (to wit)
Registered in my office as No. 80 11th October
1825 Nancy Greenwood wife of Isaac Greenwood,
a Very bright Mulatto woman with long straight
hair and hazel eyes, five feet 6 inches high,
24 years of age on the 25th of August 1825,
was born free as appears by a certificate
filed in my office.
The foregoing Register was by the Court
compared with the said Nancy and found duly

made and a copy thereof ordered to be
furnished her according to Law, done at
November Court 1825.
[In the margin] Copied.

    <u>Billy Hackly</u>, No. 81, p. 35:
Rockingham County (to wit)
Registered in my office as No. 81 11th October
1825 Billy Hackly about ... 46 years of age, a
very Dark Man, five feet 9 1/4 Inches high,
was emancipated by the will of John Hackly
deceased, all which appears by a copy of his
register heretofore Granted him, (which Copy
he has filed in my office), and also by a copy
of the Will of s'd Hackly also filed in my
office.
The foregoing register was by the County Court
this day compared with the said Billy and
found duly made, a copy thereof is ordered to
be furnished him according to Law, Done at
November Court 1825.
[In the margin] Copied & delivered to self on
the 20th day of September 1836 by D.H.
Gambill.

    <u>Samuel Madden</u>, No. 82, p. 35:
Rockingham County (To Wit)
Registered in my office as No. 82, 12 October
1825, Samuel Madden about 19 years of Age, a
dark Mulatto Five Feet 8 1/4 Inches high and
was Free Born as appears by the affidavits of
Reubin King and Wesley Landsman filed in my
office, has a Scar Crosswise on his left fore
Finger.
The foregoing Register was by the Court
Compared with the Said Samuel and found duly
made, a Copy thereof is ordered to be
furnished him according to Law, done at
November 1825 Court.
[In the margin] Copied.

    <u>Hetty Shidrack</u>, No. 83, p. 35:
Rockingham County To Wit

Registered in my office as No. 83, 12 October
1825, Hetty Shidrack about 25 Years of Age a
Mulatto Woman Five Feet 2 3/4 Inches high
[deleted: "Said Hetty has thick Bushy Hair and
a Scar on the left Side of her left foot about
Two and a half Inches from the end of her
little Toe"] and was Free Born as appears by
the affidavit of Matthew Bridges filed in my
office.
The foregoing Register was by the Court
Compared with the Said Hetty and found duly
made, a Copy thereof is ordered to be
furnished her according to Law, done at
November Court 1825.
[In the margin] Copied.

Isaac Adams, No. 84, p. 36:
Registered in my office as No. 84, 13 October
1825, Isaac Adams Twenty Two Years of Age on
the 10th day of August 1825. Isaac is rather
a dark Mulatto Man and is Five Feet 10 1/4
Inches high ... has on his left Arm the
imprission of a Cable and Anker and the
letters I.A. made by the incertion of Indian
Ink .... The Said Isaac was Freeborn as
appears by the affidavit of Joseph Cravens
filed in my office. The foregoing register
was by the Court Compared with the Said Isaac
and found duly made, a copy is ordered to be
furnished him according to law, done at
Novem'r Court 1825.
[In the margin] Copied delivered by J. Clark
8th Oct'r 1825.

Jane Givins, No. 85, p. 36:
Rockingham County (To Wit)
Registered in my office as No. 85, 13 October
1825, Jane Givins (the Wife of James Givins a
Free man of Colour). Jane is about 43 Years
of Age about 5 feet high and a light black
woman [deleted: "with rather Thick Curly hair
and is pretty well Set for her height"]. She
has a Small Scar ... above the upper Joint of

37

the Right Thumb between the Same and the fore
Finger and a Slight Scar on the left Thumb
about .... Said Jane was emancipated by the
Said James on the 14th day of October 1818 as
appears by the Records in my office. The
forgoing register was ... Court compared with
the Said Jane and found duly made, a Copy
thereof is ordered to be furnished her
according to law, done at Nov'r Court 1825.
[In the margin] Copied & Del'd son John
[Givins] 3 Nov'r 1825. H.J.G.

Hannah Givins, No. 86, p. 37:
Rockingham County (To Wit)
Registered in my office as No. 86, 13 October
1825, Hannah Givins (the Daughter of James
Givins) Aged 24 Years the 15th day of December
1824, and is 5 Feet & 1/2 an Inch high, Hannah
is a light Black Woman [deleted: "and has
tolerable thick and black Curly hair. Hannah
is not very thick or Spare for her height.
She has"] has a Small Scar on the ... fore
Finger of the Right hand and has a Scar on the
[deleted: "right Elbow occasioned by a Burn."]
She was emancipated by the Said James on the
14th day of October 1818 as appears by the
Records of my office. The foregoing register
was by the Court Compared with Said Hannah and
found duly made, a Copy thereof is ordered to
be furnished her according to law, done at
Nov'r Court 1825.
[In the margin] Cop'd & delv'd Jno. [Givins] 3
Nov. 1825. H.J.G.

Matthew alias Matthew Lewis, No. 87, p.
37:
Registered in my office as No. 87, 31 October
1825, Matthew (otherwise Called Matthew Lewis)
the Son of Milly Lewis as appears by the
affidavit of Layton Yancey filed in my office
a Free Woman of Colour. Matthew is 24 Years
of Age the 18 Inst. and Five Feet 6 1/4 Inches
high and pretty well Set for his hight and

Tolerably Black with Short Black Curly hair he
has a Scar about an Inch below the upper Joint
of his fore Finger on the right hand which is
half an Inch long and crosswise the Finger, he
has at present a Scarr on the Shin of the left
leg which has Some the appearance of Two
Scars.   The foregoing Register was by the
Court Compared with Said Matthew and found
duly made, a Copy thereof is ordered to be
furnished him according to Law, done at Nov'r
Court 1825.
[In the margin] Copy Delivered the 1st day of
November 1825 by L.W.G.

     Sally Bryant, No. 88, pp. 37-38:
Registered in my office as No. 88 the 21st day
of October 1825 Sally Bryant (a Free Woman of
Colour) about Twenty Years of Age and Five
Feet 3 3/4 Inches high.   Sally is a pale
Yellow Woman ... has rather a remarkable Scar
on the left hand on the inside of the Same,
commencing on the thick part of the hand and
extending on froward the thumb and between the
thumb & Joints of the fore finger where it
Joins the hand.   [This entry has been heavily
corrected and deleted throughout.] Said Sally
Bryant was Born Free as appears by the
affidavit of Reubin Thornhill filed in my
office.   The foregoing register was by the
Court Compared with the Said Sally and found
duly made and a Copy thereof is ordered to be
furnished her according to Law, done at Nov'r
Court 1825.
[In the margin] Copied.

     James Lowrey, No. 89, p. 38:
Registered in my office as No. 89 the 22nd day
of October 1825 James Lowrey (Free Born) aged
21 Years the 19th day of October 1825 as
appears by an Indenture of Appren[t]iceship
Made by the Overseers of the Poor of
Rockingham County Binding Said Lowrey to
Abraham Nave which Indenture is filed in my

39

office. James is a Bright Mulatto Man and
Five Feet 9 Inches high he has a Small Scar on
his right rist Just on the Joint of the Same
above the Thumb and one other Scar extending
from the left Side of the Nose to the Mouth or
very near it .... The foregoing Register was
by the Court Compared with the Said James
Lowry [sic] and found duly made, a Copy
thereof is ordered to be furnished him
according to Law, done at Nov'er Court 1825.
[In the margin] Copied, Delivered the 24th day
of December by L.W.G.

Lucey Berry, No. 90, p. 39:
Registered in my office as No. 90 the 22nd day
of October 1825 Lucey Berry the Wife of Dennis
Berry (a Free Woman of Colour). She is about
32 Years of Age and Five Feet 6 & a half
Inches high and a [deleted: "Stout large
Woman"] of pretty dark Complexion [deleted:
"with Short curly Hair and"] has a Slight Scar
on the back part of the left leg rather below
the Calf [deleted: "and an other Slight Scar
between the Shoulder rather on the left
Side"]. Said Lucy [sic] is a Free woman as
appears from the affidavits of Samuel Few and
Cordelia Hite and the Certificate of Archibald
Rutherford Esquire filed in my office. The
foregoing register was by the Court compared
with the Said Lucy [sic] and found duly made,
a Copy thereof is ordered to be furnished her
according to Law, done at Nov'er Court 1825.
[In the margin] Cop'd.

Agga, No. 91, p. 39:
Registered in my office as No. 91 the 29th day
of October 1825 [deleted: "Free born" "a Free
Woman of Colour"] Agga [deleted: "a Free Woman
of Colour"]. She is about 22 or 3 Years of
Age and Four Feet 10 3/4 Inches hig[h]
[deleted: "a thick Chunky Woman and
tolerably"] dark Complected Mulatto [deleted:
"with full round face"]. She has a Small Scar

on the ... back part of the left wrist
[deleted: "about half and Inch long and at the
broadest part about 1/4 of an Inch"] a Small
Scar rather above the right Corner of the
right Eye Two Small Scars over the right Eye
one Scar over the Left Eye .... She was free
Born as appears by the affidavit of Reubin
Thornhill filed in my office. The foregoing
Register was by the Court compared with the
Said Agga and found duly made, a Copy thereof
is ordered to be furnished her according to
Law, done at Nov'er Court 1825.
[In the margin] Cop'd.

Polly, No. 92, p. 39:
Registered in my office as No. 92 the 29th day
of October 1825 Polly [deleted: "a Free Woman
of Colour"]. She is about 22 or 23 Years of
Age and Five Feet high [deleted: "a thick
Chunky Woman"] and a dark Complected Mulatto
[deleted: "and very full faced"]. She has a
Scar over the right Corner of the right Eye
which touches the Eyebrow [deleted: "and about
1 Inch long one"] near the right Temple Slight
[deleted: "and about 1/2 an Inch"] long one
over the left Eye [deleted: "which"] is
[deleted: "in a Curved form and about 1 Inch
long"] one on the right Side of the right
Nostril and a Small Flesh mole [deleted:
"about 3/4 of an Inch by"] the left of the
left Nostril [deleted: "Two Scars on the right
arm, one of which is very near the elbow Joint
and about 1 1/2 Inches long the other which is
Slight & 2 Inches from the former and about 3
Inches long and one on the left Elbow Joint
about 1 Inch long"]. She was Free Born as
appears by the affidavit of Reubin Thornhill
filed in my office. The foregoing Register
was by the Court compared and found duly made,
a Copy thereof is ordered to be furnished her
according to Law, done at November Court 1825.

Jemima, No. 93, p. 40:

41

Registered in my office as No. 93 the 29th day
of October 1825 Jemima [deleted: "a Free Woman
of Colour"] is about 61 Or 2 years of Aag
[Age] and Five Feet 6 1/2 Inches high. She is
not veary Dark tho not a Mulatto and Sees
badly out of the Right Eye and has a
remarkable mark or Wart on the back part of
the left arm [deleted: "4 or 5 Inches below
the Elbow. The foregoing Register was by the
Court Compared and found duly made & a Copy
thereof"]. She was Emancipated by William
Ball of the County of Culpeper as appears by
the affidavit of Reubin Thornhill filed in my
office. The foregoing Register was by the
Court Compared with the Said Jemima and found
duly made, a Copy thereof is ordered to be
furnished her accord[ing] to Law done at
November Court 1825.
[In the margin] Cop'd.

Caty Back, No. 94, p. 41:
Registered in my office as No. 94 the 31st day
of October 1825 Caty Back [deleted: "Baggs (a
Free Girl of Colour)"] Twenty Three Years of
Age on the 31st day of August 1825 and Five
Feet 4 Inches high and Mulatto [deleted: "with
long hair"] and was Born Free as appears by an
Indenture of apprenticeship filed in my office
as also the Certificate of George Shaver to
whom She was Bound. The foregoing Register
was by the Court Compared with the Said Caty
Baggs [sic] and found duly made, a copy
thereof is ordered to be furnished her
according to law done at November Court 1825.
[In the margin] Copied.

Lawson Lewis, No. 95, p. 41:
Registered in my office as No. 95 the 6th day
of Decbr 1825 Lawson Lewis 21 Years of Age 5
[feet] 9 1/2 Inches high a pale Mulatto Man
and was Free Born as appears by the affidavit
of John H. Deck filed in my office and has no
particular mark on his hands Arms Face or

head. The foregoing Register was by the Court
Compared with the Said Lawson and found duly
made, a copy thereof is ordered to be
furnished to him according to Law done at
Feb'ry Court 1825.
[In the margin] Copy deliv'd to self the 16 of
Sept. 1826 by H.W.G.

Isaiah Welch, No. 96, p. 41:
Registered in my office as No. 96 the 24th
December 1825 Isaiah Welch a Dark Mulatto Man
about 28 years of age about five feet 5 inches
high, has no mark or scars on his hands or
face, has rather thick or prominent lips, was
born free as appears by a certificate of the
County Court of Orange which is filed in my
office. The foregoing Register was by the
County Cou[r]t of Rockingham compared with the
said Isaiah and found duly made, a copy
thereof is ordered to be furnished him
according to Law done at ____ Court 1826.

Litty, No. 97, p. 41-42:
Registered in my office as No. 97 the 29th day
of April 1826 Litty, about 42 Years old about
five Feet 2 Inches high and Stout made has a
Scar on the left Wrist about 2 Inches long a
Scar on the left arm not very perceivable
about half way between the Wrist and Elbow.
Said Litty was Emancipated by Ruthe Davis by
Deed dated 20th March 1826 which is of Record
in the County Court of Rockingham. The
foregoing Register was by the Court Compared
with the Said Litty and found duly made a copy
thereof is ordered to be furnished her
according to Law done at June Court 1826.
[In the margin] Cop'd.

Catharine, No. 98, p. 42:
Registered in my office as No. 98 the 29th day
of April 1826 Catharine about 24 Years old
Five Feet 9 Inches high and well Set has a
Scar on the Joint of the left Thumb and has no

43

other marks perceivable. Said Catharine was Emancipated by Ruth Davis by Deed dated 20th March 1826 which is of Record in the County Court of Rockingham. The foregoing Register was by the Court Compared with the Said Catharine and found duly made a Copy thereof is ordered to be furnished her according to Law done at June Court 1826.
[In the margin] Cop'd.

Sally, No. 99, p. 42:
Registered in my office as No. 99 the 29th day of April 1826 Sally about ... 32 Years old Five Feet 8 1/2 Inches high and rather Spare has a Scar on her forehead and a Small Scar on her Right hand on the upper Joint of the Fourth Finger and a blemish in the right Eye and no other marks perceivable. Said Sally was Emancipated by Ruth Davis by Deed dated the 20th day of March 1826 which is of Record in the County Court of Rockingham. The foregoing Register was by the Court Compared with the Said Sally and found duly made a Copy thereof is ordered to be furnished her according to Law done at June Court 1826.
[In the margin] Cop'd.

Rachael, No. 100, p. 42-43:
Registered in my office as No. 100 the 29th day of April 1826 Rachael about 22 Years old Five Feet 5 Inches high and well Set to her hight has a Scar on the left arm about 1 1/4 Inches and rather a pale Scar no other marks perceivable. Said Rachael was emancipated by Ruth Davis by Deed dated the 20th day of March 1826 which is of Record in the County Court of Rockingham. The foregoing register was Compared with the Said Rachael and found duly made a Copy thereof is ordered to be furnished her according to Law done at June Court 1826.
[In the margin] Cop'd.

George, No. 101, p. 43:

44

Registered in my office as No. 101 the 29th day of April 1826 George about 26 Years old 5 Feet 8 Inches high pretty well Set and has a Scar over his left Eye also under the Same and a Scar Crosswise his left fore Finger below the middle Joint and an other Scar occationed by a Burn on the Right arm a little below the Elbow. The Said George was Emancipated by Ruth Davis by Deed dated 20th March 1826 which is of Record in the County Court of Rockingham. The foregoing Register was by the Court Compared with Said George and found duly made a Copy thereof is ordered to be furnished him according to Law done at June Court 1826. [In the margin] Cop'd.

Robin Hood, No. 102, p. 43:
Registered in my office as No. 102 the 29th day of April 1826 Robin Hood about 48 Years old 5 Feet 2 Inches high and well Set has a mark on the Thumb of the left hand occationed by a Felon and one on the forehead about an Inch long no other mark perceivable. The Said Robin Hood was Emancipated by Ruth Davis by Deed dated the 20th March 1826 which is of Record in the County Court of Rockingham. The foregoing Register was by the Court Compared with the Said Robin Hood and found duly made a Copy thereof is ordered to be furnished him according to Law done at June Court 1826. [In the margin] Cop'd.

Freeborn Garrison, No. 103, p. 44:
Registered in my Office as No. 103 the 2nd day of June 1826 Freeborn Garrison Aged 26 Years 5 Feet 2 Inches high he has a Scar above the right Eye and an other above the left Eye a Scar on the left Cheekbone and a Scar on the back of the left hand and was Born Free as appears by the affidavit of Reubin Thornhill filed in my office. The foregoing Register was by the Court compared with Said Freeborn and found duly made a Copy thereof is ordered

to be furnished him according to Law done at June Court 1826.

Daniel alias Daniel Ransel, No. 104, p. 44:
Registered in my office as No. 104 the 3rd day of July 1826 Daniel (Alias) Daniel Ransel Aged about 22 Years 5 Feet 7 Inches high no marks or Scars perceivable and is Free as appears by the Certificates of T. Kay, Daniel Buzard and George W. Kratzer filed in my office. Daniel is pretty well Set for his hight and a Black man. The foregoing register was by the Court Compared with Said Daniel and found duly made a Copy thereof is ordered to be furnished him according to Law done at July Court 1826.
[In the margin] Copy Delivered the 25th of July 1826 to self by L.W.G.

John Givins, No. 105, p. 44:
Registered in my Office as No. 105 the 24th day of July 1826 John Givins a Free Man of Colour of Dark Complection aged 21 Years on the 13th day of April 1826 and 5 Feet 9 Inches high has a Slight Scar on Joint Bone of the Right Wrist also a Small Scar on the Uper part on the back of the Right hand and a Scar on the Fourth Finger of the left hand and a Small and Slight Scar on the Cheek bone under the left Eye and was emancipated by James Givins on the 14th day of October 1818 as appears by the Records of my Office. The foregoing Register was by the Court Compared with Said John and found duly made a Copy thereof is ordered to be furnished him according to Law done at September Court 1826.
[In the margin] Copy Delivered the 7th of Sept'r 1826 by L.W.G.

George Colley, No. 106, p. 45:
Registered in my office as No. 106 the 29th day of July 1826 George Colley a Free Mulatto Man of Tolerable bright Complection aged about

46

22 Years and Five Feet 7 1/2 Inches high he
has a Slight Scar on the Joint of the first
Finger of the left hand and no other marks or
Scars perceivable. Said George was Free Born
as appears by the Records in my office. The
foregoing Register was by the Court Compared
with Said George and found duly made a Copy
thereof is ordered to be furnished him
according to Law done at August Court 1826.
[In the margin] Copy Del'd to self the 23rd of
Nov. 1831 by L.W.G.

Abraham Colly, No. 107, p. 45:
Registered in my office as No. 107 the 29th
day of July 1826 Abraham Colly a Free Mulatto
Man of Bright Complection aged about 21 Years
and Five Feet 7 1/4 Inches high and has a Scar
on the upper lip to the left of his Nose a
Scar on the middle Joint of the little Finger
of the left hand which occations it to be a
little Crooked no other marks or Scars
perceivable and was Free Born as appears by
the Records of my office. The foregoing
Register was by the Court Compared with the
Said Abraham and found duly made a Copy
thereof is ordered to be furnished him
according to Law done at August Court 1826.
[In the margin] Copy Delivered to self the
13th of March 1830 by L.W.G. New Copy deliv'd
the 18 May 1837 by order the Court Febr'y
1837.

Noah Colly, No. 108, p. 45:
Registered in my Office as No. 108 the 29th
day of July 1826 Noah Colly a Free Mulatto Man
of rather Dark Complection aged about 20 years
and Five Feet 8 3/4 Inches high and has a
Small Scar on the upper Joint of the Thumb of
the left hand and a Small Scar above the upper
Joint of the fore Finger of the Right Hand no
other marks or Scars perceivable and was Free
Born as appears by the Records of my office.
The foregoing Register was by the Court

Compared with Said Noah and found duly made a Copy thereof is ordered to be furnished him according to Law done at August Court 1826. [In the margin] ReRegistered 3rd Feb'y 1832 as No. 155.

Betsy Colly, No. 109, p. 46:
Registered in my office as No. 109 the 29th day of July 1826 Betsy Colly a Bright Mulatto Girl aged about 18 years and Five Feet 4 Inches high has a Scar obliquely a Cross the Right hand Commencing above the Joint of the fore Finger and ending above and over the middle Finger a Small Scar on or near the upper Joint of the Right Thumb the end of the fore Finger of the Right hand injured by a Fellon no other marks or Scars perceivable and was Free Born as appears by the records of my office. The foregoing Register was by the Court Compared with the Said Betsy and found duly made a Copy thereof is ordered to be furnished her according to Law done at August Court 1826.

Isaac Harrison, No. 110, p. 46:
Registered in my office as No. 110 the 2nd day of August 1826 Isaac Harrison a Dark Mulatto Man about 23 years of Age and Five Feet 9 Inches high and has a Mole on the Right Cheek Bone and a Small Scar on the left Nostril a Small Scar between the little Finger & Fourth Finger of the left hand no other marks perceivable and was Emancipatedd by the Will of John Harrison Deceas'd as appears by the Records of my office. The foregoing Register was by the Court Compared with the Said Isaac Harrison and found duly made a Copy thereof is ordered to be furnished him according to Law done at August Court 1826. [In the margin] Cop'd & del the 6th day of August 1826.

Nelly Hackley, No. 111, p. 46-47:

48

Registered in my office as No. 111 the 21st day of October 1826 Nelly Hackley the Wife of James Hackley (a Yellow Woman about Thirty Years of Age Five Feet Three Inches high and has Three Scars one on the Breast one on the left Shoulder and one under the Chin and was Born free as appears by the Certificate of the Clerk of the County Court of Culpeper filed in my office.

Levi Lewis, No. 112, p. 47:
Rockingham County to wit,
Reregistered in my office according to Law on the 2nd day of December in the year 1826 and Numbered 112 Levi Lewis a very dark Mulatto Man about five feet ten inches high, about thirty four years of age No perticular scar or mark about him except that his right arm appears to be stiff, occasioned by its having been broke, was free born, and is a black smith to trade he was first Registered in this office the 18 August 1813 and entered in the office of Frederick County on the 10th August 1821 as appears by the Certificate of James Keith Clerk of that Court filed in my office. [In the margin] Cop'd deliv'd 2 Dec. 1826.

Peggy Jones, No. 113, p. 47:
Registered in my office according to Law on the 5th day of January 1827 and Numbered 113 Peggy Jones a Very dark Mulatto Woman Five Feet Three Inches high about Thirty Four Years of Age and has a Small Scar above the Right Eye and an other Small Scar a Cross the Nose Immediately between his Eyes and a Small Scar on the Right Cheek Bone. Said Peggy Jones was Emancipated by the last Will and Testament of Mrs. Elizabeth Baker as appears by the Records of my office. The foregoing Register was by the Court Compared with the Said Peggy Jones and found duly made a Copy thereof is ordered to be furnished her according to Law done at Febru'y Court 1827.

[In the margin] Cop'd & del. the 10th day of
Feb'y 1827.

Elvira Cross, No. 114, p. 47:
Registered in my office according to Law on
the 10th day of February 1827 and Numbered 114
Elvira Cross a Mulatto Woman Five Feet Three
Inches high about Thirty One Years of Age and
has a Small Scar on her forehead and an other
on her underlip. Said Elvira Cross was Free
Born as appears by the Affidavit of Caleb
Francis filed in my office. The foregoing
Register was by the Court Compared with the
Said Elvira Cross and found duly made a Copy
thereof is ordered to be furnished her
according to Law done at February Court 1827.
[In the margin] Cop'd.

Ford, No. 115, p. 48:
Registered in my office as No. 115 the 17th
day of July 1827 Ford a Mulatto Man aged about
35 or 36 Year and Five Feet 6 Inches high and
pretty well Set for his height and has a Scar
occationed by a Burn on the upper part of his
breast and has no other marks or Scars
perceivable and was Emancipated by the Will of
the late Jacob Bare Deceas'd which will is of
Record in my office & bears date the 17 April
1827. The foregoing Register was by the Court
Compared with the Said Ford and found duly
made a Copy thereof is ordered to be furnished
him according to Law done at August Court
1827.
[In the margin] Cop'd & del'd self the 17
August 1827 by H.J.G.

Dicey, No. 116, p. 48:
Registered in my office as No. 116 the 6th day
of August 1827 Dicey a Black Woman about 24 or
25 Years of Age Five Feet 5 1/2 Inches high
the Fingers on both her Hand[s] inclined to be
crooked with a Scar above his right Breast and
has no other marks perceivable and was

Emancipated by the Will of the late Jacob Bear
Deceas'd which Will is of Record in my office
& bears date 17 April 1827. The foregoing
Register was by the Court Compared with the
Said Dicey and found duly made a Copy thereof
is ordered to be furnished her according to
Law done at August Court 1827.
[In the margin] del'd to Ford her Husband 17
August 1827 H.J.G.

Sam, No. 117, p. 48-49:
Registered in my office as No. 117 the 3rd day
of August 1827 Sam a Black Man about 31 Years
of Age Five Feet 11 Inches high and rather
Slender made for his Hight has a Small Scar on
the Right Arm about 2 Inches from the Crook or
bint thereof below the Elbow a Small Scar on
the Face near to & on the Right Side of the
Right Nostril and an other between the Chin &
underlip about half an Inch ling and has no
other marks or Scars perceivable and was
Emancipated by the Will of the John Brock
Deceas'd which Will is of Record in my office
& bears date 4th day of April 1827. The
foregoing Register was by the Court Compared
with the Said Sam and found duly made a Copy
thereof is ordered to be furnished him
according to Law done at October Court 1827.
[In the margin] Cop'd & del. 17th Nov'r 1827.

Stephen Adams, No. 118, p. 49:
Registered in my office as No. 118 the 29th
day of September 1827 Stephen Adams a Mulatto
Man 22 Years of Age the 4th day of June 1827
and Five Feet 9 & a 1/2 Inches high. The
Third Finger of the Right hand has been Cut of
[sic] or nearly so and Sewed on (which is
perceivable) and a Small Scar over the left
Eye and was Free Born as appears by the
affidavit of Doctor Joseph Cravins filed in my
office. The foregoing Register was by the
Court Compared with the Said Stephen Adams and
found duly made a Copy thereof is ordered to

be furnished him according to Law done at November Court 1827.
[In the margin] Copy deliv'd to self on the 27th day of July 1835 D.H.G.

Betsey Boswell, No. 119, p. 49:
Registered in my office as No. 119 the 2nd day of October 1827 Betsey Boswell a light Black Woman about 45 Years of age and Five Feet 2 & a 1/2 Inches high and has a Small Scar or mark on the left Side a little above the Jaw bone occationed by a Bile and a very pale Scar on the left arm about 2 Inches above the bent of the Arm and about one Inch in length has no other marks or Scars perceivable and was Emancipated by her Husband James Boswell (a Man of Colour) as appears by the Records of my office. The foregoing register was by the Court Compared with the Said Betsey Boswell and found duly made a Copy thereof is ordered to be furnished her according to Law done at October Court 1827.

Jacob Spangler, No. 120, p. 49-50: [This entry was apparently withdrawn or rejected. It was deleted. The number (No. 120) was never re-assigned.]
Registered in my office as No. 120 the 27th day of October 1827 Jacob Spangler a Black Man about 44 Years Old Five Feet 7 & 3/4 Inches high and well Set for his hight he has a Scar on the Thumb of the left hand an[d] an other under the Right Eye about 3/4 of an Inch long and was Emancipated by Cuthbert H. Spangler as appears by the Records of my office. The foregoing Register was by the Court Compared with the Said Jacob Spangler and found duly made a Copy thereof is ordered to be furnished him according to Law done at ...

Polly Lewis, No. 121, p. 50: [This entry was deleted.]
Rockingham County To Wit on the 26th day of

52

October 1827 Polly Lewis filed in my office a Certificate of Register granted her by the Court of Hustings for the Town & Corporation of Fredericksburg Which is in the Words and figures following:
Virginia Set, No. 50
In pursuance of an Act of Assembly entitled an Act for regulating the police of Towns in this Commonwealth and to restrain the practice of Negroes going at large I Robert Smith Chew Clerk of the Court of Hustings for the Town and Corporation of Fredericksburg do hereby Certify that Polly Lewis a Mulatto Woman Aged Thirty Five Years 5 Feet 1 Inch high who was Born Free is Registered in my office agreeable to the directions of the above recited Act Certified this 9th day of June 1820 under my hand and the Seal of the Said Corporation.
R.S. Chew C.C.H.F.
Attest   Cla.   Wigglesworth   one   of   the Magistrates in the Town of Fredericksburg.
Cla. Wigglesworth

Polly Lewis, No. 121, p. 50:
Registered in my Office as No. 121 the 27th day of October 1827 Polly Lewis a Mulatto Woman 42 or 3 Years of Age 5 Feet 1 Inch high and was Free Born as appears by her former Register and Certificate of Robert Smith Chew Clerk of the Court of Hustings for the Town & Corporation of Fredericksburg Filed in my office. The foregoing register was found duly made by the Court and copy thereof is ordered to be furnished her according to Law done at November Court 1827.

James Hite, No. 122, p. 51:
Rockingham County to wit
Registered in my office as No. 122 the 1st day of March 1828 James Hite (a free Negroe) about 31 years of age, a very black man, 5 feet 6 1/2 inches high, has no mark or scare in face has a scare on the right hand near the rist,

he has a large flat nose, appears by the papers filed in my office to have been emancipated by William Dalton of Augusta County but was bound to serve untill he was 31 years of age. The foregoing Register was duly examined & compared by [sic] the said Hite by the court and found duly made and a copy thereof ordered to be furnished said Hite--done at March Court 1828.

Lucy, No. 123, p. 51:
Rockingham County to wit
Registered in my office the 1st April 1828 as No. 123 Lucy a Dark Mulatto about 30 years of age, 5 feet 5 inches high, two small scar on the left rist, the end of little finger appears to be split, she was set free by the will of David Laird deceas'd which [is] of Record in my office. The foregoing Register was duly examined & compared with the said Lucy by the Court and found duly made, and a copy thereof ordered to be furnished her done at April Court 1828.
[In the margin] Copy Delivered to the 12th of January 1829 by L.W.G.

Abbigal, No. 124, p. 51:
Rockingham County to wit
Registered in my office as No. 124 April 1st 1828 Abbigal a bright Mulatto about five feet 5 inches high, about 28 years of age, cross eyed, a small scare on the left arm just above the rist was set free by the will of David Laird, of Record in my office. The foregoing Register was duly made, a copy thereof is ordered to be delivered her, done at April Court 1828.
[In the margin] Copy Delivered the 20th of January 1829 by L.W.G.

Moses, No. 125, p. 51-52:
Rockingham County to wit
Registered in my office as No. 125 April 1st

1828, Moses a Dark Mulatto about 5 feet 3 1/2 inches high about 44 years of age, his right leg shorter than the other which occasions him to walk lame, a small scare on the chin & a small one in the left corner of his mouth, set free by the will of David Laird dec'd of Record in my office. The foregoing Register was duly examined & compared with the Moses and found duly made a copy thereof is ordered to be delivered him, done at April Court 1828. [In the margin] Copy Deliv'd the 12th of January 1829 by L.W.G.

Isaac, No. 126, p. 52:
Rockingham County to wit
Registered in my office as No. 126 1st April 1828 Isaac a Dark Mulatto about 5 feet 9 inches high about 28 years of age, a scar on the back of the right hand and a small one Just at the large rist boan of the left arm, the Little [finger] on the left hand is stiff, was set free by the will of David Laird dec'd Recorded in my office. The foregoing Register was examined and compared with the said Isaac and found duly made a copy is ordered to be delivered him, done at April Court 1828. [In the margin] Copy Del'd Isaac 10 October 1828.

Moses, No. 127, p. 52:
Rockingham County To Wit
Registered in my office as No. 127 on 25 April 1828 Moses a Black Man 5 Feet 7 Inches high and 44 Years of Age and has a Small Scar on the left arm about 3 Inches above the Wrist and nearly round about 1/2 an Inch in diameter and an other Scar on the right arm about 7 Inches above the Wrist on the inside of the arm and about one Inch long and was emancipated by a Deed dated the 5 March 1828 by William Ralston which is of Record in my office. The foregoing Register was by the Court compared with Said Moses and found duly

55

made a Copy thereof is ordered to be furnished him according to Law done at June Court 1828. [In the margin] Cop'd & ...

Rose, No. _____, p. 52-53:
The following Register was this day presented to me Clerk of Rockingham and entered according to Law to wit
Augusta County Court Clerks Office To wit (No. 70)
Rose a Mulatto Woman about Thirty Six Years of Age Five Feet five Inches high bushy hair and very black Eyes was Emancipated by John Poindexter of Louisa County as appears by the Certificate of the Clerk of the Said County dated the 12th day of November 1811 and now registered in this office.
Witness my hand with the Seal of the Court affixed the 15th day of November 1823 in the 48th Year of the Commonwealth of Virginia
Vincent Tapp D.C.A.C.
Atteste W. Boys, a Justice of the peace. The foregoing Register was presented to me Clerk of s'd County and duly entered, and certificate given the said Rose May 13, 1828.
Attest H.J. Gambill
[In the margin] entered & ... 13 May 1828.

Moses McWilliams, No. 128, p. 53:
Rockingham County to wit
Registered in my office as No. 128 on the 3rd day of June 1828 Moses McWilliams a free Man of Colour about 52 years of age 5 feet 6 inches high, Very black, a large scare a cross the right Wrist (above the bone) no other scare or mark perceavable, was emancipated by Sam'l McWilliams by Deed dated the 20 February 1816 of Record in my said County. The foregoing Register was by the Court compared with the said Moses and found duly made, a Copy thereof is ordered to be furnished him according to Law done at June Court 1828.
[In the margin] Copy delivered the 21st of

July 1828 By L.W.G.

Robert Bullet, No. 129, p. 53:
Rockingham County To Wit
Registered in my office as No. 129 the 5th day
of August 1828 Robert Bullet a Free Man of
Colour about 36 or 37 Years of Age and 5 Feet
10 Inches high his Colour very Black a Scar on
the left Thumb between the middle & upper
Joints of the Same. Also a Scar above the
upper Joint of the Same Thumb and rather
crosswise the hand no other Scars or Marks
perceivable and was emancipated by the Will of
the late Peter Higgins Deceas'd which Will is
of Record in my Said County and bears date the
17th day of September 1808. The foregoing
Register was by the Court Compared with the
Said Robert and found duly made a Copy thereof
is ordered to be furnished him according to
Law done at August Court 1828.
[In the margin] Cop'd & del'd self 9 Aug't
1828.

Henry Bullet, No. 130, p. 54:
Rockingham County To Wit
Registered in my office as No. 130 the 6th day
of August 1828 Henry Bullet a Free Man of
Colour about 32 Years of Age Five Feet Seven &
1/4 Inches high and his Colour a dark Black he
has a Small Scar on the little Finger of the
left hand between the middle and lower Joint
of the Same, and he has Also lost a part of
the Middle toe of the Right Foot Said Henry
was Emancipated by the Will of the late Peter
Higgins Deceas'd Which Will is of Record in my
Said County and bears date the 17th day of
September 1808. The foregoing Register was by
the Court Compared with Said Henry and found
duly made a Copy thereof is ordered to be
furnished him according to Law done at August
Court 1828.
[In the margin] Cop'd & Sent to J.D.W. 9
August 1828.

<u>William Bullet</u>, No. 131, p. 54:
Rockingham County To Wit
Registered in my office as No. 131 the 6th day
of August 1828 William Bullet a Free Man of
Colour about 34 Years of Age 5 Feet 8 1/4
Inches high his Colour Dark black he has a
Small Scar on the lower Joint of the little
Finger of the left hand and has also a Scar on
the middle Finger above the middle Joint of
the Same and a Mark on the Fourth Finger above
the Middle Joint all on the Same hand a Small
Scar on Ball of the Thumb of the Right hand
Said William was ... Emancipated by the Will
of the late Peter Higgins Deceas'd Which Will
is of Record in my Said County and bears date
the 17th day of September 1808. The foregoing
Register was by the Court Compared with the
Said William and found duly made a Copy
thereof is ordered to be furnished him
according to Law done at August Court 1828.
[In the margin] Cop'd & Sent to J.D.W. 9 Aug't
1828.

<u>Barney Young</u>, No. 132, p. 55:
Rockingham County To wit
Registered in my office as No. 132 the 22nd
day of August 1828 Barney Young a Free man of
Colour about 55 years of age. Five feet five
Inches high and his Colour a dark Black he has
no marks perceivable and was emancipated by
William Young of Augusta County on the 24th
day of June 1805 as appears by a copy of the
said Bill of Emancipation filed in my office.
The foregoing register was by the Court
compared with the said Barney and found duly
made a Copy thereof is ordered to be furnished
him according to Law done at September Court
1828.

<u>Lewis Bird</u>, No. 133, p. 55:
Rockingham County To Wit
Registered in my office as No. 133 the 7th day
of October 1828 Lewis Bird a Free Man of

Colour about 47 Years of Age and 5 Feet 7 & a
1/2 Inches high and is a Mulatto and has a
Scar on the end of the Finger Next the little
Finger and no other marks perceivable and was
Free Born as appears by the Affidavit of
Thomas Hord & Nathaniel Hord filed in my
office. The foregoing Register was by the
Court Compared with the Said Lewis Bird and
found duly made a Copy thereof is ordered to
be furnished him according to Law done at
November Court 1849.
[In the margin] Cop'd & del'd to self Nov'r 19
1849 J.E.C.

Rosana Green, No. 134, p. 55:
Rockingham County To Wit
Registered in my office as No. 134 the 1st day
of Decb'r 1828 Rosana Green a Free Mulatto
Woman about 43 or 44 Years of Age and 5 Feet 5
Inches high and has a Small Scar on the lower
Joint of the little Finger of the left hand,
and has also on the left arm above the Elbow a
mark occationed by Inoculation and has no
other marks perceivable and was Free Born as
appears by the affidavit of Henry Brown filed
in my office. The foregoing Register was by
the Court Compared with the Said Rosana Green
and found duly made a Copy thereof is ordered
to be furnished her according to Law done at
Decbr Court 1828.
Copy Delv'd husband the 5 Decr 1828.

Sam'l Green, No. 135, p. 56:
Rockingham County To Wit
Registered in my office as No. 135 the 1st day
of Decbr 1828 Sam'l Green a Dark Mulatto Man
[deleted: "and not of Bright Colour and"]
about 19 Years of Age and Five Feet 8 Inches
high and has a Small Scar on the left hand
above upper Joint of the Fore Finger, Scar on
the left arm below the Elbow occationed by a
Burn a Scar near his left Ear and was Free
Born as appears by the affidavit of James

59

Fulton filed in my office. The foregoing
Register was by the Court Compared with the
Said Samuel Green and found duly made a Copy
thereof is ordered to be furnished him
according to Law done at Decbr Court 1828.
[In the margin] Copy Delv'd to his father the
5 Dec. 1828.

Elizabeth Litt, formerly Green, No. 136,
p. 56:
Rockingham County To Wit
Registered in my office as No. 136 the 1st day
of Decbr 1828 Elizabeth Litt formerly Green A
Mulatto Woman about 23 Years of Age and Five
Feet 2 1/4 Inches high and has a Scar on the
upper Joint of the Fore Finger on the left
hand and a Very pale Scar on underpart of the
left arm occationed by a Burn also a Scar near
the Nose on the right Side and below the Eye
no other marks perceivable and was Free Born
as appears by the affidavit of William Bird
filed in my office the foregoing Register was
by the Court Compared with the Said Elizabeth
Litt and found duly made a Copy thereof is
ordered to be furnished her according to Law
done at Decb'r Court 1828.
[In the margin] Delivered by order of Court
Oct. 27, 1854 W.D.T.

Reubin Green, No. 137, p. 56:
Rockingham County To Wit
Registered in my office as No. 137 the 1st day
of Decbr 1828 Reubin Green A Mulatto Man about
17 Years of Age and Five Feet 4 1/4 Inches
high and has a Scar on the Upper part of the
Breast rather on the Collar Bone on the left
Side of the Th[r]ought [sic] and has also a
Scar over Two Inches, partly on the left Jaw
and partly on the neck on the left Side
thereof no other marks perceivable and was
Free Born as appears by the affidavit of James
Fulton Filed in my office the foregoing
Register was by the Court Compared with the

Said Reubin and found duly made a Copy thereof
is ordered to be furnished him according to
Law done at Decby Court 1828.
[In the margin] Copy Delv'd to father the 5
Dec'r 1828.

Jerry Bryan, No. 138, p. 57:
Rockingham County To Wit
Registered in my office as No. 138 the 6th day
of February 1829 Jerry Bryan a Black Man about
22 or 23 Years of age and Six Feet high and
has a Scar over the left Eye about one Inch
long and Cross wise his Forehead and also a
Scar on the Joint of the Thumb of the left
hand and was Free Born as appears by the
affidavit of John Crummey filed in my office.
The foregoing Register was by the Court
Compared with the Said Jerry Bryan and found
duly made a Copy thereof is ordered to be
furnished him according to Law done at
February Court 1829.
[In the margin] Copied & delivered the 5th of
June 1829. [See No. 285, p. 107.]

Jorden Cross, No. 139, p. 57:
Rockingham County To Wit
Registered in my office as No. 139 the 4th day
of May 1829 Jorden Cross a Black Man about 21
Years of Age and Five Feet 8 & a 1/4 Inches
high and has a Scar on the left Sid[e] of his
Nose occationed by a burn and an other Scar on
the Wrist of the Right Arm which was also
occationed by a Burn and was Free Born as
appears by the affidavit of Caleb Francis
filed in my office the foregoing Register was
by the Court Compared with the Said Jordon
[sic] Cross and found duly made a Copy thereof
is ordered to be furnished according to Law at
July Court 1829.
[In the margin] Cop'd & del. to J. Cross the
6th July 1829 by L.W.G.

Isaac Harrison, No. 140, p. 57:

Rockingham County to wit
Registered in my office as No. 140 the 26th day of February 1830 Isaac Harrison a Black Man between 48 & 49 years of age about 6 feet high and has a Scar in his fore head and an other on the wrist of the Right Arm and set free by deed of Emancipation from Reuben Harrison, William Bryan & Richard Custer Recorded in my office the foregoing Register was by the Court Compared with the said Isaac Harrison and found duly made a Copy thereof is ordered to be furnished him according to Law done at _____ Court 1830.

William Hite, No. 141, p. 58:
Rockingham County To Wit
Registered in my Office as No. 141 the 5th day of April 1830 William Hite Twenty Two Years of Age in March last. William Hite is a Black Man Five Feet Six Inches in hight and has a Scar on the upper lip rather on the right Side of the Mouth a Scar on the right Wrist and on the upper part of the Same and a Scar on the Breast occationed by a Burn and was Emancipated by Peachey Harrison Esq'r by Deed Recorded in my office and bears date 20th February 1830 the foregoing Register was by the Court Compared with the Said William Hite and found duly made a Copy thereof is ordered to be furnished him according to Law done at June Court 1830.
[In the margin] Copy delv'd to W. Hite the 18 April 1833 by H.J.G.

John Hite, No. 142, p. 58:
Rockingham County to wit
Registered in my Office as No. 142 the 6th day of April 1830 John Hite Sixty three years of age a Black Man Five feet five Inches in height his Fingers on the right hand Crooked and was set free by the will of his Late wife Lear Hite Deceased which is of Record in My Office the foregoing Register was by the Court

62

Compared with the said John Hite and found duly made a Copy thereof is ordered to be furnished him according to Law done at April Court 1830.

Daniel Hughs, No. 143, p. 58:
Rockingham County to wit
Registered in my office as No. 143 the 23rd day of August 1830 Daniel Hughs about 23 years of age a Black Man Six Feet one Inch high a scar on his left Thumb and also a scar on the little finger of his left hand and was free born as appears by the affidavit of Edward H. Smith Filed in my office the foregoing Register was by the Court Compared with the said Daniel Hughs and found duly made a copy thereof is ordered to be furnished him according to Law done at September Court 1830. [In the margin] Copied & ...

Essex Burks, No. 144, p. 59:
Rockingham County to wit
Registered in my office as No. 144 the 28th day of February 1831 Essex Burks about 58 years of age a Black Man Five Feet Two Inches high a Scar on the fore finger of the left hand and was emancipated by Isaac Burk by Deed of Emancipation proven in Court on this day. The foregoing Register was by the Court Compared with the said Essex and found duly made a Copy thereof is ordered to be furnished him according to Law done at March Court 1831. [In the margin] Copied & delivered the 20 Jan'y 1832.

Christian Harrison, No. 145, p. 59:
Rockingham County to wit
Registered in my office as No. 145 the 3rd day of August 1831 Christian Harrison 21 years of age on the 3rd day of April last A Mulatto Man Five feet Ten Inches high with two small scars one on the left Cheek and the other on the back of the left hand Free Born and was bound

63

by the Overseers of the Poor of Rockingham
County as appears by Indenture filed in my
office. The foregoing Register was by the
Court Compared with the said Christian and
found duly made a Copy thereof is ordered to
be furnished him according to Law done at
August Court 1831.
[In the margin] Copied & ...

Absolim Alistock, No. 146, p. 59:
Rockingham County To Wit
Registered in my office as No. 146 the 5th day
of September 1831 Absolim Alistock 51 years of
Age (A Mulatto Man) and Six Feet high and has
a Small Scar on his Forehead and a Scar a
Cross the Knuckles of the Right hand and was
Free Born as appears by the affidavit of Mary
Davis filed in my office. The foregoing
Register was by the Court Compared with the
Said Absolim Alistock and found duly made a
Copy thereof is ordered to be furnished him
according to Law done at September Court 1831.

Sally Alistock, No. 147, p. 60:
Rockingham County To Wit
Registered in my office as No. 147 the 5th day
of September 1831 Sally Alistock a Mulatto
Woman 50 Years of Age and 5 Feet 5 1/2 Inches
high and has had the left wrist broke and the
little finger on the Right hand Crooked and
was Free Born as appears by the affidavit of
Mary Davis filed in my office. The foregoing
Register was by the Court Compared with the
Said Sally Alistock and found duly made a Copy
thereof is ordered to be furnished her
according to Law--done at September Court
1831.

Fielding, No. 148, p. 60:
Rockingham County To Wit
Registered in my office as No. 148 the 4th day
of October 1831 Fielding a Black Man 37 Years
of Age and 5 Feet 2 3/4 Inches high and Well

Set to his Hight and has a Small lump on the
upper Joint of the Thumb of his right hand and
the little Finger of the left hand is Stiff
from the Middle Joint down with a Scar from
the right Corner of the Mouth down to the Chin
and a Small Scar on the Forehead above the
right Eye and was Emancipated by Joseph Mauzy
Esq'r as appears by the Records of my office.
The foregoing Register was by the Court
Compared with the Said Fielding and found duly
made a Copy thereof is ordered to be furnished
him according to Law--Done at October Court
1831.
[In the margin] Cop'd & Del'd to Fielding 4th
Octo. 1831.

Peggy Gibson, No. 149, p. 60:
Rockingham County to wit
Registered in my office as No. 149 the 24th
day of October 1831 Peggy Gibson a Mulatto
Woman 31 years of age last May and Five Feet
Six Inches high and has no scars or marks
perceivable and was Free Born as appears by
the affidavit of Joseph Cravens filed in my
office. The foregoing register was by the
Court Compared with the said Peggy and found
duly made a Copy thereof is ordered to be
furnished her according to Law Done at March
Court 1832.
[In the margin] Cop'd & del'd to ...

Elinor [Smith], No. 150, p. 61:
Rockingham County To Wit
Registered in my office as No. 150 the 29th
day of October 1831 Elinor (the Daughter of
Patty Smith who was Emancipated by James
Smith) and by the Oath of Dianah Smith which
is filed in my office the Said Elinor is
proved to be up[w]ards of 25 Years of Age, and
Five Feet Four and Three quarter Inches high
and of a Copper Colour and has a Small Pit
like that of the Small Pox on the Right Side
of the Nose nearly under the Center of the Eye

65

and no other mark perceavable. The foregoing Register was by the Court Compared with the Said Elinor and found duly made a Copy thereof is ordered to be furnished her according to Law done at November Court 1831.
[In the margin] Copied & delivered to self the 12th Novr 1831.

Jacob Spangler, No. 151, p. 61:
Rockingham County To Wit
Registered in my Office as No. 151 the 26th day of December 1831 Jacob Spangler a Black Man (and by Trade a Black Smith) about 48 Years of Age & Five Feet 7 & 3/4 Inches high and well Set for his hight, he has a Scar on the Thumb of his left hand and an other under the Right Eye about 3/4 of an Inch long, Said Jacob was Emancipated by Cuthbert H. Spangler on 16th day of February 1825 and Recorded in my office. The foregoing Register was by the Court Compared with the Said Jacob Spangler and found duly made a Copy thereof is ordered to be furnished him according to Law done at _____ Court.

Patty Smith, No. 152, pp. 61-62:
Rockingham County To Wit
Registered in my office as No. 152 the 30th day of December 1831 Patty Smith about 46 Years of Age and Five Feet Eight and a Half Inches high and of a Copper Colour and has lost a part of the Bone out of the end of the Thumb of the Right hand occationed by what is called a Bone Fellon and no other mark perceivable and was Emancipated by James Smith by his Bill of Emancipation bearing date the 20th Day of December 1803 and Recorded in my office. The foregoing Register was by the Court Compared with the Said Patty Smith and found duly made a Copy thereof is ordered to be furnished her according to Law done at January Court 1832.
[In the margin] Copied & delivered to self the

66

13th of January 1832.

Thompson Tyree, No. 153, p. 62:
Rockingham County To Wit
Registered in my office as No. 153 the 2nd day
of January 1832 Thompson Tyree free Negroe
about 22 years of age five feet 8 inches high,
dark complexion, two scars on his forehead one
on his right arm, all which appears by a
Register of the said Thompson Tyree taken by
the Clerk of Albemarle County on the 7th day
of June 1830 which Register by which it also
appears that he is free is filed in my office.
The foregoing Register was by the Coutrt
Compared with the Said Thompson Tyree and
found duly made a Copy thereof is ordered to
be furnished him according to Law done at
January Court 1832.
[In the margin] Copy delv'd to Thompson 7 June
1832 by H.J.G.

Martin Cauly, No. 154, p. 62:
Rockingham County To Wit
Registered in my office as No. 154 the 27th
day of January 1832 Martin Cauly (a free
Negroe) about 62 years of age five feet 7 1/2
inches high has a small scar on his left cheek
bone is a bright Mulatto, black eyes, and is
very gray, was born free as appears by
evidence filed in my office. The foregoing
register was by the court compared with the
said Martin and found duly made a copy thereof
is ordered to be furnished him according to
Law done at February Court 1832.
[In the margin] Copied & delivered to Self the
...

Noah Colly, No. 155, p. 62:
Rockingham County To Wit
Registered in my Office as No. 155 the 3rd day
of February 1832 Noah Colly (a Free [deleted:
"Negroe"] Mulatto) Aged about 26 Years and
Five Nine & 3/4 Inches high and has a Small

67

Scar on the upper Joint of the Thumb of the
left hand and a Small Scar above the upper
Joint of the forefinger of the right hand no
other marks or Scars perceivable and was Free
born as appears by the Records of my office.
The foregoing Register was by the Court
Compared with the Said Noah and found duly
made a Copy thereof is ordered to be furnished
him according to Law done at Febr'y Court
1832.
[In the margin] Copied & delivered to self
10th Febr'y 1832 L.W.G.

William Bundy alias William Lewis, No.
156, p. 63:
Rockingham County To Wit
Registered in my office as No. 156 the 3rd day
of February 1832 William Bundy (Alias William
Lewis) a Free Mulato Man of rather dark
Complection about 22 or 23 years of Age and
Five Feet Six Inches high and has a Scar on
the forefinger of the left hand between the
middle and upper Joints of the Same and which
Scar also extends across Said finger to the
middle finger and has a lump on the Joint of
the elbow of the left arm which is out of
Joint at this time no other marks perceivable
Said William is a Free Man as appears by the
Affidavit of George Clarke Esq'r filed in my
office.   The foregoing Register was by the
Court Compared with Said Wm. Bundy and found
duly made a Copy thereof is ordered to be
furnished him according to Law done at April
Court 1832.
[In the margin] Copied & delivered to Bundy
the 2 July 1832 H.J.G.

Augustus, No. 157, p. 63:
Rockingham County To Wit
Registered in my office as No. 157 the 4th day
of February 1832 Augustus a very Black Man
about 22 or 23 years of Age and Five Feet
Seven and a 1/4 Inches in hight and was Free

Born as appears by the affidavit of Archibald
Hopkins filed in my office. Augustus has a
Small Scar on the left Side of the head about
an Inch from his Eye and a Small Scar on the
forehead over the Right Eye and a large scar
Just below the elbow on the left arm and no
other marks perceivable. The foregoing
Register was by the Court Compared with the
Said Augustus and found duly made a Copy
thereof is ordered to be furnished him
according to Law done at February Court 1832.
(See Page 121)
[In the margin] Copy Delivered to self 10th
Febr'y 1832 L.W.G.

Malinda, No. 158, p. 63:
Rockingham County To Wit
Registered in my office as No. 158 the 4th day
of February 1832 Malinda a Black Woman 23 or
24 Years of Age and Five Feet and One Fourth
of an Inch high and was Free Born as appears
by the affidavit of Archibald Hopkins filed in
my office. Malinda's Right Shoulder is
disjointed or out of place and a small scar
over the right Eye and no other mark or Scar
perceivable. The foregoing Register was by
the Court Compared with Said Malinda and found
duly made a Copy thereof is ordered to be
furnished her according to Law done at
February Court 1832.
[In the margin] Copy & delivered to self the
25 of Febr'y 1832 L.W.G.

Maria, No. 159, p. 64:
Rockingham County To Wit
Registered in my office as No. 159 the 4th day
of February 1832 Maria a Black Woman 20 or 21
years of Age and Five Feet Four Inches high
and was Free Born as appears by the affidavit
of Archibald Hopkins filed in my office.
Maria has a Small Scar on the left arm about
Two Inches above the Wrist and no other marks
or Scars perceivable. The foregoing Register

was by the Court Compared with Said Maria and found duly made a Copy thereof is ordered to be furnished her according to Law done at Feb'y Court 1832.
[In the margin] Copy Delivered to self the 5th of May 1832 L.W.G.

Esther alias Esther Hopkins, No. 160, p. 64:
Rockingham County To Wit
ReRegistered in my office as No. 160 the 4th day of February 1832 Esther Commonly Called Esther Hopkins a Black Woman Said to be 41 Years of Age in March last (and was Free Born) and Five Feet Three Inches high. The end of the little Finger of the left hand appears to have been Split She says with a Sickle and no other Scars perceivable. The foregoing Register was by the Court compared with the Said Esther and found duly made a Copy thereof is ordered to be furnished her according to Law done at March Court 1832.
[In the margin] Copied & deliv'd to ...

John Holman, No. 161, p. 64:
Rockingham County To Wit
Registered in my office as No. 161 the 9th day of February 1832 John Holman a Black Man between 21 & 22 years of Age and was Free Born as appears by the affidavit of William J. Smith filed in my office, and 5 Feet 8 Inches high and has a Slight Scar on the forefinger of the left hand between the middle and upper Joints of the Same and a Slight Scar on upper part of the Right hand on the back of the Same and a Scar on his Chin. The foregoing Register was by the Court Compared with the Said John and found duly made a Copy thereof is ordered to be furnished him according to Law done at February Court 1832.
[In the margin] Copied & delv'd to self the 5th of June 1832 L.W.G.

Rebecca Allen alias Rebecca Holman, No.
162, pp. 64-65:
Rockingham County To Wit
Registered in my office as No. 162 the 9th day
of February 1832 Rebecca Allen alias Holman
aged 32 years in September last and was Born
Free as appears by the affidavit of Dinah
Allen filed in my office. Said Rebecca is 5
Feet 7 Inches and 3/4 of an Inch high and a
Black Woman and has a Small Mole under her
Right Eye and one larger on the Right Side of
her Nose [and] a Small Scar on the back of
each of her Rists occationed by a Knife. The
foregoing Register was by the Court Compared
with Said Rebecca and found duly made a Copy
thereof is ordered to be furnished her
according to Law done at February Court 1832.
[In the margin] Cop'd & delv'd self 21 July
1838 by H.J.G.

Hannah Airtrip, No. 163, p. 65:
Rockingham County To Wit
Registered in my office as No. 163 the 9th day
of February 1832 Hannah Airtrip a Mulatto
Woman about 45 or 46 Years of Age and 5 Feet 3
Inches high and has a Scar on the back of the
left hand and a Slight Scar near the upper
Jo[i]nt of the Thumb of the Same hand and also
an other Slight Scar near the upper Joint of
the Right hand and a Slight Scar on the left
Side of her face no other marks perceivable
and is Registered on the proof of her Freedom
by Abraham Strickler made in open Court. The
foregoing Register was compared by the Court
with Said Hannah and found duly made a Copy
thereof is ordered to be furnished her
according to Law done at February Court 1832.
[In the margin] Cop'd & delv'd to self the 15
September 1834 H.J.G.

Hannah Fortuna, No. 164, p. 65:
Rockingham County to wit
Registered in my office as No. 164 Hannah

Fortuna 11th February 1832 a black Woman about five feet 4 1/2 inches high, with 2 large scars on the right arm, one Joint of the forefinger of the left hand off which makes it smaller than the other occasioned by a fellon, was free born as appears by satisfactory evidence filed in my office. The foregoing Register was compared by the court with the said Hannah and found duly made a copy thereof is ordered to be delivered her in the manner prescribed by Law done at March Court 1832. [In the margin] Copied & delivered to self the 20th of March 1832.

Lucinda Belcher, No. 165, p. 65:
Rockingham County to wit
Registered in my office as No. 165 the 11th day of February 1832 Lucinda Belcher a Dark Mulatto about 18 years of age five feet 2 1/2 inches high, with a small scar on the left arm and a small black Mole on the left Cheak, was born free as appears by satisfactory evidence filed in my office. The foregoing Register was by the court compared with the said Lucinda and duly made a copy thereof is ordered to be delivered her in the manner prescribed by Law done at March Court 1832. [In the margin] Copied & delivered to self the 5th of May 1832 L.W.G.

Patsy Belcher, No. 166, p. 66:
Rockingham County to wit
Registered in my office as No. 166 Patsy Belcher 11th February 1832 a very Dark Mulatto Woman inclining to be black, about 20 years old 5 feet 6 inches high has a remarkable large scar on the left side of her Neck Just below the ear, also a small scar on the forehead, was born free as appears by satisfactory evidence filed in my office. The foregoing Register was by the Court compared with the said Patsy and found duly made a copy thereof is ordered to be furnished her in the

manner prescribed by Law, done at March Court
1832.
[In the margin] Cop'd & delivered to self the
24th of March 1832 L.W.G.

Rebeccah Belcher, No. 167, p. 66:
Rockingham County to wit
Registered in my office as No. 167 11th of
February 1832 Rebeccah Belcher a Dark Mulatto
Woman about 21 years of age, five feet high,
with a small scar in her forehead Nearly
between her eyes, she inclin[e]s to be thick,
no other scar or Mark discovered, was born
free as appears by satisfactory evidence filed
in my office. The foregoing Register was by
the court compared with the said Rebecah
[sic], and found duly made, a copy thereof is
ordered to be furnished her in the manner
prescribed by Law, done at March Court 1832.
[In the margin] Copied & delivered to self the
20th of March 1832 L.W.G.

Zachariah, No. 168, p. 66:
Rockingham County to wit
Registered in my office as No. 168 11th of
February 1832 Zachariah a very black man,
about 16 years of age, five feet 10 inches
high a handsome boy, has a small scar on the
back of his right hand near the rist, a large
scar on his left arm, with several whitish
looking spots on his face occasioned as he
says by a ringworm,--was born free as appears
by satisfactory evidence filed in my office.
The foregoing register was by the court
compared with the said Zachariah and found
duly made a copy thereof is ordered to be
furnished him in the manner directed by Law,
done at March Court 1832.
[In the margin] Cop'd & delv'd to self the
24th of March 1831 L.W.G.

Sally Peters formerly Sally Fortuna, No.
169, pp. 66-67:

Rockingham County to wit
Registered in my office as No. 169 11th of
February 1832 Sally Peters formerly Sally
Fortuna, a very black woman, about 43 years of
age, about 5 feet 2 1/2 inches high, has a
small scar on her left cheak, and a small mole
on the left side of her nose and some small
scars on both hands, was born free being the
Daughter of a free woman as appears by
satisfactory evidence. The foregoing Register
was by the court compared with the said Sally
and found duly made a copy thereof is ordered
to be furnished her in the manner directed by
Law, done at March Court 1832.
[In the margin] Cop'd & delv'd to ...

Stephen Adams, No. 170, p. 67:
Rockingham County to wit
Registered in my office as No. 170 the 28th
day of February 1832 Stephen Adams a Mulatto
Man 27 years of age on the 4th day of June
Next Five Feet Nine Inches high the third
Finger of the right hand has been cut off or
nearly so and Sewed on (which is perceivable)
and a small scar over the left Eye and was
Free Born as appears by the affidavit of
Doctor Joseph Cravens filed in my office. The
foregoing register was by the Court comparted
with the said Stephen Adams and found duly
made a Copy thereof is ordered to be furnished
him according to Law done at March Court 1832.
[In the margin] Cop'd & delv'd to ...

Freeborn Garrison, No. 171, p. 67:
Rockingham County to wit
Registered in my office as No. 171 the 28th of
February 1832 Freeborn Garrison a black Man
Aged about 32 years old Five Feet 2 Inches
high he has a scar above the right Eye and an
other above the left Eye a Scar on the left
Cheek bone and a scar on the back of the left
hand and was Free Born as appears by the
affidavit of Reuben Thornhill filed in my

office. The foregoing register was by the
Court Compared with the said Freeborn Garrison
and found duly made a Copy thereof is ordered
to be furnished him according to Law done at
March Court 1832.
[In the margin] Cop'd & delv'd to ...

    Fanny Artrip, No. 172, p. 67:
Rockingham County to wit
Registered in my office as No. 172 the 1st day
of March 1832 Fanny Artrip Daughter of Hannah
Artrip about 23 years of age 5 feet 2 1/2
Inches high has a small scar on the right hand
near where the thumb Joins the hand, a bright
Mulatto rather handsome no other scars or
marks perceivable and was Free Born as appears
by the affidavit of Sally Michael filed in my
office. The foregoing register was by the
Court Compared with the said Fanny Airtrip
[sic] and found duly made a Copy thereof is
ordered to be furnished her according to Law
done at March Court 1832.
[In the margin] Cop'd & delv'd to Jno. Rush
Jr. 15 Sept'r 1834 H.J.G.

    Maria Artrip, No. 173, p. 68:
Rockingham County to wit
Registered in my office as No. 173 the 1st day
of March 1832 Maria Artrip Daughter of Hannah
Artrip Between 21 & 22 years of age 5 feet 1
1/2 Inches high has a Large Scar on her breast
occasioned by a burn Two Small scars on the
back of her left hand also a small one on the
back of the right hand a Bright Mulatto and
was free Born as appears by the affidavit of
Sally Michael filed in my office. The
foregoing register was by the Court Compared
with the said Maria Artrip and found duly made
a Copy thereof is ordered to be furnished her
according to Law done at March 1832.
[In the margin] Cop'd & delv'd to ...

    William Webb, No. 174, p. 68:

75

Rockingham County to wit
Registered in my office as No. 174 The 13th
day of March 1832 William Webb A Black Man
Between 21 and 22 years of age 6 feet 1 Inch
high has a small scar on his nose between his
Eyes and a scar on his Chin also a scar on the
little finger of the right hand and a scar on
the left wrist and walks lame occasioned by
his loosing the first Joint off of each big
toe and was free Born as appears by Evidence
filed in my office. The foregoing register
was by the Court Compared with the said
William Webb and found duly made a Copy
thereof is ordered to be furnished him
according to Law done at March Court 1832.
[In the margin] Cop'd & delv'd to ...

Barbary Pence, No. 175, p. 68:
Rockingham County to wit
Registered in my office as No. 175 the 16th
day of March 1832 Barbary Pence A Bright
Mulatto Woman 37 years of age 5 feet 5 1/2
Inches High the little finger on the right
hand Stiff a small scar on her Chin also a
small scar on the little finger of the left
hand Free Born Daughter of Patty Adams. The
foregoing register was by the Court Compared
with the said Barbary Pence and found duly
made a Copy thereof is ordered to be furnished
her according to Law done at March Court 1832.
[In the margin] Cop'd & delv'd to ...

Nancy alias Nancy Hopkins, No. 176, p.
69:
Rockingham County to wit
Registered in my office as No. 176 the 20th
day of March 1832 Nancy Commonly Called Nancy
Hopkins a Black Woman about 48 years of age
about 5 feet 3 1/2 Inches high has a scar over
her right Eye and a scar on the Knuckle of the
middle finger of the right hand was born free
but bound to serve a certain Number of years
as appears by the Records of my said County.

76

The Foregoing register was by the Court Compared with the said Nancy Hopkins and found duly made a Copy thereof is ordered to be furnished her according to Law done at April Court 1832.
[In the margin] Copied & Delivered to self the 18th of April 1832 L.W.G.

Lewis Byrd, No. ____, p. 69: [Deleted from the register with no explanation.]
In the Clerks office of the County Court of Rockingham March 22nd 1832, This day Lewis Byrd presented to me Clerk of said County the following Register, to wit No. 85. Lewis Byrd about 38 years old a light Mulatto with short bushy hair a dark mark extending from the top extremity of the Nose next the forehead, along the right side, & some distance a cross the right Cheek, occasioned by the stroke of a Switch--also another scar, occasioned by a Warte on the end of the fourth finger of the right hand--his eyes a light blue or grey--five feet seven & a quarter inches high--born free & registered in my office this 9th day of August 1819. Stafford County Court August the 9th 1819. The ...

Delilah Morris, No. 177, p. 69:
Rockingham County to wit
Registered in my office as No. 177 the 27th day of March 1832 Delilah Morris formerly Delilah Peters a Dark Mulatto about 25 years of age 5 feet 1 Inch high has a small scar on the right side of the Neck and a scar on the Knuckle of the middle finger of the left hand Free Born as appears by Evidence filed in my office. The foregoing Register was by the Court Compared with the said Delilah Morris and found Duly made a Copy thereof is ordered to be furnished her according to Law done at April Court 1832.
[In the margin] Copied & delivered to self the 28 Nov. 1834 H.J.G.

77

<u>Lucinda Peters</u>, No. 178, p. 70:
Rockingham County to wit
Registered in my office as No. 178 the 27th
day of March 1832 Lucinda Peters a Black Girl
Between 23 & 24 years of age Five Feet 1 1/2
Inches high has a scar on her forehead and one
on her Chin and a large scar on the right
wrist Free Born as appears by Evidence filed
in my office. The foregoing register was by
the Court compared with the said Lucinda
Peters and found duly made a Copy thereof is
ordered to be furnished her according to Law
done at April Court 1832.
[In the margin] Copied & delivered to ...

<u>Joshua Peters Jr.</u>, No. 179, p. 70:
Rockingham County to wit
Registered in my office as No. 179 the 27th
day of March 1832 Joshua Peters Jr. a Black
Man Between 22 & 23 years of age Five feet 3
Inches high has a scar on the right Cheek and
one on the left Cheek and a large scar on the
breast and a scar on the back of the right
hand and on the right wrist and Two on the
left wrist Free Born as appears by the
affidavit of John Crumney filed in my office.
The foregoing register was by the Court
compared with the said Joshua Peters Jr. and
found duly made a Copy thereof is ordered to
be furnished him according to Law done at
April Court 1832.
[In the margin] Copied & delivered to self.
And March Court 1835 another Copy Delivered
him by order of the Court.

<u>Jessee Parrott alias Jessee Dunken</u>, No.
180, p. 70:
Rockingham County to wit
Registered in my office as No. 180 the 14th
day of April 1832 Jessee Parrott alias Dunken
about 34 years of age a Very black Man about 5
feet 11 1/2 Inches high, a large Nose rather
inclined to be flat, his mouth rather

78

prominant, has a small scar on the inside of
his left rist, Just where it Joins the hand[,]
his Chin an[d] necke, very full of what is
call'd currage bumps, was set free by Jehue
Guin executor of Jacob Parrott deceas'd by
Deed dated the 19th day of March 1832 and
Recorded in my office. The foregoing register
was by the Court compared with the said Jessee
and found duly made a copy thereof is ordered
to be furnished him according to Law, done at
April Court 1832.
[In the margin] Copied & delivered to ...

Isaac Brock, No. 181, p. 71:
Rockingham County to wit
Registered in my office as No. 181 The 23rd
day of April 1832 Isaac Brock a Black Man 25
years of age 5 feet 7 1/2 Inches high a small
scar on the back of the right hand and also a
small a scar on the Knuckle of the forefinger
of the same hand and a large scar on the
little finger of the same hand and a scar on
the Knuckle of the forefinger of the left hand
and one or two small scars on his forehead and
a noose on the right side of his face and was
emancipated by the will of John Brock deceased
which is of Record in my office. The
Foregoing Register was by the Court compared
with the said Isaac Brock and found duly made
a Copy thereof is ordered to be furnished him
according to Law done at May Court 1832.
[Cop'd & deliv'd to self the 28th of May 1832
L.W.G. At Nov'r Court 1832 the Clerk was
directed to furnish s'd Isaac with a duplicate
register which was done accordingly. The
original being left with the clerk.

John Moore, No. 182, p. 71:
Rockingham County to wit
Registered in my office as No. 182 The 21st
day of May 1832 John Moore a Black Man Between
43 and 44 years of age Five feet Ten Inches
high and has a small scar at the Corner of his

79

right Eye and also a scar on his chin and no
other marks or scars perceivable and was
Emancipated By the Widow and Executor of
Thomas Moore Deceased which is of record in my
office. The foregoing Register was by the
Court Compared with the said John Moore and
found duly made a Copy thereof is ordered to
be furnished him according to Law done at May
Court 1832.
[In the margin] Cop'd & delivered to self the
22nd of May 1832.

Delilah Young, No. 183, p. 71:
Rockingham County to wit
Registered in my office as No. 183 The 23rd
day of May 1832 Delilah Young a Bright Mulatto
Woman 22 years of age Five Feet Three Inches
high and has a small scar or Mark on her neck
and also a scar on the little finger of the
left hand and also one on the right Thumb of
the same hand and also Three scars on the
right arm and one on the right hand and a
blemish on the ball of the right eye and was
Free Born as appears by Evidence filed in my
office. The Foregoing register was by the
Court compared with the Delilah Young and
found duly made a Copy thereof is ordered to
be furnished her according to Law done at May
Court 1832.
[In the margin] deliv'd to self the ...

Isaiah Welch, No. 184, p. 72:
Rockingham County to wit
Registered in my office as No. 184 the 30th
day of May 1832 Isaiah Welch a Dark Mulatto
Man about 34 years of age Five Feet Seven
Inches high and has a small scar on his left
cheek and a scar on the inside of the left
hand or Thumb and was free born as appears by
a Certificate of the County Court of Orange as
filed in my office. The foregoing Register
was by the Court Compared with the said Isaiah
Welch and found Duly made a Copy thereof is

ordered to be furnished him according to Law done at ____ Court 1832.

Harvy Smith alias Harvy Young, No. 185, p. 72:
Rockingham County to wit
Registered in my office as No. 185 the 18 of June 1832 Harvy Smith alias Harvy Young said to be 23 years of age, about 5 feet 7 1/2 inches high a Dark Mulatto, a small scare on the left cheak near the ear, and also a Very small scare on the back of the left hand, a spar man, rather handsome than otherwise, was emancipated by Daniel Smith by Deed dated the 25 day of May 1832, which is of Record in my office. The foregoing Register was by the court compared with the said Harvey [sic] Smith alias Harvy Young and found duly made a copy thereof is ordered to be furnished him, according to Law done at June Court 1832.
[In the margin] Copied & Delivered to self the ...

William Vaughn, No. 186, p. 72:
Rockingham County to wit
Registered in my office as No. 186 the 21st day of August 1832 William Vaughn a Dark Mulatto about 22 years of age Five Feet Seven Inches high and has a small scar over the left Eye Brow and a scar on the Knuckle of the fore finger on right hand and a scar on the little finger of the left hand, and was free born as appears by the affidavit of George Clarke filed in my office. The foregoing register was by the Court Compared with the said William Vaun [sic] and found duly made a Copy thereof is ordered to be furnished him according to Law done at August [Court] 1832.
[In the margin] Cop'd & delv'd 10 Sept'er 1832 [to] self.

Judy, No. 187, p. 73:
Rockingham County to wit

81

Registered in my office as No. 187 the 17th
day of September in the year 1832 Judy a very
Dark Woman about 5 feet one and a half inches
high, about 22 years of age, was born free as
appears by evidence filed in my office, has a
small scare on the elbow of the left arm, and
a small scare on the left hand near where the
Little finger Joins the hand, no other mark
perceivable. The foregoing Register was by
the County Court of Rockingham Compared with
the said Judy and found duly made a copy
thereof is ordered to be furnished her,
according to Law done at ____ Court 1832.
[In the margin] Cop'd and delv'd to Judy 21
Sept'er 1832 by H.J.G.

Lydia, No. 188, p. 73:
Rockingham County to wit
Registered in my office as No. 188 the 17th
day of September in the year 1832, Lydia a
Mulatto Girl about five feet 3 inches high,
about 19 years of age, has a small scare a
cross her Nose (appears to have been a cut)
and also a small scare high up on the rist of
the left arm, dark eyes, she was born free, a
appears by evidence filed in my office. The
foregoing Register was by the Court of the
said County Compared with the said Lydia and
found duly made a copy thereof is ordered to
be furnished her according to Law, done at
Septemnber Court 1832.
[In the margin] Cop'd & delv'd self the 17
September 1832 by H.J.G.

Alferd, No. 189, p. 73:
Rockingham County to wit
Registered in my office as No. 189 the 17
September 1832 Alferd a Dark Mulatto man about
25 years of age five feet 7 inches high, has a
scare on the thumb of the left hand and a
scare in the palm of the same hand, and has
also two scars on the forehead, one very small
about the center an[d] the other on the right

side of the forehead, above the temple, he was emancipated by James Walters by Deed Recorded in my office. The foregoing Register was by the Court of said County Compared with the said Alferd and found duly made a copy thereof is ordered to be furnished him according to Law, Done at September Court 1832.
[In the margin] Cop'd & delv'd self 17 September 1832 by H.J.G.

William Airtrip, No. 190, p. 73:
Rockingham County to wit
Registered in my office as No. 190 the 24 September 1832 William Airtrip, a son of Hannah Airtrip, who says he is about 25 years of age, a very Dark Mulatto, five feet 7 1/2 inches high, has a scare on the little finger of the left hand, appears to be a cut, he has also a scare on the inner part of the left leg below the calf, he has no other scare, he is a handsome face boy, he was born free, being the child of a free Woman, as appears by satisfactory evidence filed in my office. The foregoing Register was by the Court of said County Compared with said William and found duly made a copy thereof is ordered to be furnished him according to Law, done at October Court 1832.
[In the margin] Copied & delivered to self the 20th of Oct'ber 1832 L.W.G. Renwd Feb'y of 1861 & copy delv'd.

William Brock, No. 191, p. 74:
Rockingham County to wit
Registered in my office as No. 191 the 16th day of April 1833 William Brock A Black Man about 25 years of age Five Feet 7 1/2 Inches high and has a scar on the forefinger of the right hand and one on the middle finger of the Same hand and one on the Knuckle of the forefinger of the same hand and a scar on the Palm of the left hand and a scar on the little finger of the Same hand and was emancipated by

83

the Will of John Brock Deceased which is of
Record in my Office. The foregoing Register
was by the Court Compared with the said
William Brock and found duly made and a Copy
thereof is ordered to be furnished him
according to Law done at April Court 1833.
[In the margin] Cop'd & Delv'd self 1st July
1834.

Fritz, No. 192, p. 74:
Rockingham County to wit
Registered in my office as No. 192 the 16th
day of April 1833 Fritz A Mulatto Man ...
Between Forty Five and 50 years of age Five
Feet Six Inches high and has Two Scars on the
back of the right hand and was emancipated by
Andrew Lags by Deed of Emancipation bearing
the date the 15th of April 1833 and of Record
in my office. The foregoing Register was by
the Court Compared with the said Fritz and
found duly made and a Copy thereof is ordered
to be furnished him according to Law done at
April Court 1833.
[In the margin] Copy Delv'd to the s'd Fritz
16 April 1833.

Robert Hoover, No. 193, p. 74:
Rockingham County to wit
Registered in my office as No. 193 the 20th
day of May 1833 Robert Hoover a Black Man
about 33 years of age Five feet Six Inches
high and has a long scar on the left Cheek &
Two Scars one on the right Tumb and one on the
left and was emancipated by the will of John
Hoover which is of Record in my office his
freedom to be by said will on the 1st of
January 1833. The foregoing register was by
the Court Compared with the said Robert Hoover
and found duly made and a Copy thereof is
ordered to be furnished him according to Law
done at May Court 1833.
[In the margin] Copy delv'd Robert 27 May
1833.

84

Matilda Moore, No. 194, p. 75:
Rockingham County to wit
Registered in my office as No. 194 the 15th
day of July 1833 Matilda Moore A Black Girl
about 24 years of age Five Feet Four Inches
high and has a Scar on her right Cheek and one
on the back of the left hand and was
Emancipated by the will of Thomas Moore
Deceased which is of record in my office. The
Foregoing register was by the Court Compared
with the said Matilda Moore and found duly
made and a Copy thereof is ordered to be
furnished her according to Law done at July
Court 1833.
[In the margin] Cop'd & ...

Rachael Moore, No. 195, p. 75:
Rockingham County to wit
Registered in my office as No. 195 the 15th
day of July 1833 Rachael Moore a Black Woman
Between 35 and 36 years of age about 5 feet
high and has a small scar on her forehead and
a scar on the right arm Just above the wrist
and was emancipated by the will of Thomas
Moore Deceased which is of Record in my
office. The foregoing Register was by the
Court Compared with the said Rachael Moore and
found duly made and a Copy thereof is ordered
to be furnished her according to Law done at
July Court 1833.
[In the margin] Cop'd & ...

Alexander Moore, No. 196, p. 75:
Rockingham County to wit
Registered in my office as No. 196 the 15th
day of July 1833 Alexander Moore a Black Man
Between 51 and 52 years of age 5 Feet 5 1/2
Inches high and has a scar on his Forehead
Just above the left Eye and one on his Chin
and a scar on the left wrist and Two on the
back of the left hand and the little finger of
the left hand Stiff and has had his right arm
broke and was emancipated by the will of

Thomas Moore Deceased which is of Record in my office. The foregoing Register was [by] the Court Compared with the said Alexander Moore and found duly made and a Copy thereof is ordered to be furnished him according to Law done at July Court 1833.
[In the margin] Cop'd & delivered to self the 11th of April 1835 L.W.G.

Archibald, No. 197, p. 76:
Rockingham County to wit
Registered in my office as No. 197 the 21st day of August 1833 Archibald a free boy of Colour about 21 or 22 years of age, he is Dark Mulatto, five feet 10 inches high, has a scar on the left cheak Near the corner of his Mouth, also a scar on the chin, and a scar on the Middle finger of the left hand, and one on the Knuckle of the forefinger of the same hand, was free born, and bound an apprentice by the overseers of the poor, as appears by his indenture filed in my office. The foregoing Register was by the Court Compared with the said Archibald and found duly made a Copy thereof is ordered to be furnished said Archibald as the Law direts, done at August Court 1833.
[In the margin] Cop'd & delivered to self on the 22nd of Aug't 1833 by L.W.G.

Sevena, No. 198, p. 76:
Rockingham County to wit
Registered in my office as No. 198 the 1st day of October 1833 Sevena a very dark Mulatto (Nearly a black woman) about 5 feet 7 1/2 inches high, has a small scare on the right side of her Neck, occasioned by a burn, no other mark perceavable, she is a straight handsom woman, said to be 26 years of age last Chrismas, was born free as appears by the affidavit of Peachy H. McWilliams filed in my office. The foregoing register was by the Court Compared with the said Sevena and found

86

duly made a copy thereof is ordered to be
furnished said Sevena as the Law direts done
at March Court 1834 [1833 was corrected to
1834].
[In the margin] Cop'd & delv'd to s'd Sevena
the 15 Nov'ber 1845 by H.J.G.

Armstead alias Armstead Gardner, No. 199,
p. 76:
Rockingham County to wit
Registered in my office as No. 199 the 21st
day of October 1833 Armstead alias Armstead
Gardner about 50 years of age A Black Man 5
feet 7 Inches high and has a scar on the right
side of his Nose and a scar on the third
finger of the left hand and one on the Knuckle
of the forefinger of the right hand and was
Emancipated by Henry Bear by deed bearing date
the 16th of May 1833 and of record in my
office. The foregoing register was by the
County Court Compared with the said Armstead
and found duly made a Copy thereof is ordered
to be furnished said Armstead as the Law
directs at October Court 1833.
[In the margin] Copied & delivered to self
L.W.G.

Zachariah McCoy, No. 200, p. 77:
Rockingham County to wit
Registered in my office as No. 200 the 18th
day of November 1833 Zachariah McCoy A Mulatto
Man 22 years of age the 2nd day of December
Next Five feet Eight and a half Inches high
and has a small scar near the Corner of the
right Eye and the little finger of the left
hand Crooked occasioned by a Cut and was free
born as appears by the Certificate of Thomas
Buck who was formerly and [sic] Overseer of
the Poor for said County and also by the
affidavit of Henry Martz to whom the said
Zachariah was bound which Certificate and
affidavit is filed in my office. The
foregoing Register was by the Court Compared

87

with the said Zachariah McCoy and found duly
made a Copy thereof is ordered to be furnished
the said Zachariah as the Law directs done at
November Court 1833.
[In the margin] Copied & delivered to Self the
19th of Nov'er 1833 L.W.G. [See No. 284, p.
106.]

Abraham Jackson, No. 201, p. 77:
Rockingham County to wit
Registered in my office as No. 201 the 18th
day of February 1834 Abraham Jackson A Black
Man 30 years of age Five Feet Six Inches high
and has three Scars on the back of the right
hand and one on the Knuckle of the forefinger
of the left hand occasioned by a Cut and was
emancipated by the will of Philip Koontz
Deceased which is of Record in my office. The
foregoing Register was by the Court Compared
with the said Abraham Jackson and found duly
made a Copy thereof is ordered to be furnished
the [said] Abraham as the law directs done at
February Court 1834.
[In the margin] Cop'd & deliv'd to Abraham the
4 Dec'r 1834 by H.J.G.

Jessee, No. 202, pp. 77-78:
Rockingham County to wit
Registered in my office as No. 202 the 18th of
April 1834 Jessee a very Black Man about 29 or
30 years of age 6 feet 1 inch high, several
small scars on his ... right hand, a cut on
the four finger of the left hand, and also a
cut on the rist of the left arm, a strigh[t]
good looking man, he was emancipated by Deed
of Record in the Clerks office of the county
Court of Rockingham, which deed bears date the
_____ day Mar'h 1834. The foregoing register
was by the court compared with the said Jessee
and found duly made a copy thereof is ordered
to be furnished him as the Law direts at April
Court 1834.
[In the margin] Cop'd & deliv'd to Jessee 22

April 1834 by H.J.G.

   Adam, No. 203, p. 78:
Rockingham County to wit
Registered in my Office as No. 203 the 25 day
of August 1834 Adam a Very black Man about 5
feet 7 inches high, has a white speck near the
Center of the right eye, which causes him to
be nearly blind of that eye (so he says), his
little finger on the left hand is crooked
occasioned by a cut near the Joint, the toes
of both feet are crooked, perticularly those
on the left foot and it appears that the
little toe on that foot has been turned, and
has Grown to the side of the foot, he is said
to be about 40 years of age, was emancipated
by Jno. Carpenter by Deed dated the 18 August
1834 and Recorded in the Clerks office of said
County. The foregoing register was compared
by the Court with the said Adam and found duly
made a copy thereof is ordered to be furnished
the said Adam as the Law direts done at
Septem. Court 1834.
[Cop'd & deliv'd to Jno. Carpenter for Adam
the 20 Sept'er 1834 by H.J.G.

   Necy Lewis, No. 204, p. 78:
Rockingham County to wit
Registered in my office as No. 204 the 3rd of
September 1834 Necy Lewis a Daughter of Milly
Lewis a dark Mulatto about 25 years of old
[sic] in June last, five feet 4 1/2 inches
high has a small black mole on the right side
of her Neck and a small scare on the rist of
the right arm near the ... hand, was born
free, as appears by a certificate of freedom
filed in my office. The foregoing register
was compared by the court with the said Necy
and found duly made, a copy thereof is ordered
to be furnished the said Necy as the Law
direts done at Sept'er Court 1834.
[In the margin] Cop'd & delv'd self the 20
Sept'er 1834 by H.J.G.

<u>Darkey Lewis</u>, No. 205, pp. 78-79:
Rockingham County to wit
Registered in my office as No. 205 the 3rd of
September 1834 Darkey Lewis a light Mulatto
between 16 and 17 years of age has a small
scare on the right hand Just above where the
Thumb Joins the hand, no other scare or mark
perceavable was born free as appears [by] a
certificate of freedom filed in my office.
The foregoing Register was compared by the
court with the said Darkey and found duly
made, a copy thereof is ordered to be
furnished the said Darkey as the Law dirts,
done at September Court 1834.
[In the margin] Cop'd & delv'd self the 20
Sept'ber 1834 by H.J.G.

<u>George Harrison</u>, No. 206, p. 79:
Rockingham County to wit
Registered in my Office as No. 206 the 6th of
September 1834, George Harrison, a Dark
Mulatto Near 22 years of age about 5 feet 2
1/2 Inches high, has a cut Near the end of the
3rd finger on the right hand, also a scare on
the first finger of the right hand, a very
large cut on the calf of the right leg, has
two small black moles on each side of his
Nose, large Nostrels, was born free as appears
from evidence on record in my office. The
foregoing register was compared with the said
George and found duly made a copy thereof is
ordered to be furnished the said George as the
Law directs, done at September Court 1934.
[In the margin] Cop'd & Delivered to self on
the 19th Sept'r 1834 by H.J.G.

<u>Allen Colley</u>, No. 207, p. 79:
Rockingham County to wit
Registered in my Office as No. 207 the 14th
day of September 1834, Allen Colley (a
Mulatto) about 23 years of age about five feet
4 1/2 inches high has a large scare on the
back of the left hand, has also a small scare

90

on the first Joint of the fore finger of the
right hand, has also a black mole between the
eyes. Rather a handsome face with large
Nostrels, was born free, as appears from
evidence filed in my office. The foregoing
Register was compared with the said Allen &
found duly made a copy thereof is ordered to
be furnished the said Allen as the Law
directs, done at September Court 1834.
[In the margin] Cop'd & delv'd self the 15
Sept. 1834 by H.J.G.

Stapleton Airtrip, No. 208, p. 79:
Rockingham County to wit
Registered in my office as No. 208 the 15th
day of September 1834 Stapleton Airtrip, a
dark Mulatto, about 22 years of age, 5 feet 4
inches high, a scar in the palm of the left
hand, has a small mole or tit on the left side
of his face near the ear, also a small mole on
the Chin, he is rather a handsome boy man, was
born free, as appears by proper evidence
thereof filed in my office. The foregoing
Register was compared with the said Stapleton
and found duly made a copy thereof is ordered
to be furnished the said Stapleton as the Law
directs, done at September Court 1834.
[In the margin] Cop'd & delv'd self the 20
Sept'er 1834 by H.J.G.

Nancy Dungan, No. 209, p. 80:
Rockingham County to wit
Registered in my office as No. 209 the 15th
September 1834 Nancy Dungan dark Mulatto about
44 years of age, five feet two Inches High, a
scar on the upper joint of the right arm and a
scar on the wrist of the right arm, was
emancipated by John Sellars of the County of
Rockingham in the State of Virginia as appears
by his Deed of Emancipation recorded in this
Court and filed in my office. The foregoing
Register was compared by the Court with the
said Nancy and found duly made a copy thereof

is ordered to be furnished to the said Nancy as the Law directs, done at September Court 1834.
[In the margin] Cop'd & delv'd self the 25 Sept'er 1834 by H.J.G. Fee paid.

Willoughby Greenby, No. 210, p. 80:
Rockingham County to wit
Registered in my office as No. 210 the 1st day of October 1834 Willoughby Greenby at this time about 42 years of age 5 feet 6 inches high, a very black man, has a large Scare on the back of the right hand occasioned by a burn (as he says), has also a scare on the forehead, a dent in the Chin, was born free as appears by satisfactory evidence filed in my office. The foregoing Register was compared by the Court with the said Willoughby and found duly made a copy thereof is ordered to be furnished the said Willoughby as the Law direts done at October Court 1834.
[In the margin] Cop'd & delv'd to Greenby the 18 October 1834.

George Byrd, No. 211, p. 80:
Rockingham County to wit
Registered in my office as No. 211 the 8th day of October 1834 George Byrd supposed to be about 37 years of age, 5 feet 11 inches high a very dark Mulatto, has a large mark or scare a cross his breast & small one above the first also a small scare between his eye brows he was born free as appears by satisfactory evidence filed in my office. The foregoing register was compared with the said George and found duly made a copy thereof is ordered to be furnished him as the Law direts done at October Court 1834.
[In the margin] Cop'd and delv'd self the 28 October 1834.

Jerry Moore, No. 212, p. 81:
Rockingham County to wit

92

Registered in my office as No. 212 the 3rd day
of October 1834 Jerry Moore, supposed to be 53
years of age, 5 feet 4 1/2 inches high a very
dark Mulatto, has a scare on the side of his
left cheek bone also a small scare on the fore
finger of the right hand above the first
Joint, also a scare on the little finger of
the left hand, he was emancipated by Deed
recorded in my office, dated the 20th day of
October 1834.   The foregoing Register was
compared by the court with the said Jerry and
found duly made a copy thereof is ordered to
be furnished him as the Law direts done at
November Court 1834.
[In the margin] Delv'd to self 28 August 1834.

Daniel Hurley, No. 213, p. 81:
Rockingham County to wit
Registered in my office as No. 213 the 17th of
November 1834 Daniel Hurley about 21 or 22
years of age 6 feet and one half inch high, a
Dark Mulatto has a large scare on the right
cheak bone a scare on the breast, also on[e]
on the thumb of the left hand (appears to be a
cut) he was born free as appears by
satisfactory evidence filed in my office. The
foregoing Register was compared by the Court
with the said Daniel and found duly made a[nd]
a copy thereof is ordered to be furnished the
said Daniel as the Law direts done at November
Court 1834.
[In the margin] Copy delv'd to self 12 Sept'er
1835 by H.J.G.

George, No. 214, p. 81:
Rockingham County to wit
Registered in my office as No. 214 the 19th of
November 1834 George a free Negroe, about 50
years of age, a black man 5 feet 8 inches
high, a little pock marked, a small scare over
the left eye, a little Grey, no other marks
perceavable, who was emancipated by George W.
Piper Jr. by Deed dated the _____ day of 1834

93

of record in my office. The foregoing
Register was compared by the court with the
said George and found duly made a copy thereof
is ordered to be furnished him as the Law
direts done at December Court 1834.

Abraham Lowderbery, No. 215, pp. 81-82:
Rockingham County to wit
Registered in my office as No. 215 the 24th
day of November 1834 Abraham Lowderbery a Dark
or black man, about 5 feet 1 1/2 inches high,
a small scare on the forehead, he is a black
Smith to trade, and has several small scars on
his hands, he says he is about 39 years of
age, was set free by James Magell Sr. (the
elder) by his Last will of Record in my
office. The foregoing Register was by the
court compared with the said Abraham and found
duly made a copy thereof is ordered to be
furnished him as the Law direts done December
at Court 1834.

Isaac Lowderbery, No. 216, p. 82:
Rockingham County to wit
Registered in my office as No. 216 the 24th
day of November 1834 Isaac Lowderbery a Dark
or black man about 36 or 37 years of age,
about 5 feet 5 1/4 inches high, a tolerable
large scare on the back of the left hand,
sevel small bumps on his face, and also
several small scars on his hands occasioned by
burning, he being a black Smith, he was set
free by James Magell the Elder dec'd by his
Last will of Record in my office. The
foregoing Register was compared with the said
Isaac and found duly made a copy thereof is
ordered to be furnished him as the Law direts,
done at December Court 1834.

Patsey Gilmore, No. 217, p. 82:
Rockingham County to wit
Registered in my office as No. 217 the 15th
day of January 1835 Patsey Gilmore a Mulatto

Woman about 33 or 34 years of age Five feet
four Inches high and has a small scar on the
Left Arm in the bend of the arm and also a
mole on her Chin and was set free by Mary P.
Gilmore by deed of Emancipation which is of
Record in my office which deed also includes
her 3 children Ann, Milly, & Jessee. The
foregoing Register was compared with the said
Patsey Gilmore and found duly made a Copy
thereof is ordered to be furnished her as the
Law directs done at January Court 1835.
[In the margin] Copy delv'd to said Patsy
[sic] the 23 Jan'y 1835 by H.J.G.

William Hackley, No. 218, p. 82:
Rockingham County to wit
Registered in my office as No. 218 the 14th
day of January 1835 William Hackley a Dark
Mulatto man about 24 years of age Five feet
Five Inches high and has a scar on the left
side of his neck Just under the ear and also a
scar on the left wrist and was free Born as
appears by the affidavit of Mildred Wollidge
filed in my office. The foregoing register
was compared with the said William Hackley and
found duly made a Copy thereof is ordered to
be furnished him as the Law directs done at
February Court 1835.
[In the margin] Cop'd & delv'd to Hackly [sic]
the 18 April 1835 H.J.G.

John Hackley, No. 219, p. 83:
Rockingham County to wit
Registered in my office as No. 219 the 4th day
of March 1835 John Hackley a Dark Mulatto man
about 27 years of age Five feet Ten Inchesd
high and has a scar in the right Eye Brow and
one near the Corner of the left Eye and also a
scar on the left Cheek near his mouth and also
a scar on the Wright [sic] wrist and was free
born as appears by the affidavit of Mildred
Wollidge filed in my office. The foregoing
register was compared with the said John

95

Hackley and found duly made a Copy thereoof is ordered to be furnished him as the Law directs done at March Court 1835.
[In the margin] Copy delivered to self the 3rd of August 1835 L.W.G.

John Coffman, No. 220, p. 83:
Rockingham County to wit
Registered in my office as No. 220 the 14th day of March 1835 John Coffman A Mulatto man about 21 years of age Five Feet Five Inches high and has a small scar on the left cheek bone and also a scar on the back of the left hand and was free born as appears by his Indenture of apprenticeship filed in my office. The foregoing register was compared with the said John Coffman and found duly made a Copy thereof is ordered to be furnished as the Law directs done at March Court 1835.
[In the margin] Copied and delivered to self the 11th of May 1835 L.W.G.

John Harvey Lewis, No. 221, p. 83:
Rockingham County to wit
Registered in my office as No. 221 the 14th day of March 1835 John Harvey Lewis a Dark Mulatto man about 22 years of age Five Feet Eleven Inches high and has a small scar or dent in his forehead and one on the left cheek and Two scars on the fore finger of the left hand and also a scar on the right Thumb and was free born as appears by satisfactory evidence filed in my office. The foregoing register was compared with the said John Harvey Lewis and found duly made a Copy thereof is ordered to be furnished him as the Law directs done at August Court 1835.
[In the margin] Copied & delivered to self the 18th of August 1835 L.W.G.

William, No. 222, p. 84:
Rockingham County to wit
Registered in my office as No. 222, the 7th

96

day of September 1835 William, a very Dark
Mulatto man, about 23 years of age, 5 feet 4
1/4 inches high, has a scare in his forehead
Just between his eyes, has also a scare on the
left hand, back and a cross the thumb, a small
piece appears to have been cut off the middle
finger of the right hand, rather a handsome
man, was emancipated by Elizabeth Erwin by
Deed dated the 13th November 1818 and of
Record in the Clerks office of Rockingham
County. The foregoing Register was compared
with the said William and found duly made a
copy thereof is ordered to be furnished him
according to Law, done at September Court
1835.

Milly Vaughn formerly Milly Hackley, No.
223, p. 84:
Rockingham County to wit
Registered in my office as No. 223 the 9th of
September 1835 Milly Vaughn formerly Milly
Hackley 5 feet 2 1/2 inches high about 23
years of age, has a scare over the left eye
near the temple, has a scare on the elbow of
the left arm, and also a mark a cross the
right arm, below the elbow, she was born free
as appears by satisfactory evidence filed in
my office. The foregoing Register was
compared with the said Milly and found duly
made a copy thereof is ordered to be furnished
her according to Law done at September Court
1835.
[In the margin] Cop'd & delv'd Self on the
14th of October 1836 by D. H. Gambill.

John Deck, No. 224, p. 84:
Rockingham County to wit
Registered in my office as No. 224 the 15th
day of September 1835 John Deck A Mulatto Man
Between 21 and 22 years of age Five Feet 6 1/2
Inches high has a scar across the Knuckle of
the fore finger of the left hand and also a
scar on the left side of his nose and was

emancipated by Mathias Doubt Deceased by Deed of Emancipation recorded in my office. The foregoing Register was compared with the said John Deck and found duly made a Copy thereof is ordered to be furnished him according to Law done at September Court 1835.

Mary Hackley, No. 225, p. 85:
Rockingham County to wit
Registered in my office as No. 225 the 21st day of September 1835 Mary Hackley a Daughter of Nelly Hackley about 21 years old, a very Dark Woman, 5 feet 2 inches high, a small scare on the thick part of the right hand, and also black mark on the same hand between the thumb & finger appears to have a mark near the left eye on the cheak bone, was born free as appears by satisfactory evidence filed in my office. The foregoing Register was compared with the said Mary and found duly made a copy thereof is ordered to be furnished her according to Law done at September Court 1835. [In the margin] Copyed & delivered to self on 26th day of October 1836 by D.H.G.

Mary Webb, No. 226, p. 85:
Rockingham County to wit
Registered in my office as No. 226 the 22nd day of December 1835 Mary Webb about 21 years of age a verry Dark Woman 5 feet 5 inches high a small scare on the right side of her Cheak bone and a scare on the left arm above the elbow and also two scares on the right arm and is free born as appears by the satisfactory evidence filed in my office. The foregoing Register was compaired with the said Mary and duly made a Copy thereof is ordered to be furnished her according to Law done at December Court 1835.
[In the margin] Copied & Delivered to self the 27th of May 1845 L.W.G.

Kitty Webb, No. 227, p. 85:

Rockingham County to wit
Registered in my office as No. 227 the 22nd of
December 1835 Kitty Webb about 21 years of age
a verry Darke Woman 5 feet 4 1/2 inches high
has a scare on the left rist she was born free
as appears by satisfactory evidence filed in
my office. The foregoing Register was
compared with the said Kitty and found duly
made a copy thereof is ordered to be furnished
her according to Law done at December Court
1835.
[In the margin] Copyed & ...

<u>James Gorden</u>, No. 228, p. 86:
Rockingham County to wit
Registered in my office as No. 228 the 18
January 1836 James Gorden a free Negroe about
20 years of age, a verry black man about 6
feet & 1/2 inch high, a scare on the right
rist, and a scare on the back of the left
hand, he was emancipated by Annis, Mary,
Sarah, Ruth, & Jane Gorden by Deed dated the
15 December 1835 and Recorded in my office.
The foregoing Register was compared with the
said James and found duly made a copy thereof
is ordered to be furnished him as the Law
directs done at January Court 1836.
[In the margin] Made out & delivered to self.

<u>Isaac Gorden</u>, No. 229, p. 86:
Rockingham County to wit
Registered in my Office as No. 229 the 18
Janu'y 1836 Isaac Gorden a free Negroe about
29 years of age, Very dark or black man, 5
feet 8 1/2 inches high a scare on the left
side of his cheak bone, and two scars on the
left hand one on the inside and the other on
the out side Near the thumb, he was
emancipated by Annis Gorden & Sisters by Deed
dated the 15 December 1835, and Recorded in my
Office. The foregoing Register was compared
with the said Isaac and found duly made a copy
thereof is ordered to be furnished him as the

99

Law direts, done at Janu'y Court 1836.
[In the margin] Made out & delv'ed to self.

William Gorden, No. 230, p. 86:
Rockingham County to wit
Registered in my Office as No. 230 the 18
Janu'y 1836 William Gorden, a free Negroe
about 32 years of age, a Very Darke or black
Man, 5 feet 8 1/4 inches high, has a scare on
his forehead and also one on the right cheak
bone below the eye, and also one on the Out
side of the left rist, he was emancipated by
Annis Gorden & Sisters by Deed dated the 15
December 1835 and Recorded in my Office. The
foregoing Register was compared with the said
William and found duly made, a copy thereof is
ordered to be furnished him as the Law direts,
done at Jan'y Court 1836.
[In the margin] Made out & Delv'ed to self.

Moses Gorden, No. 231, p. 87:
Rockingham County to wit
Registered in my Office as No. 231 the 18
January 1836 Moses Gorden a free Negroe, about
25 years of age, a Very Dark Mulatto, about 5
feet 9 inches high, has a scare on the Left
side of his face near the cheak bone below the
eye, also a scare on the left hand on the back
part thereof, was emancipated by Annis Gorden
& Sisters by Deed dated the 15 December 1835
and Recorded in my Office. The foregoing
Register was compared with the said Moses and
found duly made, a copy thereof is ordered to
be furnished him as the Law direts, done at
Janu'y Court 1836.
[In the margin] Made out & delivered to self.
1851 Jan'y Court new regit ord'd & copy delv'd
to. Age 48 years.

Stephen, No. 232, p. 87:
Rockingham County to wit
Registered in my office as No. 232 the 16th
April 1836 Stephen a free Negroe about 21

years of age a dark Mulatto about 5 feet 7
inches high has a scare on the Left side of
his Cheek and a scare on his right arm above
the elbow occuationed by a burn and was free
born as appears by the evidence filed in my
office. The foregoing Register was compared
with the said Stephen and found duly made, a
copy thereof ordered to be delivered him as
the Law direts done at April Court 1836.
[In the margin] Made out & delivered to
Stephen the 22 Ap'l 1836 by H.J.G.

Julia Cochran, No. 233, p. 87:
Rockingham County to wit
Registered in my office as No. 233 the 2nd
August 1836 Julia Cochran a Dark Mulatto Girl
about 24 years of age, 5 feet 3 1/2 Inch high,
has a scare on forehead, one under her chin,
and one on the first Joint of the forefinger
of the Left hand, a sprightly handsome woman.
She was emancipated by Elizabeth Irvin, by
Deed bearing date the 13 of November 1818
Recorded in the Clerks office of my said
County. The foregoing Register was compared
with the said Julia and found duly made, a
copy thereof ordered to be Delivered her as
the Law direts done at August Court 1836.
[In the margin] Cop'd & delv'd self the 20 Jun
1840 H.J.G.

Ann Hackley, No. 234, pp. 87-88:
Rockingham County to wit
Registered in my office as No. 234 the 10th
August 1836 Ann Hackley, a light Mulatto
Woman, about 27 years of age (as she says),
five feet 3 3/4 inches high, has a remarkable
scare on her right breast & small one on her
forehead, she was born free as appears by
satisfactory evidence filed in my office. The
foregoing Register was compared with the said
Ann, and found duly made, a copy thereof is
ordered to be furnished her as the Law direts,
done at August Court 1836.

[In the margin] Cop'd & delv'd self on the 7th day of Sept. 1836 by D.H.G.

<u>Loundon Briggs</u>, No. 235, p. 88:
Rockingham County to wit
Registered in my office as No. 235 this 9th day of September 1836 Loundon Briggs a dark Mulatto Man about 52 years of age five feet six inches high has a scar on thick part of Left hand and a scar on his left thumb and little gray and was Emancipated by Henry Miller as appears by the recordes of my office. The foregoing was compared with the said Loundon [and found] duly made a copy thereof ordered to be delivered him as the Law directs done at September Court 1836.
[In the margin] Cop'd & delv'd self 19 Sept'r 1836.

<u>James Hackley</u>, No. 236, p. 88:
Rockingham County to wit
Registered in my office as No. 236 The 14th day of September 1836 James Hackley a black Man about 46 years of age five feet six inches & 1/2 high has four scars on his breast one on the right thumb and also a scar on his right arm above the elbow. The said James Hackly [sic] was emancipated by the will of John Hackly Dec'd in Culpeper. The foregoing register was compared with the said James [and found] duly made a copy thereof ordered to be delivered him as the Law directs done at September Court 1836.
[In the margin] Cop'd & delivered to self on the 21st day of October 1836 by D.H. Gambill.

<u>Stephen Brock</u>, No. 237, p. 89:
Rockingham County to wit
Registered in my office as No. 237 the 17th day of September 1836 Stephen Brock a verry Black Man about 26 years of age five feet six inches high with Large prominent eyes has two scares on his breast and a scar on his right

102

thumb on the right hand and a scar on the
right fore finger on the right hand and a scar
on the Little finger on the same hand no other
marks perceavable and is the same Man that was
emancipated by the will of John Brock Deceased
as appears by the records of my office.   The
foregoing was Compared with the said Stephen
[and found] duly made a Copy thereof ordered
to be delivered him as the Law directs done at
Sept. Court 1836.
[In the margin] Copied & delivered to self on
the 28th day of October 1836 D.H.G.

William Strother, No. 238, p. 89:
Rockingham County to wit
Registered in my office as No. 238 the _____
day of September 1836 William Strother A
Mulatto Man about Forty one years of age five
six and a fourth inches high has Two small
Scras above the wrist on the Left arm
including a Cross and one other Lengthwise and
near one of the other Scars and is rather dim
Sighted in the Left Eye and was Set free by
the will of George Carpenter Deceased as
proved by the affidavit of John Carpenter
filed in my office.   The foregoing register
was compared with the said William duly made a
Copy thereof ordered to be delivered him as
the Law directs done at Sept. [deleted] Court
1836.

Milly Gains alias Milly Moore, No. 239,
pp. 89-90:
Rockingham County to wit
Registered in my office as No. 239 the 19th
day of September 1836 Milly Gains alias Milly
Moore now the wife of Loundon Briggs a verry
bright Mulatto Woman about 41 years of age
five feet seven & a half inches high has a
scar on the right side of her neck and a scar
on the side of her head back of the right ear
and a Scar on the back of the Left hand and is
verry deff and was free born as appears by the

evidence filed in my office. Foregoing register was compared with the said Milly duly made a copy ordered to be delivered to her as the Law directs done at Sept. Court 1836.
[In the margin] Cop'd & dev'd self the 19 Sept. 1836.

Eliza Moore alias Eliza Gains, No. 240, p. 90:
Rockingham County to wit
Registered in my office as No. 240 the 19th day of September 1836 Eliza Moore or Eliza Gains said to be daughter of Milly Moore a free Woman & wife of Loundon Briggs a Mulatto Girl about 17 years of age five feet five inches high has a scar on the first joint of the forefinger on the right hand. She was free born as appears by satisfactory evidence filed in my office. Foregoing register was compared with the said Eliza duly made a copy ordered to be delivered to her as the Law directs done at ... September Court 1836.
[In the margin] Copy'd & dev'd self the 19 Sept'er 1836.

William Peters, No. 242, p. 90:
Rockingham County to wit
Registered in my office as No. 242 the 19th day of September 1836 William Peters a verry Black Man about 19 years of age five feet 7 1/2 inches high has two scars on the Left arm below the elbow and a ... scar above the Left eye and scar on the right hand Hand was free born as appears by the evidence filed in my office. Foregoing registered [sic] was compared with the said William duly made a copy ordered to be delivered to him as the Law directs done at September Court 1836.
[In the margin] Copy'd & delivered to self on the 3rd day of October 1836 by D.H.G.

James Holman, No. 243, p. 91:
Rockingham County to wit

Registered in my office as No. 243 the 14th
day of October 1836 James Holman a Mulatto Man
about Twenty Two years of age six feet high
has a Scar on the uper part of the Left arm
and a scar on the right wrist and is free born
as appears by evidence filed in my office.
Foregoing register was compared with the said
James duly made a Copy ordered to be delivered
to him as the Law directs done at October
Court 1836.
[In the margin] Copy'd & Delivered to self on
the 23rd of October 1836 by D.H.G.

Nelly Hackley, No. 244, p. 91:
Rockingham County to wit
Registered in my office as No. 244 the 14th
day of October 1836 Nelly Hackley the wife of
James Hackley a yellow Woman about Forty Three
years of age Five Feet Three Inches high has
Three scars one on the Breast one on the Left
Shoulder and one under the Chin and was Born
free as appears by the Certificate of the
Clerk of the County Court of Culpeper filed in
my office. Foregoing register was compared
with the said Nelly duly made a Copy ordered
to be delivered to her as the Law directs done
at October Court 1836.
[In the margin] Copy'd & delivered to self on
the 21st day of October 1836 by D.H.G.

Elizabeth Hackly, No. 245, p. 91:
Rockingham County to wit
Registered in my office as No. 245 this 15th
day of October 1836 Elizabeth Hackly Daughter
of Nelly Hackley [sic] about 19 years of age a
verry Dark Mulatto Girl Five feet four inches
high has a Scar under her Chin and a Scar on
the Left Thumb and is free Born as appears by
evidence filed in my office. Foregoing
register was compared with the said Elizabeth
duly made a Copy ordered to be delivered to
her as the Law directs done at October Court
1836.

[In the margin] Cop'd & delivered to self on the 23rd October 1836 by D.H.G.

Levi, No. 244, p. 92:
Rockingham County to wit
Registered in my office the 17 October 1836 as No. 246 Levi a Verry dark Mulatto or black Man over 21 years of age, about 5 feet 11 Inches high, has a mole one above the right eye, and a small scare over same eye, and a small scar on the left rist above the Joint and a scar on the Little finger of the left hand near the end. He his [sic] a Verry Likely [sic] Man, he was emancipated by Judge Smith & William Cravens but bound to serve until 21 years of age, and is now free having served out his term, as appears by certificate of Judge Smith filed in my office. The foregoing Register was compared with the said Levi and found duly made, a copy thereof is ordered to be furnished him as the Law direts. Done at October Court 1836.
[In the margin] delv'd to s'd Levi the 18 October 1836 H.J.G.

Sam'l, No. 247, p. 92:
Rockingham County to wit
Registered in my office the 10th October 1836 as No. 247 Sam'l a Dark Mulatto or black man about 28 years of age five feet 6 1/2 inches high has a scar on his Little finger on the Left hand and a scar on the third finger of the same hand his right wrist is verry large was produced by a strain and was emancipated by Joseph Coffman by Deed of Record ... in my office. The foregoing Register was compared with the said Sam and found duly made a Copy thereof is ordered to be furnished him as the Law directs done at December Court 1836.
[In the margin] Copyed & Delivered to Sam the 9 Jan'y 1837 by H.J.G.

Philip, No. 248, pp. 92-93:

Rockingham County to wit
Registered in my office the 19th November 1836
Philip as No. 248 about 41 years of age a
black man five feet 11 Inches high, has two
Scars on ... the thick part of the left hand
Near the thumb and one also warts on each
Little finger of his hand--a Verry high
forehead he was set free by David Smith esqr.
by Deed the 19 Nov'er 1836 and of Record in my
office. The said Philip was compared with the
said Register and found duly made, a copy
thereof is ordered to be furnished him as the
Law direts, done at December Court 1836.
[In the margin] Delivered to Self on the 17th
day of January 1837 by D.H. Gambill.

Peachey Swingler, No. 249, p. 93:
Rockingham County to wit
Registered in my office the 17th day of June
1837 as No. 249, Peachey Swingler a Dark
Mulatto Man about 23 years of age five feet 9
inches high has a Scar on the Left Side of his
neck and a Scar on the ... thumb of the right
hand on the Second joint and was free born as
appears by evidence filed in my office. The
foregoing register was compared with the Said
Peachey duly made a copy ordered to be
delivered to him as the Law directs done at
_____ Court 1837.

Polly Byrd, No. 250, p. 93:
Rockingham County to wit
Registered in office the 16th day of August
1837 as No. 250 Polly Byrd a Mulatto Girl
about 21 years of age Five feet five inches
high and was free born as appears by evidence
filed in my office. The foregoing Register
was compared with the Said Polly and found
duly made a Copy thereof is ordered to be
furnished her as the Law directs done at
August Court 1837.

Betsey Byrd, No. 251, pp. 93-94:

107

Rockingham County to wit
Registered in my office the 16th day of August
1837 as No. 251 Betsey Byrd a Mulatto Girl
about 22 years of age Five Feet 4 1/2 inches
high has a Scar on the back of her neck and a
mole above the Left eye and is free born as
appears by evidence filed in my office. The
foregoing Register was compared with the Said
Betsey and found duly made a copy thereof is
ordered to be furnished her as the Law directs
done at August Court 1837.
[In the margin] Copied & delivered to said
Betsey Byrd the 26th Mar'h 1849 by E.C.

Polly Bundy, No. 252, p. 94:
Rockingham County to wit
Registered in my office as No. 252 the 19th
day of August 1837 Polly Bundy a Daughter of
Willis Bundy Verry black at about 23 years of
age 4 feet 11 1/2 Inches high, has a small
scare on the Joint of the thumb on left hand
and a small scare above the Left eye, was born
free as appears by a certificate filed in my
Office. The foregoing Register was compared
with the Said Polly and found duly made a copy
thereof is ordered to be furnished her as the
Law direts done at August Court 1837.
[In the margin] Reregistered on the 24th of
February 1846.

Eliza Bunday, No. 253, p. 94:
Rockingham County to wit
Registered in my office as No. 253 the 14th
day of September 1837 Eliza Bunday a Daughter
of Willis Bunday a Dark Mulatto Girl about 18
years of age Five feet high has a scar in the
corner of the wright eye, and a scar on the
wright rist and is free born as appears by
evidence filed in my office. The foregoing
Register was compared with the said Eliza and
found duly made a copy thereof is ordered to
be furnished her as the Law directs done at
_____ Court 1837.

[In the margin] Copyed & delivered to ...

Eliza, No. 254, pp. 94-95:
Rockingham County to wit
Registered in my office as No. 254 the 18th
day of September 1837 Eliza a Dark Mulatto
Woman about 27 years of age Five feet 4 inches
high has a scar on the back part of her right
hand and was set free by Jacob Claypole as
appears by his bill of Sale filed in my
office. The foregoing register was compared
with the said Eliza and found duly made a copy
thereof is ordered to be furnished her as the
Law directs done at September Court 1837.
[In the margin] Copyed & Delivered to self on
the 19th day of September 1837 by D.H.G.

Sally Brock, No. 255, p. 95:
Rockingham County to wit
Registered in my office as No. 255 the 14th
day of April 1838 Sally Brock a verry black
Negroe about 25 years of age 5 feet 2 1/2
inches high has a scar on the left seide of
her face and a Small Scare on the right wrist
and was emancipated by the will of John Brock
Deceased Recorded in Clerkes office at May
Court 1827. The foregoing register was
Compared with the said Sally and found duly
made a Copy thereof is ordered to be furnished
her as the Law directs done at April Court
1838.
[In the margin] Delivered self 8 October 1838
by H.J.G.

Christopher Shiderick, No. 256, p. 95:
Rockingham County to wit
Registered in my office on the 16th June 1838
as No. 256 Christopher Shiderick a Dark
Mulatto Man about 21 years of age Five feet 8
1/2 inches high a scar above the Left eye on
his forehead and also a Scare on the Joint of
the third finger on the Left hand and is free
born as appears by evidence filed in the

Clerks office. The foregoing register was
Compared with the said Christopher and found
duly made a Copy thereof is ordered to be
furnished her [sic] as the Law directs done at
June Court 1838.
[In the margin] Cop'd & dev'd to Shadrik [sic]
20 Nov'er 1838 by H.J.G.

George, No. 257, p. 96:
Rockingham County to wit
Registered in my office on the 4th day of July
1838 as No. 257 George a darke Mulatto Man
about 28 years of age Five feet 4 1/2 inches
high has a Scar above the right eye and a Scar
in the corner of the Left eye and a Scar on
the Left hand between his Little finger and
third finger and is verry bowl Legged and was
emancipated by the will of David Laird
deceased Recorded in the Clerks office at
April Court 1828. The foregoing register was
compared with the said George and found duly
made a Copy thereof is ordered to be furnished
him as the Law directs done at July Court
1838.
[In the margin] Cop'd & Delv'd to Geo. by
H.J.G.

Peachey Gordon, No. 258, p. 96:
Rockingham County to wit
Registered in my office on the 17th day of
August 1838 as No. 258 Peachey Gordon a
Mulatto Man about 24 years of age Five feet 10
inches has a scar in the right Corner of his
right eye and a scar on the third fore finger
of the right hand between the first and second
joints and a scar on the right thumb and is
free born as appears by evidence filed in my
office. The foregoing Register was Compared
with the said Peachey and found duly made a
Copy thereof is ordered to be furnished him as
the Law directs, done at August Court 1838.
[In the margin] Copyed & ...

Reuben Cross, No. 259, pp. 96-97:
Rockingham County to wit
Registered in my office on the 18th day of
August 1838 as No. 259 Reuben Cross a Dark
Mulatto Boy about 22 years of age Five feet 3
inches high has a scar on his Left Ceeck boan
and a scar on the first joint of the little
finger on right hand and is free born as
appears by evidence filed in my office. The
foregoing Register was compared with the said
Reuben and found duly made a copy thereof is
ordered to be furnished him as the Law directs
done at August Court 1838.
[In the margin] Copyed & delv'd self the 11th
Sept'er 1838 by H.J.G.

John Bundy, No. 260, p. 97:
Rockingham County to wit
Registered in my office on the 20th day of
August 1838 as No. 260 John Bundy a Mulatto
Boy about 22 years of age Five feet 6 inches
has a scar on the Left hand of the fore finger
on the first joint and is free born as appears
by evidence filed in my office. The foregoing
Register was compared with the said John and
found duly made a copy thereof is ordered to
be furnished him as the Law directs done at
August Court 1838.
[In the margin] Copyed & delivered to self on
the 20th day of August 1838 by D.H.G.

Harrison Burk, No. 261, p. 97:
Rockingham County to wit
Registered in my office on the 20th day of
August 1838 as No. 261 Harrison Burk a bright
Mulatto man about 22 years of age, five feet
10 1/2 inches high, has a small scare on his
forehead, and scare on the left hand, Just
above the Thumb Joint, a verry handsom[e] Man,
he was born free, as appears by satisfactory
evidence filed in my Office. The foregoing
Register was compared with the said Harrison
and found duly made a copy thereof is ordered

111

to be furnished him as the Law directs done at
August Court 1838.
[In the margin] Cop'd & delv'd the 5 October
1838.

Harrison Vine, No. 262, pp. 97-98:
Rockingham County to wit
Registered in my office as the 22nd day of
August 1838 as No. 262 Harrison Vine a Dark
Mulatto Man about 23 years of age Five feet 9
inches high has a Scar on the back part of his
neck and was occationed by a burn and is free
born as appears by evidence filed in my
office. The foregoing register was compared
with the said Harrison and found duly made a
copy thereof is ordered to be furnished him as
the Law directs done at August Court 1838.
[In the margin] Copied & delivered to self on
the 22nd day of August 1838 by D.H.G.

Lucinda Let, No. 263, p. 98:
Rockingham County to wit
Registered in my office as No. 263 the 17th
September 1838 Lucinda Let a verry bright
Mulatto about 19 or 20 years of age, five feet
2 inches high, has two scars, one [on] the
left arm, the other on the first Joint of the
forefinger, and also a small scare on the left
Jaw bone, was born free as appears by
satisfactory evidence filed in my office. The
foregoing register was compared with the
[said] Lucinda Let, and found duly made a copy
thereof is ordered to be furnished her in the
Manner directed by Law done at September Court
1838.
[In the margin] Copyed & Delivered to Self on
the 18th day of September 1839 by D.H.G.

Dice, No. 264, p. 98:
Rockingham County to wit
Registered in my office on the 19th day of
January 1839 as No. 264 Dice a Dark black
woman about 28 years of age five feet 1 inch

112

high has no scars perceable was emancipated by
Reuben Harrison by Deed Recorded in my office
but bound to serve a certain Number of years
as appears [deleted: "by evidence filed in my
office."] The foregoing register was compared
with the said Dice and found duly made a copy
thereof is ordered to be furnished her in the
manner directed by Law done at January Court
1839.
[In the margin] Copyed & Delv'd to self 27
Feb'y 1839 by H.J.G.

Elbert Smith, No. 265, pp. 98-99:
Rockingham County to wit
Registered in my office on the 21 Janu'y 1839
No. 265 Elbert Smith a free boy of Colour (a
Verry black man) about 21 years of age, 5 feet
5 inches high has no scars, was emancipated by
Hon'ble Dan'l Smith & W. Cravens but bound to
serve until 21 years of age, as appears by the
records of my office. The foregoing register
was compared with the said Elbert and found
duly made a copy thereof is ordered to be
furnished him in the manner directed by Law
done at Janu'y Court 1839.
[In the margin] Copyed & Delv'd to self the
3rd of September 1842 L.W.G.

Richard White alias Dick Rife, No. 266,
p. 99:
Rockingham County to wit
Registered in my office as No. 266 Richard
White sometimes called Dick Rife the 21 Jan'y
1839 a black man about 50 years of age 5 feet
6 3/4 inches high, baldhead, has a scare on
the left hand above the uper Joint of the
Little finger, he was emancipated by deed
date[d] on this day by Hon'ble Dan'l Smith
which is recorded in my office. The said
Register was compared with the said White
alias Rife and duly made a copy thereof is
ordered to be furnished him as the Law direts
done at Janu'y Court 1839.

113

[In the margin] Copyed & Delivered to Self on the 17th day of May 1839 D.H.G.

Milly Hubbard, No. 267, p. 99:
Rockingham County to wit
Registered in my office as No. 267 the 16th February 1839 Milly Hubbard (the wife of Jacob) a Dark Mulatto woman about 29 years of age 5 feet 6 1/4 inches high, has a small scar on the left side of her face appears to have been occasioned by a burn, a large woman, was born free as appears by satisfactory evidence filed in my office. The foregoing Register was compared with the said Milly and found duly made a copy thereof is ordered to be furnished her according to Law, done at Febru'y Court 1839.

John White, No. 268, p. 99:
Rockingham County to wit
Registered in my office as No. 268 John White, a bright Mulatto man about 27 years of age, 6 feet 1 1/4 inches high has a dark spot over the left eye, and a scare on the Little finger of the left hand (the finger appears to have been broke) he was born free as appears by satisfactory evidence filed in my office. The foregoing register was compared with the said John White and found duly made a copy thereof is ordered to be furnished him according to Law, done at Febru'y Court 1839.
[In the margin] Copy delv'd to White the 15 Nov'er 1839 by H.J. Gambill.

Rebeccah Allen, No. 269, p. 100:
Rockingham County to wit
Registered in my office as No. 269 the 16th February 1839 Rebeccah Allen a Mulatto woman, said to be about 35 years of age, 5 feet 7 inches high, has no scars either on her face or hands (except that finger Nale of the Little finger on the left hand appears to have been split) as she say with a reap hook, she

114

was born free, as appears by evidence filed in my office. The foregoing Register was compared with the said Rebeccah and found duly made a copy thereof is ordered to be delivered her as the Law directs done at Febru'y Court 1839.
[In the margin] Cop'd & dev'd self the 13th March 1839 by H.J.G.

Alexander Moore, No. 270, p. 100:
Rockingham County to wit
Registered in my office as No. 270 the 15th February 1839 Alexander Moore a Dark Mulatto Man about 21 years of age 6 feet high has a scar above the right eye no other marks perseavible he was free born as appears by evidence filed in my office. The foregoing Register was Compared with the said Alexander and found duly made a copy thereof is ordered to be delivered him as the Law directs done at _____ Court.
[In the margin] Copyed & delivered.

John Anderson, No. 271, p. 100:
Rockingham County to wit
Registered in my office as No. 271 the 16th of September 1839 John Anderson a Mulatto man, 25 years old the 7th of January (1839) last, has a remarkable scare on the middle finger of the right hand occasioned by a cut through the Nail (a part of a Nail appears to have grown in the place where the cut was) has also a small scare on the Little finger of the Left hand, across the first Joint, he was emancipated by James Walters but bound to serve Alexander Smith untill 25 years of age, as appears ... by written evidence filed in my office. The foregoing register was compared with the said John and found duly made, a copy thereof ordered to be delivered him as the Law directs, done at September Court 1839.
[In the margin] Cop'd & delv'd self the 17 Sept'er 1839 by H.J.G.

John Gibson, No. 271 [sic], p. 101:
Rockingham County to wit
Registered in my office as No. 271 the 19th
day October 1839 John Gibson a Mulatto Man
about 21 years of age 5 feet 7 inches high has
a scar on the fore finger of the Left hand on
the first joint no other marks perciable, he
was born free as appears by evidence filed in
my office.   The foregoing Register was
compared with the said John and found duly
made a Copy thereof is ordered to be furnished
him as the Law directs done at October Court
1839.
[In the margin] Cop'd & delv'd to Jno. 7
October 1841 by D.H. Gambill.

Fielding Cochran, No. 272, p. 101:
Rockingham County to wit
Registered in my office as No. 272 the 18th
day of October 1840 Fielding Cochran a Dark
Mulatto Man about 22 years of age 5 feet 9
inches high has a scar on the first joint of
the forefinger of the right hand and a scar on
the Left hand near the first joint of his
Thumb no other marks perciable, he was born
free as by evidence filed in my office.   The
foregoing Register was compared with the said
Fielding and found duly made a copy thereof is
ordered to be furnished him as the Law directs
done at February Court 1840.
[In the margin] Copyed & Delivered to Self on
the 18th day of Feberuary 1840 by D.H.G.

John Poindexter, No. 273, pp. 101-103
[sic, 102]:
Rockingham County to wit
Registered in my office as No. 273 the 17th
day of April 1840, John Poindexter a Dark
Mulatto Man about 29 years of age 5 feet 8 1/2
inches high has a scar on his forehead above
the Left eye and a scar on the wright rist no
other marks persiable he was born free as by
evidence filed in my office.   The foregoing

116

Register was compared with the said John and found duly made a copy thereof is ordered to be delivered to him as the Law directs done at April Court 1840.
(See page 186: At April Court 1851 the said John Poindexter was registered by an order [of] Court made at that time & Copy Delivered to him the 23rd of April 1851.)
[In the margin] Copyed & Delivered to Self on the 17th day of April 1840 by D.H.G.

Mima, No. 274, p. 103 [sic]:
Rockingham County to wit
Registered in my office as No. 274 the 30th day of July 1840 Mima a verry Black Woman said to be 30 years old about first day of May last, about 4 feet 10 1/2 inches high has a small scare on the first finger of the left hand near the end, and also a small scare on the bone of the Joint of the rist of the right arm, no other mark or scare perceavable, said Mima was set free by the Will of George Carpenter deceased but bound to serve till 30 years of age, which will is of Record in the Clerks Office of said County. The foregoing Register was compared with the said Mima and found duly made a copy thereof is ordered to be delivered her as directed by Law done at May Court 1842 [corrected from 1840].
[In the margin] Copied & Delivered to Self the 18 of May 1842 L.W.G.

John Holeman, No. 275, p. 103:
Rockingham County to wit
Registered in my office as No. 275 the 9th day of August 1840 John Holeman a Verry black Man 6 feet 3 1/2 inches high, says he is about 48 or 49 years of age, his left eye appears to be defective having a small lump in the corner next his Nose, has a scare on the thumb of the left hand, the little finger on the left hand crooked, was born free as appears by satisfactory evidence filed in my office. The

117

foregoing Register was compared by the Court with the said John and found duly made a copy thereof is ordered to be delivered him, as directed by Law done at ____ Court 1840.
[In the margin] Copy delv'd to J. Holeman the 19 August 1840 by H.J.G.

Eliza Beasley, No. 276, pp. 103-104:
Rockingham County to wit
Registered in my office as No. 276 the 8th day of February 1841 Eliza Beasley a verry Bright Mulatto Girl about 5 feet 3 inches high she says that she is about 25 years of age has a Small scar over each eye has a small scar on her thumb of the left hand. By the order of the County Court of Rockingham made at January Court 1841 the said Eliza was directed to be Registered by the Clerk of said County, it appearing to the Court that she was free. The foregoing Register was Compared by the Court with the said Eliza and found duly made a copy Thereof is ordered to be delivered her as directed by Law done at February Court 1841.
[In the margin] Copyed & Delivered to Self on the 15th day of February 1841 by D.H.G.

Benjamin Curtis, No. 277, p. 104:
Rockingham County to wit
Registered in my office as No. 277 The 13th day of February 1841 Benjamin Curtis a verry Black man about 5 feet 8 inches high he says that he is about 26 years of age has a scar on the left arm above the rist was born free as appears by evidence filed in my office. The foregoing Register was compared by the Court with the said Benjamin Curtis and found duly made a copy Thereof is ordered to be delivered him as directed by Law done at February Court 1841.
[In the margin] Copyed & delivered to self Sept. 10 1849 J.G.C.

Harvey Curtis, No. 278, p. 104:

Rockingham County to wit
Registered in my office as No. 278 the 13th
day of February 1841 Harvey Curtis a verry
Black Man about 5 feet 4 1/2 inches high he
says that he is about 24 years of age has a
scar on the Left wrist was born free as
appears by evidence filed in my office. The
foregoing Register was compared by the Court
with the said Harvey and found duly made a
copy Thereof is ordered to be delivered him as
directed by Law done at February Court 1841.
[In the margin] Copy'd & Delivered Self on the
13th of April 1841 by D.H.G.

Morgan Curtis, No. 279, pp. 104-105:
Rockingham County to wit
Registered in my office as No. 279 the 13th
day of February 1841 Morgan Curtis a verry
Black Man about 5 feet 3 inches high he says
that he is about 22 years of age has on his
breast something Like a vein and a scar on the
right hand was free born as appears by
evidence filed in my office. The foregoing
Register was compared by the Court with the
said Morgan and found duly made a copy Thereof
is ordered to be delivered him as directed by
Law done at February Court 1841.
[In the margin] Copyed & Delivered to Self on
the 12th of June 1849 J.N.

Cloe Curtis, No. 280, p. 105:
Rockingham County to wit
Registered in my office as No. 280 the 13th
day of February 1841 Cloe Curtis a Verry Black
Girl about 5 feet 2 inches high she says that
she is about 27 years of age has a scar on the
Left arm was free born as appears by evidence
filed in my office. The foregoing Register
was compared by the Court with the said Cloe
and found duly made a copy Thereof is ordered
to be delivered to her as directed by Law done
at February Court 1841.
[In the margin] Copyed & Delivered to self the

John Bachus, No. 281, pp. 105-106:
Rockingham County to wit
Registered in my office as No. 281 the 17th
day of April 1841 John Bachus a verry Black
Man about 5 feet 2 inches high he says that he
is about 25 years of age has a scar above the
right eye and a scar on the second joint of
third finger on the left hand and a scar on
the fat part of the same hand was free born as
appears by evidence filed in my office. The
foregoing Register was compared by the Court
with the said John and found duly made a copy
Thereof is ordered to be delivered him as
directed by Law done at May Court 1841.
[In the margin] Copyed & Delivered to Self on
the 14th day of June 1842 by D.H.G.

John P. Anderson, No. 282, p. 106:
Rockingham County to wit
Registered in my office as No. 282 the 22nd
day of June 1841 John P. Anderson a verry
Bright Mulatto Man about 5 feet 6 inches high
he says that he is about 21 years of age has a
scar on his forehead was born free as appears
by evidence filed in my office. The foregoing
register was compared by the Court with the
said John and found duly made a copy Thereof
is ordered to be delivered him as directed by
Law done at June Court 1841.
[In the margin] Copyed & Delivered to Self on
the 22nd day of November 1841 by D.H.G.

Zachariah McCoy, No. 284 [sic, 283;
misnumbered in the margin], p. 106:
Rockingham County to wit
Registered in my office according to Law as
No. 283 [correct within the body of the text]
the 30th of June 1841 Zachariah McCoy a
Mulatto man about 31 years of age the 2nd
December Next, about five feet 8 1/2 inches
high, has a small scar near the corner of his

right eye, the Little finger of the left hand crooked occasioned by a cut, was born free, as appears by his freedom paper heretofore filed in my office. (This man was Registered in my office on the 18 November 1833 & a certificate Granted him as No. 200) which has been delivered up to the clerk & destroyed. The foregoing re-register was compared by the court with the said Zachariah and found duly made, a copy thereof is ordered to be delivered him as directed by Law, done at _____ Court 1841.
[In the margin] Copyed & ...

Jerry Bryan, No. 285, p. 107:
Rockingham County to wit
Registered in my office as No. 285 the 14th day of August 1841 Jerry Bryan a Black Man about 35 years of age, and six Feet high and has a scar over the left Eye about one Inch Long and Crosswise his Forehead and also a Scar on the Joint of the Thumb of the left hand and was born free as appears by his freedom papers heretofore filed in my office on the 6th day of February 1829 and a certificate granted him as No. 138 which has been delivered up to the Clerk and destroyed as directed by Law. The foregoing register was compared by the Court with the said Jerry and found duly made a copy thereof is ordered to be Delivered him as directed by Law done at _____ Court 1841.
[In the margin] Copyed & Delivered ...

Dennis alias Dennis Hews, No. 286, p. 107:
Rockingham County to wit
Re-Registered in my office as No. 286 the 18th day of September 1841 Dennis, otherwise Cal[l]ed Dennis Hews, A Black Man Sixty years old Five Feet Six Inches & Three quarters high pretty well set for his hight he has a Small scar over the Left eye and another of the

121

Right corner of the right Eye and a Scar on
the back part of the left wrist immeadiately
on the joint and was emancipated by William
Hughes in the year 1804 which is of Record in
the County Court of Rockingham. The foregoing
Register was by the Court compared with Said
Dennis and a copy thereof ordered to bbe
furnished him done at October Court 1841.
[In the margin] Copyed & Delivered to Self the
14 November 1845 L.W.G. [See No. 74, p. 32.]

William Bundy, No. 287, p. 108:
Rockingham County to wit
Registered in my office as No. 287 this 5 day
of January 1842 William Bundy a Dark Mulatto
21 years of age in April next about 5 Feet 7
Inches high and has a scar across the Corner
of the left Eye and scar on the Chin also a
scar on the left arm or wrist and was free
born as appears by the affidavit of Thomas
Bohanon filed in my office. The foregoing
Register was compared by the Court with the
said William Bundy and found duly made a copy
thereof is ordered to be delivered to him as
directed by Law done at January Court 1842.
[In the margin] Copied & Delivered to Self the
18th day of January 1842 L.W. Gambill.
Renewed by order of Ct. at Aug't 1855 with age
of 35 yrs & Delivered to self the 12th of
February 1856 L.W.G.

Anthony Rice, No. 288, p. 108:
Rockingham County to wit
Registered in my office as No. 288 this 19th
day of February 1842 Anthony Rice A Black Man
59 years of age about 5 Feet 5 1/2 inches high
has a scar on his breast and was emancipated
by Peachey Rice on the 17th day of January
1842 which Deed is of Record in the County
Court of Rockingham. The foregoing Register
was by the Court Compared with the said
Anthony and a copy thereof ordered to be
furnished him done at February Court 1842.

[In the margin] Copyed & Delivered to Anthony Rice June 6th 1851 J.G.C.

Thornton Boswell, No. 289, pp. 108-109:
Rockingham County to wit
Registered in my office as No. 289 this 19th day of March 1842 Thornton Boswell a Mulatto Man 24 Years of age in June Next Five Feet Eleven Inches high and has a small scar on the left Eye Brow and was Emancipated by James Boswell a free man of Color by Deed of Emancipation recorded in my office. The foregoing Register was by the Court compared with the said Thornton Boswell and found duly made a Copy thereof is ordered to be furnished him according to Law done at March Court 1842. [In the margin] Copied & delivered to self the 29th of March 1842 L.W. Gambill.

Samuel Lewis, No. 290, p. 109:
Rockingham County to wit
Registered in my office as No. 290 This 1st day of April 1842 Samuel Lewis a Mulatto man Between 21 and 22 years of age a little upwards of Six foot high and has a scar on the Corner of the right Eye Brow and a small scar on the right thumb and also one on the right wrist and the Middle Joint of the little finger on the left hand out of place and was free Born as appears by the affidavit of Mary Long filed in my office. The Foregoing register was by the Court compared with the said Samuel Lewis and found duly made a Copy thereof is ordered to be furnished him according to Law done at August Court 1842. [In the margin] Copyed & Delivered to Self on the 18th day of May 1844 by D.H.G.

Aggy, No. 291, p. 109:
Rockingham County to wit
Registered in my office as No. 291 This 16 day of April 1842 Aggy a dark Mulatto Girl 25 years of age on the 1st day of this Month Five

Feet Four Inches high and has a small scar on the left side of her face Just below the Cheek Bone and the little finger on the left hand stiff and was emancipated by the will of John Brock Deceased of Record in my office. The foregoing Register was by the Court compared with the said Aggy and found duly made a Copy thereof is ordered to be furnished him according to Law done at April Court 1842.
[In the margin] Copyed & Delivered self the 5 of May 1845 L.W.G.

James Williamson, No. 292, p. 110:
Rockingham County to wit
Registered in my office as No. 292 This 16th day of June 1842 James Williamson a dark Mulatto or black man Between 22 & 23 years of age Five Feet 7 1/2 Inches high and has a small scar on the left Cheek bone a small scar near the left ear a scar on the middle Joint of the left forefinger and a scar on the middle finger of the left hand and a scar on the left thumb inside of the hand and a scar on the forefinger of the right hand and also a scar on the thumb of the right hand and was free born as appears by the affidavit of George Campbell filed in my office. The foregoing Register was by the Court compared with the said James Williamson and found duly made a Copy thereof is ordered to be furnished him according to Law done at July Court 1842.
[In the margin] Copyed & Delivered to self the 23rd of Dec'r 1843 L.W.G.

William F. Bryan, No. 293, p. 110:
Rockingham County to wit
Registered in my office as No. 293 This 16 day of July 1842 William F. Bryan A Dark Mulatto Man about 21 years of age Six Feet Three inches high has a scar on the Left Corner of the right Eye and a Scar on the Back of his right hand and a Scar on the fore finger of the second joint on the Left hand and is free

born as appears by evidence filed in my office. The Foregoing register was by the Court compared with the said William and found duly made a copy thereof is ordered to be furnished him according to Law done at July Court 1842.
[In the margin] Copyed & Delivered the 29th of July 1842 L.W.G.

Allen Bryan, No. 294, pp. 110-111:
Rockingham County to wit
Registered in my office as No. 294 This 16th day of July 1842 Allen Bryan A Dark Mulatto Man about 19 years of age Five Feet Nine Inches high has a scar on the right corner of the Left eye and a scar on the second joint of the Little finger on the Left hand and was free born as appears by evidence filed in my office. The Foregoing register was compared with the said Allen and found duly made a copy thereof is ordered to be furnished him according to Law done at July Court 1842.
[In the margin] Copyed & Delivered to self the 2nd of Sept'er 1842 L.W.G.

Evaline Bozwell formerly Peters, No. 295, p. 111:
Rockingham County to wit
Registered in my office as No. 295 This 16th of July 1842 Evaline Bozwell formerly Peters a Mulatto Woman about 24 years of age Five Feet one Inch high has a scar on the Left arm above the rist and is free born as appears by evidence filed in my office. The Foregoing register was compared with the said Evaline and found duly made a copy thereof is ordered to be furnished her according to Law done at July Court 1842.
[In the margin] Examined & Delivered to self the 7th July 1843 L.W.G.

Louisa Peaters, No. 296, pp. 111-112:
Rockingham County to wit

Registered in my office as No. 296 This 16th
of July 1842 Louisa Peaters A Dark Mulatto
Woman about 15 years of age Five Feet high has
a scar on the right side of her neck was born
free as appears by evidence filed in my
office. The Foregoing register was compared
with the said Louisa Peaters and found duly
made a copy thereof is ordered to be furnished
her according to Law done at July Court 1842.
[In the margin] Examined & Delivered to self
the 8th of July 1843 L.W.G.

Angelina Heath, No. 297, p. 112:
Rockingham County to wit
Registered in my office as No. 297 This 14th
day of September 1842 Angelina Heath a black
Woman 5 Feet 1 1/2 Inches high who was 20
years old on the 1st day of March 1835 the
little Finger of the right hand Crooked full
eyes and thick projecting lips free Born as
appears by a Copy of a Former Register Taken
in the County of Page and filed in my Office.
The Foregoing Register was compared with the
said Angelina Heathe [sic] and found duly made
a copy thereof is ordered to be furnished her
according to Law Done at ____ Court 184_.

Lemuel Herring, No. 298, p. 112:
Rockingham County to wit
Registered in my office as No. 298 This 14th
day of September 1842 Lemuel Herring A Black
Man Between 42 and 43 years of age 6 Foot High
and has a small scar on the left side of his
nose and a small scar on the little Finger of
the left hand and a scar on the Middle Finger
of the same hand and the first Joint of the
same Finger Stiff and was Emancipated by
Abraham Smith by Deed of Emancipation recorded
in my Office. The Foregoing Register was by
the Court Compared with the said Lemuel
Herring and found duly made a copy thereof is
ordered to be furnished him according to Law
done at the November Court 1842.

126

[In the margin] Examined & Delivered to Self on the 2nd day of December 1842 by D.H. Gambill.

Sinclair Gibson, No. 299, p. 113:
Rockingham County to wit
Registered in my office as No. 299 This 16th day of September 1842 Sinclair Gibson a Bright mulatto Man about 21 years of age 5 Feet 7 1/2 Inches high and has a scar on his Forehead Just above the Temple also a scar on the right Wrist also a scar on the Middle Finger of the right hand and the first Joint of the same finger Stiff also a scar on the back of the left hand Free Born as appears by the Affidavit of Augustus Waterman filed in my Office. The Foregoing Register was by the Court compared with the said Sinclair Gibson and found duly made a copy thereof is ordered to be furnished him according to Law done at September Court 1842.
[In the margin] Examined & Delivered to self the 26th of Sept. 1842 L.W.G.

Charlotte Russell, No. 300, p. 113:
Rockingham County to wit
Registered in my office as No. 300 This 19th day of September 1842 Charlotte Russell a Dark Mulatto Girl about 20 years of age 5 Feet 2 1/2 Inches high has a Small Scar above the right Eye and a large lump on the fore finger of the right hand between the First and second Joint and set free by the will of Peter Koontz Deceased which is of Record in my office. The Foregoing Register was by the Court compared with the said Charlotte and found duly made a copy thereof is ordered to be furnished her according to Law done at September Court 1842.
[In the margin] Examined & Delivered to Self on the 19th day September 1842 by D.H.G.

Lucretia Henderson, No. 301, p. 114:
Rockingham County to wit

127

Registered in my office as No. 301 This 12th
day of January 1843 Lucretia Henderson a Black
Woman 39 years of age Five Feet Seven and a
half Inches high and has a small scar on the
back of her right hand and was Emancipated by
the will of Thomas McKinsey Deceased which is
of record in my office and also proved to be
the same by the affidavit of John Paulser
filed in my office. The foregoing Register
was by the Court compared with the said
Lucretia Henderson and found duly made a Copy
thereof is ordered to be furnished her
according to Law done at Janu'y Court 1843.
[In the margin] Copied & delivered to self the
19th of January 1844 L.W.G.

George T. Bird, No. 302, p. 114:
Rockingham County to wit
Registered in my office as No. 302 This 16th
day of February 1843 George T. Bird a Mulatto
Man Between 21 and 22 years of age Five Feet 9
Inches high and has a scar on his chin and
also a scar on the Middle Joint of the third
Finger of the right hand and a scar or wart on
the Knuckle of the Middle finger of the same
hand and also a scar on the left wrist and
appears by the records filed in my office that
the said George T. Bird was free born. The
foregoing register was by the Court compared
with the said George T. Bird and found duly
made a Copy thereof is ordered to be furnished
him according to Law done at February Court
1843.
[In the margin] Copy Delivered to self the
27th of Febr'y 1843 L.W.G.

St. Clair Poindexter, No. 303, p. 114:
Rockingham County to wit
Registered in my office as No. 303 This 13th
day of March 1843 St. Clair Poindexter A Black
Man Five Feet 3 Inches high 27 years of Age in
June Next and has a small scar near the Corner
of the left Eye and a small scar or mark on

128

the right Cheek bone and a scar on the right
wrist and was free Born as appears by the
affidavit of John Fisher filed in my office.
The Foregoing register was by the Court
compared with the said St. Clair Poindexter
and found duly made a Copy thereof is ordered
to be furnished him according to Law done at
March Court 1843.
[In the margin] Copy & Delivered to self the
21st of May 1845.

Ledirey Holman, No. 304, p. 115:
Rockingham County to wit
Registered in my office as No. 304 This 15th
day of July 1843 Ledirey Holman a Verry dark
Mulatto woman about 5 feet 7 Inches high says
herself to be 26 years of age in March 1844
has a small scare on the right arm, appears to
have been a burn, has also a small scare on
the Thumb of the left hand, and a small one on
the end of the first finger on the left hand,
appears to be from a cut, has a small black
mole on her forehead, and also a small one on
her Nose, she was born free, as appears from
satisfactory evidence on file in my office.
The foregoing Register was by the Court
compared with the said Ledirey and found duly
made a copy thereof is ordered to be furnished
her as the Law directs done at July Court
1843.
[In the margin] Delivered to self the 1st
Nov'r 1843 L.W.G.

Maria Miller, No. 305, p. 115:
Rockingham County to wit
Registered in my office as No. 305 Maria
Miller a Mulatto Woman very large, about 5
feet 3 1/2 Inches high, appears to be about 23
or 24 years of age, has several scars on the
back of her Neck, [h]as a Very prominant mole
on the left side of her Neck, has two scars on
the left arm, has a small one on the 3rd
finger of the left hand, and also a small one

129

on the first finger of the same hand on the
first Joint, was born free, and bound out by
the overseers of the [poor] until she was 18
years of age as appears by the records of my
office. The foregoing Register was by the
court compared with the said Maria and found
duly made a copy thereof was ordered to be
furnished her as the Law directs, done at a
July Court 1843.

Peter Harrison, No. 306, p. 116:
Rockingham County to wit
Registered in my office as No. 306 This 21st
day of August 1843 Peter Harrison A Black Man
6 Foot High about Thirty years of age. The
Forefinger of the left hand Crooked and has a
scar on the Third finger of the same hand near
the middle Joint and the End of the Third
finger of the right hand very large occasioned
by a fillon as [sic] was free born as appears
by the affidavit of David Harrison filed in my
office. The Foregoing register was by the
Court compared with the said Peter Harrison
and found duly made a Copy thereof is ordered
to be furnished him as the Law directs done at
August Court 1843.
[In the margin] Examined & copy Delivered to
self the 22nd of August 1843 L.W.G. Register
ret'd & renewed at Dec'r Ct 1855 with age of
42 years. Delv'd Dec. 18th 1855 W.S.T.

Miller Harrison, No. 307, p. 116:
Rockingham County to wit
Registered in my office as No. 307 This 21st
day of August 1843 Miller Harrison 22 years of
age in May Next 6 Feet One and a half inches
high has a small scar in the right Eye Brow
and the end of the left Thumb very large
occasioned by a fillon and a small scar on the
right wrist and was free born as appears by
the affidavit of Michael Sellars filed in my
office. The Foregoing Register was by the
Court Compared with the said Miller Harrison

and found duly made a Copy thereof is ordered
to be furnished him according to Law done at
August Court 1843.
[In the margin] Examined & Copy Delivered to
self the 22nd day of Aug. 1843 L.W.G.

   Peachy Swingler, No. 308, p. 116:
Rockingham County to wit
Registered in my Office as No. 308 This 23rd
day of August 1843 Peachy Swingler a Dark
Mulatto Man about 29 years of age Five Feet
Nine Inches high and has a small scar near the
Corner of the right Eye and also a scar on the
First Joint of the left Thumb and was free
Born as appears by Evidence filed in my
Office. The foregoing Register was by the
Court Compared with the said Peachy Swingler
and found duly made a Copy thereof is ordered
to be furnished him according to Law done at
August Court 1843.
[In the margin] Examined & Copy Delv'ed to
self the 4th of Sept'er 1843 L.W.G.

   Eliza Swingler formerly Bundy, No. 309,
p. 117:
Rockingham County to wit
Registered in my Office as No. 309 The 23rd
day of August 1843 Eliza Swingler formerly
Eliza Bundy Five foot High A Black or Dark
Mulatto about 24 years of age and has a scar
in the Corner of the right Eye and also a scar
on the right wrist and was free Born as
appears by Evidence filed in my office. The
foregoing Register was by the Court Compared
with the said Eliza and found duly made a Copy
thereof is ordered to be furnished her
according to Law done at August Court 1843.
[In the margin] Examined & Delivered to self
the 11th Sept'r 1843 L.W.G.

   James Holeman, No. 310, p. 117:
Rockingham County to wit
Registered in my office as No. 310 The 15th

day of November 1843 James Holeman A Mulatto
Man 29 years of age Six Feet high has a scar
on the up[p]er part of the left arm and a scar
on the right wrist and also a large scar
across his neck below the left ear and was
free Born as appears by evidence filed in my
office. The foregoing register was by the
County Court Compared with the said James
Holeman and found duly made a Copy thereof is
ordered to be furnished him according to Law
done at November Court 1843.

Zachariah McCoy, No. 311, pp. 117-118:
Rockingham County to wit
Registered in my office as No. 311 The 18th
day of November 1843 Zachariah McCoy A Mulatto
Man 32 years of age the 2nd day of December
Next, Five Feet Eight and a half Inches high
and has a Small scar near the corner of the
right Eye and the little finger of the left
hand crooked occasioned by a cut and was free
born as appears by the Certificate of Thomas
Buch who was formerly an overseer of the Poor
for said County and also by the affidavit of
Henry Martz to whom the said Zachariah was
bound which certificate and affidavit is filed
in my office. The foregoing Register was by
the Court Compared with the said Zachariah
McCoy and found duly made a copy thereof is
ordered to be furnished the said Zachariah as
the Law directs done at November Court 1843.
[In the margin] Examined & Delivered to Self
on 21st of November 1843 by D.H.G. Renewed by
order of the May Term 1854 & Co. Delivered.

Catharine Moore, No. 312, p. 118:
Rockingham County to wit
Registered in my office as No. 312 The 20th
day of February 1844 Catharine Moore Five Feet
4 Inches high A Black or Dark Mulatto about 24
years of age and has a scar on the Little
finger of the Left hand and was set free by
the will of Thomas Moore Deceased of Record in

132

my office. The foregoing Register was by the Court compared with the said Catharine and found duly made a copy thereof is ordered to be furnished her according to Law done at January Court 1846 [corrected from 1844].
[In the margin] Examined & Delivered to Self on the 3rd of March 1846 D.H.G.

Alexander Moore, No. 313, p. 118:
Rockingham County to wit
Registered in my office as No. 313 The 20th day of February 1844 Alexander Moore a Dark Mulatto Man about 25 years of age 6 feet high has a scar above the right eye and a scar on the end of the third finger on the left hand, no other marks perseaviable he was free born as appears by evidence filed in my office. The foregoing Register was by the Court compared with the said Alexander and found duly made, a copy thereof is ordered to be furnished him according to Law done at February Court 1844.
[In the margin] Copyed & Delivered to Self on 9th of August 1847 by D.H.G.

Daniel Jackson, No. 314, p. 119:
Rockingham County to wit
Registered in my office as No. 314 The 12th day of April 1844 Daniel Jackson a Mulatto Man about 21 years of age Five Feet Four Inches high and has a scar on the inside of his left hand on Thumb and has a scar on the left wrist and was free born as appears by Evidence filed in my office. The Foregoing Register was by the Court Compared with the said Daniel Jackson and a copy thereof is ordered to be furnished him according to Law done at April Court 1844.
[In the margin] Copyed & Delivered to Self on the 1st day of April 1847 by D.H. Gambill.

Jerry Henderson, No. 315, p. 119:
Rockingham County to wit

133

Registered in my office as No. 315 the 11th day of May 1844 Jerry Henderson A verry Black Man about 37 years of age 5 feet 7 inches high has a scar on the back of the right hand and a scar on the right cheak boan, and was set free by Deed of emancipation from David Stinespring bearing date the 15th of April 1844 and record[ed] in the Clerks office of said County. The foregoing register was by the court compared with the said Jerry and a copy thereof is ordered to be furnished him according to Law done at May Court 1844.
[In the margin] Copyed & Delivered to self the 19th Sept'r 1845 D.W.G.

<u>James Peters</u>, No. 316, p. 119:
Rockingham County to wit
Registered in my office as No. 316 the 22nd day of May 1844 James Peters A Black Man about 20 years of age 5 feet 7 inches high has a scar in the corner of the Left eye and was free born as appears by evidence filed in my office. The Foregoing Register was by the court compared with the said James and a copy thereof is ordered to be furnished him according to Law done at May Court 1844.
[In the margin] Copyed & Delivered to self the 16th of December 1845 L.W. Gambill.

<u>Abraham McCourland</u>, No. 317, p. 120:
Rockingham County to wit
Registered in my office as No. 317 The 19th day of October 1844 Abraham McCourland A Black Man Between 45 and Fifty years of age Five Feet Five and a half inches high and has a scar on the left cheek a small scar in the Forehead a scar around the front of his left Thumb a scar on the little Finger of the left hand and also a scar on the third finger of the left hand and was emancipated by the will of William McCourland Deceased which is of record in my office. The Foregoing register was by the Court Compared with the said

134

Abraham McCourland and found duly made a Copy thereof is ordered to be furnished him according to Law done at October Court 1844. [In the margin] Copy Delivered to self the 23rd of October 1844 L.W.G.

James McCourland, No. 318, p. 120:
Rockingham County to wit
Registered in my Office as No. 318 the 19th day of October 1844 James McCourland A Black Man Between 41 and Forty Two years of age Five Feet Four and a half inches high and has a scar on his forehead and a scar near the right side of his nose a scar on the right side of his chin the first Joint of the forefinger of the right hand has been broken and a scar on the third Joint of the forefinger of the left hand and a scar on the back of the right hand and was emancipated by the will of William McCourland deceased which is of Record in my office. The foregoing Register was by the Court Compared with the said James McCourland and found duly made a Copy thereof is ordered to be furnished him according to Law done at October Court 1844.
[In the margin] Copy Delivered to self the 23rd of October 1844 L.W.G.

Levi Lewis, No. 319, p. 120:
Rockingham County to wit
Registered in my office as No. 319 the 19th day of October 1844 Levi Lewis A Black Man Between 26 and 27 years of age 5 Feet 4 Inches high has a scar across his nose and a scar on the right side of his right eye and a scar on the left eye Brow and was free Born as appears by the affidavit of James Hopkins filed in my office. The foregoing register was by the Court compared with the said Levi Lewis and found duly made a copy thereof is ordered to be furnished him according to Law done at ____ Court 1844.

<u>Nancy Bundy</u>, No. 320, p. 121:
Rockingham County to wit
Registered in my office as No. 320 This 14th
day of March 1845 Nancy Bundy A Black Woman
Between 29 & 30 years of age, and has a scar
on the inside of the left wrist her eye sight
Bad occassioned by the Scrofula and was free
Born as appears by the affidavit of Thomas
Bohanon filed in my office. The foregoing
Register was by the Court compared with the
said Nancy Bundy and found duly made a Copy
thereof is ordered to be furnished her
according to Law done at March Court 1845.
[In the margin] Examined & Delivered to self
the 3rd of May 1845 L.W.G.

<u>Matilda Amos</u>, No. 321, p. 121:
Rockingham County to wit
Registered in my office as No. 321 The 20th
day of May 1845 Matilda Amos A Dark Mulatto
Girl 18 years of age Five Feet high and a
small scar on the right Cheek Bone and a scar
on the back of the left hand and was Free Born
as appears by the affidavit of Elizabeth
Stevens filed in my Office. The foregoing
Register was by the Court compared with the
said Matilda and found duly made a Copy
thereof is ordered to be furnished her
according to Law done at May Court 1845.
[In the margin] Copied & Delivered to self the
22nd of May 1845 L.W.G.

<u>Augustus</u>, No. 322, pp. 121-122:
Rockingham County to wit
Registered in my office as No. 322 The 22nd
day of July 1845 Augustus a verry Black Man
about 35 years of age and Five Feet Seven and
a fourth Inches high and was Free Born as
appears by the affidavit of Archibald Hopkins
filed in my office. Augustus has a Small Scar
on left side of the head about an Inch from
his Eye and a Small Scar on the forehead over
the right eye and a lump on the forehead and a

large Scar just below the elbow on the left arm and no other marks perceable. The foregoing register was by the Court compared with the said Augustus and found duly made a copy thereof is ordered to be furnished him according to law done at September Court 1845. [In the margin] Copyed & Delivered to ...

Henry Bundy, No. 323, p. 122:
Rockingham County to wit
Registered in my office the 16th day of August 1845 as No. 323 Henry Bundy a handsome black man Straight & well-made about 5 feet 4 inches high, has a scare on the inside of his left rist, and a scare on the back of the left hand, 21 years old about the 8th day of August 1845 (as he says), he was born free as appears by satisfactory evidence filed in my office. The foregoing Register was by the Court compared with the said Henry Bundy and found duly made, a copy thereof ordered to be furnished him as the Law directs done at November Court 1845.
[In the margin] Copyed & Delivered to 21st of January 1846 by D.H.G.

Synthia, No. 324, p. 122:
Rockingham County to wit
Registered in my office as No. 324 the 19th day of August 1845 Synthia a verry dark Mulatto Girl 22 years old in May last (as she says) 5 feet 3 inches high, has a scare on the lower part of the thumb on the right hand on[e] other scare perceavable, she was set free by Thomas Rice her late Master by Deed of emancipation dated the _____ day of October 1844 and of Record in my office. The foregoing Register was compared by the Court with the said Synthia and found duly made, a copy thereof is ordered to be furnished her, as the Law directs done at August Court 1845.
[In the margin] Copied and delivered to self the 27th of August 1845 L.W. Gambill

Sam Null, No. 325, pp. 122-123:
Rockingham County to wit
Registered in my office as No. 325 the 29th
September 1845 Sam Null, about 40 years of age
a verry Black man 5 feet 8 Inches high, No
scars either on his breast, face or hands
perceavable, rather handsom[e], was
emancipated by Leonard Null by deed date[d]
19th August 1845, and Recorded in my office.
The foregoing Register was compared by the
Court with the said Sam and found duly made a
copy thereof was ordered to be furnished him
in the manner directed by Law done at October
Court 1845.
[In the margin] Copied & Delivered to self the
1st of October 1846 L.W.G.

Levi Null, No. 326, p. 123:
Rockingham County to wit
Registered in my office as No. 326 the 29th
September 1845 Levi Null about 25 years of
age, a dark Mulatto, about 5 feet 9 Inches
high, has a small scare on the fore finger of
the left hand (appears to have been by a cut)
no other scare perceavable a verry likely man,
he was emancipated by Leonard Null, by deed of
Record in my Office dated the 19th August
1845. The foregoing Register was compared by
the court with the said Levi, and found duly
made a copy thereof was ordered to be
delivered him as the Law directs done at
October Court 1845.
[In the margin] Copied & Delivered to self
[deleted: 20th of October 1845] July 1846
L.W.G.

Robert Null, No. 327, p. 123:
Rockingham County to wit
Registered in my office as No. 327 29
September 1845 Robert Null about 20 years of
age, a verry dark Mulatto about 5 feet 11 1/2
Inches high, has a scare on the outside of the
Little finger of the left hand, and a small

138

one across the Knuckel of the fore finger of
the Right hand, was emancipated by Leonard
Null by deed of Record in my said Office dated
the 19th August 1845. The foregoing register
was this day compared by the Court with the
said Robert and found duly made, a copy
thereof was ordered to be delivered the said
Robert, as the Law directs done at October
Court 1845.
[In the margin] Copied & Delivered to self 20
of [deleted: October 1845] July 1846 L.W.G.

Mary Null, No. 328, p. 124:
Rockingham County to wit
Registered in my Office (No. 328) the 29th
September 1845 Mary Null about 23 years of age
a dark Mulatto about 5 feet 5 Inches high a
small scare on the rist of the left hand or
arm, also a [deleted: large] scare on her
breast Occasioned by a burn, no other marks
perceavable, a likely woman, she was
emancipated by Leonard Null by deed Recorded
in my Office dated the 19th August 1845. The
foregoing Register was this day compared by
the Court with the said Mary and found duly
made a copy thereof was ordered to be
delivered her, as the Law directs done at
October Court 1845.
[In the margin] Copied & delivered [deleted:
to self ____ of October 1845] 20th July 1846
L.W.G.

Rachael Null, No. 329, p. 124:
Rockingham County to wit
Registered in my office (No. 329) the 29th
September 1845 Rachael Null about 21 years of
age, a dark Mulatto 5 feet 4 inches high, has
a small scare on the upper Lip near the right
corner of her mouth no other mark or scare
perceavable, a likely woman, she was
emancipated by Leonard Null by deed dated the
19th of August 1845 and Recorded in my office.
The foregoing Register was compared by the

court with the said Rachael and found duly
made a copy thereof was ordered to be
furnished her by the Clerk as the Law directs,
done at October Court 1845.
[In the margin] Copied & [deleted: delivered
to self ____ of October 1845] delivered to
self the 20th July 1846 L.W.G.

Matilda McCausland, No. 330, p. 124:
Rockingham County to wit
Registered in my office as No. 330 20th day of
October 1845 Matilda McCausland about 29 years
of age, a very black Woman 5 feet 5 inches
high, has scare on the back of the left hand
Near the Joint of the finger, No other mark or
scare visable rather a likely woman was
emancipated by the will of William McCausland
Recorded in my office. The foregoing Register
was compared by the Court with the said
Matilda and found duly made a copy thereof was
ordered to be furnished her by the clerk as
the Law directs done at October Court 1845.
[In the margin] Copied & delivered to self the
[deleted: ____ of October 1845] 10th March
1846 L.W.G.

Rachael Jane McCausland, No. 331, pp.
124-125:
Rockingham County to wit
Registered in my office as No. 331 the 20th
October 1845 Rachael Jane McCausland about 41
years of age a Mulatto Woman 5 feet 4 1/2
Inches high, a scare on the Right hand
Occasioned by the Nail of the Little finger
being defective, has no other scare or mark
Visable, a likely woman, she was emancipated
by the will of William McCausland deceased
which is of Record in my office. The
foregoing Register was compared by the Court
with the said Rachael Jane, and found duly
made, a copy thereof was ordered to be
furnished her by the Clerk of the Court, as
directed by Law, done at October Court 1845.

[In the margin] Copied & delivered to self
[deleted: ____ of October 1845] the 10th March
1846 L.W.G.

George Gordon, No. 332, p. 125:
Rockingham County to wit
Regtistered in my Office as No. 332 the 18th
day of November 1845 George Gordon A Dark
Mulatto Man about 36 years of age Five Feet
Ten Inches high has a Scar on the back of the
right hand also Two Scars on the left arm or
wrist A large Scar across the Eye Brow of the
left Eye and a small scar above the same Eye
and a small Scar near the Right Corner of the
Mouth and was emancipated by the Will of
Philip Koontz Deceased which is of Record in
my office. The foregoing Register was by the
Court Compared with the said George Gordon and
found duly made. A Copy thereof is ordered to
be furnished the said George Gordon as the law
directs done at November Court 1845.
[In the margin] Copied & Delivered to self the
29th September 1846 L.W.G.

Polly Bundy, No. 333, p. 125:
Rockingham County to wit
Registered in my office as No. 333 the 24th
day of February 1846 Polly Bundy A Black Woman
between 31 and 32 years of age 4 feet 11 1/2
Inches high, has a small scar on the Joint of
the Thumb on the left hand and a small Scar
above the left Eye was born free as appears by
a Certificate filed in my office. The
foregoing Register was by the Court Compared
with the said Polly Bundy and found duly made
A Copy thereof is ordered to be furnished the
said Polly Bundy as the Law directs done at
March Court 1846.
[In the margin] Copied & Delivered to self the
18th of March 1846 L.W.G.

Nelly Null, No. 334, p. 126:
Rockingham County to wit

141

Registered in my office as No. 334 the 12th day of August 1846 Nelly Null A Dark Mulatto Woman Between 43 & 44 years of age Five Feet Three and a half Inches high has a thick Neck and a Mole above the right Eye Brow and a Scar on the back of the little finger of the left hand and was emancipated by Leonard Null by Deed of Emancipation of Record in my office dated the 19th day of August 1845. The foregoing Register was by the Court Compared with the said Nelly Null and found duly Made A Copy thereof is ordered to be furnished the said Nelly as the Law directs done at August Court 1846.
[In the margin] Copied & Delivered to self the 18th of August 1846 L.W.G.

Lewis Byrd, No. 335, p. 126:
Rockingham County to wit
Registered in my office as No. 335 the 12th day of September 1846 Lewis Byrd a Mulatto Man about 65 years of age Five Feet Seven Inches high has a mark or scar on the End of the fourth finger of the right hand and was free born as appears by a former Register of his Freedom from the County of Stafford filed in my office. The Foregoing Register was by the Court compared with the said Lewis Byrd and found duly made. A Copy thereof is ordered to be furnished the said Lewis as the Law directs done at _____ Court 184_.

Martha Ann Craig, No. 336, p. 126:
Rockingham County To wit
Registered in my office as No. 336 the 13th day of February 1847 Martha Ann Craig a Dark Mulatto Girl about Twenty Years of age Five Feet Two inches high has no marks and was free born as appears by evidence filed in my office. The Foregoing Register was by the Court Compared with the said Martha and found duly made. A Copy thereof is ordered to be furnished the said Martha as the Law directs

142

done at February Court 1847.
[In the margin] Copyed & Delivered to ...

   Levi Lewis, No. 337, p. 337:
Rockingham County To wit
Registered in my office as No. 337 The 16th
day of March 1847 Levi Lewis A Black Man
Between 26 and 27 years of age 5 Feet 4 Inches
high has a Scar across his nose and a scar on
his forehead a scar on the right side of his
right eye and a scar on the left eye Brow and
was free Born as appears by the affidavit of
James Hopkins filed in my office. The
foregoing register was by the Court Compared
with the said Levi Lewis and found duly made a
copy thereof is ordered to be furnished him
according to Law done at May [deleted: March]
Court 1847.
[In the margin] Copyed & Delivered to self
20th October 1848 E.C.

   Harry Sellers, No. 338, p. 127:
Rockingham County To wit
Registered in my office as No. 338 The 9th day
of April 1847 Harry Sellers A Black Man about
45 years of age Five Feet Ten inches high has
a large scar on the Thum[b] of the left hand,
a scar on the wright eye Brow and is the same
Man that was emancipated by the Eve Sellars
Dec'd as appears by the records of my office.
The foregoing register was by the Court
Compared with the s'd Harry Sellars [sic] and
was found duly made a copy thereof is ordered
to be furnished him according to Law done at
April Court 1851 [deleted 1847].
[In the margin] Examined & Delivered to self
Ap'l 22nd 1851 J.G.C.

   Lucretia, No. 339, p. 127-128:
Rockingham County to wit
Registered in my office as No. 339 the 26th
April 1847 Lucretia a verry Dark Mulatto or
Black Woman about 24 years of age, five feet 7

143

Inches high has a scare on the top of the
right rist supposed to be occasioned by a
burn, has prominent mouth no other marks or
scare perceavable, she has an Infant Male
Child with her who[se] name she says is Santa
Anna. The foregoing register was made in my
office on the day of its date, but as the said
Woman wanted to go with her Mother to
Pennsylvania, I delivered her a copy with the
seal of my office & which was attested by W.G.
Stevens a justice of the peace for this county
in which certificate all the facts and
circumstances was [sic] set forth at large,
etc.
[In the margin] A copy delv'd to Lucretia etc.

Harrison Parriott, No. 340, p. 128:
Rockingham County To wit
Registered in my office as No. 340 The 13th
day of May 1847 Harrison Parriott A Black Man
about 23 years of age 19th Feb'ry 1847 Five
Feet 7 inches high, a scar on the left cheek,
and a scar on the right thumb and is free born
as appears by evidence filed in my office.
The foregoing register was by the court
compared with the said ... Harrison Parriott
and found duly made a copy thereof is ordered
to be furnished him according to Law done at
May Court 1847.
[In the margin] Copyed & Delivered to self on
the 18th day of May 1847 D.H.G. Renewed at
Aug't Ct. 1857 & delv'd on Nov. 7, 1957 L.W.G.

Lydia Ann Lewis, No. 341, p. 128:
Rockingham County To wit
Registered in my office as No. 341 Lydia Ann
Lewis A Bright Mulatto Woman 23 years of age
Five Feet 8 inches high a scar on the left eye
brow, and a scar on the middle finger of left
hand, and is free born as appears by evidence
filed in my office. The Court is refered to
the foregoing register and was by the court
compared with the said Lydia Ann and found

144

duly made, a copy thereof is ordered to be furnished her according to Law done at May Court 1847.
[In the margin] Copied & Delivered to self on the 5th of June 1847 D.H.G.

Abraham Brock, No. 342, p. 129:
Rockingham County To wit
Registered in my office as No. 342 This 14th May 1847 Abraham Brock A Black Man Between Twenty Five and Twenty Six years of age Five Feet 8 inches high a scar under his chin, and a scar on the fore finger of the left hand, and was set free as appears by the last will of John Brock Dec'd. The Court is refered to the foregoing register and was by the court compared with the said Abraham and found duly made a copy thereof and is ordered to be furnished him done at May Court 1847.
[In the margin] Copied & Delivered to Self on the 5th June 1847 D.H.G.

Barbara Pence, No. 343, p. 129:
Rockingham County To wit
Register[ed] in my office as No. 343 This 14th May 1847 Barbara Pence a Bright Mulatto Woman 47 years of age Five Feet 5 1/2 inches high a scar on her chin and the Little finger on the right hand Stiff, a small Scar on the little finger of the left hand Free born, Daughter of Polly Adams. The Foregoing register was by the court compared with the Said Barbara Pence and found duly made a copy thereof is ordered to be furnished her done at May Court 1847.
[In the margin] Copied & Delivered to Self on the 6th of June 1847 D.H.G. Fee Paid.

Gabril Lewis, No. 344, p. 130:
Rockingham County to wit
Registered in my office as No. 344 This 17th day of May 1847 Gabril Lewis 17 years of age Five Feet 9 inches high a scar on the left Arm, and a Scar on the left thumb, and is free

145

born as appears by evidence filed in my office. The court is refered to the foregoing register and was by the court compared with the said Gabril Lewis and found duly made a copy thereof and is ordered to be furnished him done at May Court 1847.
[In the margin] Copyed & Delivered to Self on the 6th of June 1847 by D.H.G.

George Lewis, No. 345, p. 130:
Rockingham County To wit
Registered in my office as No. 345 This 21st day of May 1847 George Lewis a Dark Mulatto Man 21 years of age 6 Feet high and has a small scar Just above the right Thumb on the right hand and a scar near the Corner of the right Eye caused by a burn. Free Born as appears by the affidavit of John Dixon filed in my office. The foregoing register was by the Court Compared with the said George Lewis and Found duly made a copy thereof is ordered to be furnished him according to Law done at June Court 184_.
[In the margin] Copyed & Delivered to Self on the 5th of June 1847 D.H.G.

John Flory, No. 345, pp. 130-130 [sic, 131]:
Rockingham County to wit
Registered in my office as No. 345 This 21st day of June 1847 John Flory a Black Man about 21 years of age 5 feet 8 inches high a scar on the Right Thumb and a scar on his forhead above the right eye and was born free as appears by evidence filed in my office. The court is refered to the foregoing register was by the court compared with the said John and found duly made a copy thereof and is ordered to [be] furnished him done at June Court 1847.
[In the margin] Copyed & Delivered to self the 22nd of December 1847 L.W.G.

Rebecca Noel, No. 347, p. 130 [sic, 131]:

146

Rockingham County To wit
Registered in my office as No. 347 The 22nd
day of June 1847 Rebecca Noel a Bright Mulatto
Girl about 21 years of age Five feet 8 inches
high has a scar on the Thumb of the left hand
and was free born as appears by evidence filed
in my ... office. The Court is refered to the
foregoing register was by the court compared
with the said Rebecca and found duly made a
copy thereof and is ordered to be furnished
her done at June Court 1847.
[In the margin] Copyed & Delivered to Self on
6th of June 1847 D.H.G.

Mary Holeman, No. 348, p. 130 [sic, 131]:
Rockingham County To wit
Registered in my Office as No. 348 The 17th
day of August 1847 Mary Holeman a Black Woman
Thirty Five years of age Five Feet Three
Inches High has a small scar on the back of
the left wrist and also a small scar on the
third finger of the left hand and was free
born as appears by the affidavit of Reuben
Kingree filed in my office. The foregoing
register was by the Court compared with the
said Mary Holeman and found duly made a Copy
thereof is ordered to be furnished her
according to Law done at August Court 1847.
[In the margin] Examined Copyed & Delivered to
...

Jerry Holly, No. 349, pp. 130 [sic,
131]-131:
Rockingham County To wit
Registered in my office as No. 349 The 16th
day of October 1847 Jerry Holly A Black Man
about Thirty Five years of age Five Feet Nine
inches high has a scar on the left side of his
face upon the uper and lower lip also a scar
behind his right ear and is free born as
appears by evidence filed in my office. The
foregoing register was by the court compared
with the said Jerry and found duly made a copy

147

thereof and is ordered to be furnished him done at October Court 1847.
[In the margin] Copyed & Delivered to self the 2nd day of November 1849 J. Coffman.

Shederick Holly, No. 350, p. 131:
Rockingham County to wit
Registered in my office as No. 350 The 16th of October 1847, Shederick Holly A Black Man about 26 years of age Six feet one inch high has a lump in the left corner of his lower lip and is free born as appears by evidence filed in my office. The foregoing register was by the Court compared with the said Shederick and found duly made a copy thereof and is ordered to be furnished him done at October Court 1847.
[In the margin] Copyed & Delivered to ...

Thornton Spangler, No. 351, p. 131:
Rockingham County To wit
Registered in my office as No. 351 The 7th day of July 1848 Thornton Spangler a dark Mulatto Boy 21 years of age in August Next Five Foot Nine Inches high and has a small scar above the Corner of the right Eye near the Temple and also a scar on the inside of the right Thumb and severall small scars on the back of the left hand also a scar near the left Temple and a scar behind the left ear and was free Born as appears by the affidavit of Daniel Leedy filed in my office. The foregoing register was by the Court compared with the said Thornton Spangler and found duly made a Copy thereof is ordered to be furnished him according to Law done at July Court 1848.
[In the margin] Copied & delivered to self July 17 1848 E.C.

Daniel Veny, No. 352, p. 132:
Rockingham County to Wit
Registered in my Office as No. 352 the 21st day of August 1848 Daniel Veny a black man

Twenty two years of age Five feet eleven 1/2
inches high a scar above the first joint of
the right thumb a large scar on the left arm
below the shoulder and was free born as
appears by the affidavit of Alex'r Chrisman
filed in my office. The foregoing register
was by the court compared with the said Daniel
Veny and found duly made--a copy thereof is
ordered to be furnished him according to law
Done at August Court 1848.
[In the margin] Copyed & Delivered to Self on
21st of Aug 1848 S.H.

William Hughs, No. 353, p. 132:
Rockingham County to wit
Registered in my Office as No. 353 the 21st
day of August 1848 William Hughs a Mulatto
Twenty five years of age, Five feet Seven &
1/2 inches high, has a small scar on the left
ankle and was free born as appears by the
affidavit of Elisha Bryan filed in my office.
The foregoing register was by the Court
compared with the said William Hughs and found
duly made--a copy thereof is ordered to be
furnished him according to law Done at August
Court 1848.
[In the margin] Copyed & Delivered to Self on
Oct 26, 1849 J.G.C.

Lewis Bird, No. 354, p. 132:
Rockingham County to Wit
Registered in my Office as No. 354 the 5th day
of _____ 184_ Lewis Bird a Free Man of Colour
about 67 years of age, and 5 Feet 7 & 1/2
Inches high and is a Mulatto and has a Scar on
the end of the Finger Next the Little Finger,
and a Small scar on the Forehead, and no other
marks perceivable and was Free Born as appears
by the affidavits of Thomas Hord & Nathaniel
Hord filed in my office & The Foregoing
Register was by the County Court of Rockingham
compared with the said Lewis Bird and found
duly made a copy thereof was ordered to be

149

furnished him as the Law directs, done at ____
Court 184_.

Nancy Henry, No. ____, p. 133:
The following Register was this day presented
to Mr. Erasmus Coffman Clerk of Rockingham
County and entered according to Law to Wit:
State of Virginia Clerks Office Rockbridge
County August 6th 1844
Registered Nancy Henry a free woman of colour
aged twenty three years since December last
five feet 4 3/4 inches high, black bushy hair,
has a scar on the nose, also a scar on the
wrist of the right arm abov[e] the thumb--was
free born in Augusta County and daughter of
Suckey Morris, who is a free woman which
appears by a certificate from the Clerk of
Augusta County.
                    Teste Dan'l Hutchison D.C.
A Rockbridge County Court August 6th 1844
The Register of which the abov[e] is a true
copy was produced in Court and the said Nancy
Henry being examined it was ordered to [be]
certified that said Register was truly made.
In testimony whereof I Samuel McD. Reid Clerk
of Rockbridge County Court in said State have
hereto subscribed my name and affixed the seal
of said County at Lexington this tenth day of
April 1848 and in the 72nd year of the
Commonwealth
                    Sam'l D. Reid
                    By Dan'l Hutchison D.C.
                    Atteste John Ruff J.P.
Rockingham County to Wit
The foregoing Register was presented to me
Erasmus Coffman Clerk of the said County and
certificate given the said Nancy Henry October
23rd 1848.
                    Atteste E. Coffman C.R.C.

Caroline Craig, No. 355, p. 133:
Rockingham County to Wit
Registered in my Office as No. 355 on the 16th

150

day of December 1848 Caroline Craig a free
woman a dark mulatto about 21 years of age 5
feet 6 inches high has a scar on the joint of
the left wrist occasioned by a burn, very
thick lips of slender person and delicate
appearance and was free born as appears by the
affidavit of Frances B. Beirm filed in my
office. The foregoing register was by the
County Court of Rockingham compared with the
said Caroline Craig and found duly made a copy
thereof was ordered to be furnished her as the
Law directs. Done at December Court 1848.
[In the margin] Copy'd & Delv'd to Self on
18th of Dec. 1848 S.H.

Dianna Cook, No. 356, p. 134:
Rockingham County to wit
Registered in my office as No. 356 on the 18th
day of December 1848, Dianna Cook a free
woman, a mulatto about 21 years of age--4 feet
10 inches high, and was free born as appears
by the affidavit of Andrew J. Huffman filed in
my office. The foregoing register was by the
county court of Rockingham compared with the
said Dianna Cook and found duly made a copy
thereof was ordered to be furnished her as the
law directs. Done at December Court 1848.
[In the margin] Copyed & delivered to self the
18th Dec. 1848   S. Henry.

Frances Cook, No. 357, p. 134:
Rockingham County to wit
Registered in my office as No. 357 on the 18th
day of December 1848 Frances Cook a free
woman--a mulatto 5 feet high and about 24
years of age, and was free born as appears by
the affidavit of Sarah Miles--filed in my
Office. The foregoing register was by the
county court of Rockingham compared with the
said Frances Cook and found duly made a copy
thereof was ordered to be furnished her as the
law directs. Done at December Court 1848.
[In the margin] Copyed & delivered to self the

18th of Dec. 1848 S. Henry.

Lawson Lewis, No. 358, p. 135:
Rockingham County to wit
Registered in my office as No. 358 on the 17th
of Dec'r 1848 Lawson Lewis a pale mulatto man
about 44 years of age, 5 feet 7 1/2 inches
high, has a scar on the top of his forehead,
no other marks perceivable, and was free born
as appears by the affidavit of John H. Deck
filed in my office. The foregoing register
was by the county court of Rockingham compared
with the said Lawson Lewis and found duly made
a copy thereof was ordered to be furnished him
as the Law directs. Done at January Court
1849.
[In the margin] Copy'd & deliv'd to Self on
the 14th day of July 1849 S. Henry. May 4th
1855 copy made out according to order made of
March Ct 1855 with addition of "about 50 years
of age."

William Cooke, No. ____, p. 135:
The following Register was this day presented
to me Clerk of Rockingham County and entered
according to Law to wit:
Register No. 215 of William Cooke a dark
mulatto man, five feet five and a half inches
high about Thirty Six years of age and has a
scar on his breast occasioned by a burn, made
satisfactory evidence to the Court that he was
born free and is registered by an order of the
Court this 10th day of September 1838.
                    Geo. Grandstaff
Virginia, Shenandoah County to Wit:
At a Court held for the County of Shenandoah
on Monday the 10th of September 1838 the
abov[e] Register No. 215 of William Cooke was
produced, examined by the Court and ordered to
be certified as truly made.
In testimony whereof I have hereunto set my
hand and affixed the seal of said County the
day and date aforesaid.

P. Williams S.C.
Rockingham County to wit:
The foregoing Register was presented to me
Erasmus Coffman Clerk of the said County and
certificate given the said William Cooke
February 24th 1849.

Atteste E. Coffman C.R.C.
[In the margin] Copy'd & Deliver'd to Self on
the 24th of Febr'y 1849 E.C.

Eliza Tate, No. _____, p. 136:
Rockingham County to wit
The following Register was this day presented
to me Erasmus Coffman Clerk of Rockingham
County, and entered according to Law to wit:
Register No. 216 of Eliza Tate a Mulatto woman
five feet three Inches high, about Thirty two
years of age and has two small marks or scars
on the left side of the Neck made satisfactory
evidence to the Court that she was born free
and is reregistered by an order of Court this
10th day of September 1838.

Geo. Grandstaff
Virginia, Shenandoah County to wit:
At a Court held for the County of Shenandoah
on Monday the 10th day of September 1838 the
above register No. 216 of Eliza Tate was
produced, examined by the Court and ordered to
be certified as truly made.
In Testimony whereof I have hereunto set my
hand & affixed the seal of said County the day
and date aforesaid.

P. Williams C.L.S.C.
Rockingham County to wit:
The foregoing register was presented to me
Erasmus Coffman Clerk of said County and
certificate given the said Eliza Tate the 24th
day of September 1849.

William Bailey, No. 359, p. 137:
Rockingham County to wit:
Registered in my Office as No. 359 on the 17th
day of March 1849 William Bailey a free Black

153

Man Five Feet Nine Inches high, has a scar on the Middle finger of the left hand, also the thumb of the left hand out-of-place & a very small scar on the Forehead. Aged about Twenty-three years of age. And was free born as appears by the affidavit of Cyrus Rhodes filed in my office. The foregoing Register was by the County Court of Rockingham compared with the s'd William Bailey and found duly made. A copy thereof was ordered to be furnished him as the Law directs. Done at March Court 1847.
[In the margin] Copy'd & Delv'd to Self on the 19th of March 1849 S.H. Renewed March Ct 1855 with addition of 28 years. Delv'd Dec. 20 1855.

Jacob Hackley, No. 360, p. 137:
Rockingham County to wit
Registered in my office as No. 360 on the 16th day of June 1849 Jacob Hackley a black boy--27 years old 1st of March 1849, has a scar on the forefinger of the left hand & a small scar on the inside of the left hand near the wrist & a scar across the ankle of the right foot, 5 feet 10 inches high. And was free born as appears by the affidavit of Wm. C. Harrison filed in my office. The foregoing register was by the County Court of Rockingham compared with the s'd Jacob Hackley and found duly made. A copy thereof was ordered to be furnished him as the Law directs--done at June Court 1849.
[In the margin] Copy'd & Delv'd to self August 2nd 1849 J.E.C.
Jacob Hackley's register renewed by an order of Court made at the August term 1855 with the addition 33 years old 1st March 1855.

Gabriel Hackley, No. 361, pp. 137-138:
Rockingham County to wit
Registered in my office as No. 361 on the 16th day of June 1849 Gabriel Hackley a black boy

about 21 years of age, has a scar above the first joint of the thumb on the left hand. Also one on the right hand near the wrist & the end of the forefinger of the right hand disfigured--5 feet 11 inches high--and was free born as appears by the affidavit of Wm. C. Harrison filed in my office. The foregoing register was by the county court of Rockingham compared with the said Gabriel Hackley and found duly made, a copy thereof was ordered to be furnished him as the law directs. Done at June Court 1849.
[In the margin] Copy'd & Delv'd to self the 17th of July 1854 L.W.G.

Frances Armstrong, No. 362, p. 138:
Rockingham County to wit
Registered in my office as No. 362 on the 16th day of June 1849, Frances Armstrong a dark Mulatto woman about 21 years of age has a protuberance on each of her little fingers & 5 feet 6 inches high--and was free born as appears by the affidavit of Mrs. Mary Harrison filed in my office. The foregoing register was by the County Court of Rockingham compared with the said Frances Armstrong and found duly made a copy thereof was ordered to be furnished her as the Law directs--done at June Court 1849.
[In the margin] Copy'd & Delv'd to self the 27th July 1849 L.W.G.

Hannah Armstrong, No. 363, p. 138:
Rockingham County to wit
Registered in my office as No. 363 on the 16th day of June 1849 Hannah Armstrong a Mulatto woman between 50 & 60 years of age, has a scar on the left side of the nose about the Middle, has lost her front teeth above & below, 5 feet 5 inches high--and was free born as appears by the affidavit of Abr'm Smith filed in my office. The foregoing register was by the county court of Rockingham compared with the

said Hannah Armstrong and found duly made. A copy thereof was ordered to be furnished her as the Law directs--done at June Court 1849. [In the margin] Copy'd & Delv'd to self the 27th July 1849 L.W.G.

Harrison Armstrong, No. 364, pp. 138-139:
Rockingham County to wit
Registered in my office as No. 364 on the 16th day of June 1849 Harrison Armstrong a dark Mulatto man between 27 & 28 years of age--5 feet 11 inches high-- has a small scar on the back of the left hand & a scar on the top of the left shoulder and was free born as appears by the affidavit of Abr'm Smith filed in my office--the foregoing register was by the county court of Rockingham compared with the s'd Harrison Armstrong and found duly made--a copy thereof was ordered to be furnished him as the Law directs done at June Court 1849. [In the margin] Copy'd & Delv'd to self the 27th July 1849 L.W.G.

Jos. Armstrong, No. 365, p. 139:
Rockingham County to wit
Registered in my office as No. 365 on the 16th day of June 1849 Jos. Armstrong a dark Mulatto Man about 22 years of age--5 feet 11 inches high--has a scar on the right side of the forehead, near the hair--a scar on the right cheek about 1/2 an inch from the nose--a scar on the right leg above the knee--and was free born as appears by the affidavit of Abr'm Smith filed in my office--the foregoing register was by the county court of Rockingham compared with the s'd Jos. Armstrong and found duly made--a copy thereof was ordered to be furnished him as the Law directs--done at June Court 1849. [In the margin] Copy'd & Delv'd to self the 27th July 1849 L.W.G.

Jacob Curtis, No. 366, p. 139:

Rockingham County to wit
Registered in my office as No. 366 on the 16th
day of June 1849--Jacob Curtis--a black boy
about 22 years of age--has two small scars on
the forefinger of the left hand--5 feet 7
inches high--and was free born as appears by
the affidavit of Abr'm Smith filed in my
office. The foregoing register was by the
county court of Rockingham compared with the
s'd Jacob Curtis and found duly made--a copy
thereof was ordered to be furnished him as the
Law directs--done at June Court 1849.
[In the margin] Copy'd & Deliv'd to self June
23rd 1849.

   Polly Armstrong, No. 367, p. 139:
Rockingham County to wit
Registered in my office as No. 367 on the 16th
day of June 1849--Polly Armstrong a black
woman about 23 years of age--5 feet high--has
a scar on the right side of the forehead, a
small mole on the right side of the upper lip
near the nose & a thick neck--and was free
born as appears by the affidavit of Abr'm
Smith filed in my office. The foregoing
register was by the county court of Rockingham
compared with the s'd Polly & found duly made
a copy thereof was ordered to be furnished her
as the Law directs, done at June Court 1849.
[In the margin] Copy'd & Delv'd.

   Hannah Curtis, No. 368, p. 140:
Rockingham County to wit
Registered in my office as No. 368 on the 16th
day of June 1849 Hannah Curtis a dark Mulatto
Woman about 20 years of age--has a scar on the
back of the right hand--5 feet 6 inches high.
And was free born as appears by the affidavit
of Francis McIrvine filed in my office. The
foregoing register was by the county court of
Rockingham compared with the s'd Hannah Curtis
and found duly made--a copy thereof was
ordered to be furnished her as the Law

157

directs, done at June Court 1849.
[In the margin] Copy'd & Delv'd to self August
24th 1849 J.E.C.

Harrison Pearcey, No. 369, p. 140:
Rockingham County to wit
Registered in my office as No. 369 on the 16th
day of June 1849 Harrison Pearcey a tolerably
dark Mulatto boy--about 22 years of age--has a
scar on the wrist of the left hand, the end of
the forefinger of the left hand disfigured,
caused by a felon. A scar on the left foot, 5
feet 8 Inches high. And is free born as
appears by the affidavit of John Cannoe filed
in my office. The foregoing register was by
the county court of Rockingham compared with
the Said Harrison Piercy [sic, deleted
Curtis], and found duly made. A copy thereof
was ordered to be furnished him, as the Law
directs. Done at June Court 1849.
[In the margin] Copy'd & Delv'd to self the 8
Sept 1849 L.W.G.

Catharine Colly, No. 370, pp. 140-141:
Rockingham County to wit
Registered in my Office as No. 370 on the 18th
day of June 1849 Catharine Colly a black Girl
4 feet 1 3/4 Inches high has a Scar on the
right hand & side of the forehead near the
hair about 19 years old. And is free born as
appears by the affidavit of Dr. S.M. Hunter
filed in my office. The foregoing Register
was by the County Court of Rockingham compared
with the said Catharine Colly and found duly
made. A copy thereof was ordered to be
furnished her, as the Law directs. Done at
June Court 1849.
[In the margin] Copy'd & Delv'd to self July
20 1849 J.E.C.

John Peters, No. 371, p. 141:
Rockingham County to wit
Registered in my office as No. 37 on the 18th

158

of June 1849 John Peters a black boy 28 years
old 5 feet 9 1/2 Inches high, has a small scar
near the left eye. And a small scar on the
right side of the nose. And is free born as
appears by the affidavit of Daniel Witts filed
in my office. The foregoing Register was by
the County Court of Rockingham compared with
the said John Peters and found duly made. A
Copy thereof was ordered to be furnished him
as the Law directs, done at June Court 1849.
[In the margin] Copy'd & Delv'd.

Peter Armstrong, No. 372, p. 141:
Rockingham County to wit
Registered in my Office as No. 372 on the 18th
of June 1849 Peter Armstrong A Mulatto Boy
about 15 years old 5 feet 7 inches high has no
visible marks and was free born as appears by
the affidavit of John Camick filed in my
office. The foregoing Register was by the
County Court of Rockingham compared with the
said Peter Armstrong and found duly made. A
copy thereof was ordered to be furnished him
as the Law directs, done at June Court 1849.
[In the margin] Copy'd & Delv'd to self on the
16th of July 1849 S.H.

Mary Armstrong, No. 373, p. 141:
Rockingham County to wit
Registered in my office as No. 373 on the 18th
day of June 1849 Mary Armstrong a mulatto
woman about 18 years of age--has a small scar
on the back of the left hand. No other marks
visible, 5 feet 4 inches high. And was free
born as appears by the affidavit of John
Cammack filed in my office. The foregoing
Register was by the County Court of Rockingham
compared with the said Mary Armstrong and
found duly made. A copy thereof was ordered
to be furnished her as the Law directs, done
at June Court 1849.
[In the margin] Copy'd & Delv'd to self the
27th July 1849 L.W.G.

<u>Julia Curtis</u>, No. 374, p. 142:
Rockingham County to wit
Registered in my office as No. 374 on the 18th
day of June 1849 Julia Curtis a dark Mulatto
Woman about 22 years of Age has a Small Scar
on the forehead has no other marks visible 5
feet 6 inches high and was free born as
appears by the affidavit of John Cammack
[deleted: Abr'm Smith] filed in my office.
The foregoing Register was by the County Court
of Rockingham compared with the s'd Julia
Curtis, and found duly made, a copy thereof
was ordered to be furnished as the Law
directs--done at June Court 1849.
[In the margin] Copy'd & Delv'd to self on the
10th day of Sept. 1849 J.G.C.

<u>Marcellus Lewis</u>, No. 375, p. 142:
Rockingham County to Wit
Registered in my office as No. 375 on the 12th
day of July 1849 Marcellus Lewis--a free black
boy 21 Years of age 5 feet 8 inches high--has
a Scar on his right wrists and was free born
as appears by the affidavit of Henry Hulva
filed in my office. The foregoing register
was by the county court of Rockingham compared
with the said Marcellus Lewis, and found duly
made a copy thereof was ordered to be
furnished him as the Law directs, done at July
Court 1849.
[In the margin] No. 375 Copied & delivered to
self May 30, 1850 E.C.

<u>Yancey Veney</u>, No. 376, pp. 142-143:
Rockingham County To wit
The following Register was this day presented
to me Clerk of Rockingham County the 21st day
of August 1849 and entered according to Law as
No. 376 To wit as is Persuant to an act of the
General Assembly passed the Second day of
March One thousand eight hundred & nineteen
entitled an act reducing into one the several
acts Concerning Slaves Free Negroes and

Mulattoes. I William J. Menefee Clerk of the
County Court of Rappahannock do Certify that
Yancey Veney a brown Coloured man five Feet
Six & three quarter inches high Twenty One
years of age on the 22nd day of April 1845
with a scar on the right side of the face,
supposed to be occasioned by a scratch and no
other apparent mark or scar on his head face
or hands & Was born free as appears from the
Certificate of Thomas Harris here produced &
dated the 10th day of November 1845 and is
registered in my office according to Law.
In Testimony whereof I have hereunto
subscribed my name and affixed the seal of the
said County this 11th day of November in the
year One thousand Eight Hundred & Forty Five
and in the 70th year of the Commonwealth, W.J.
Menefee Clerk
Attest M. Miller a Justice of the Peace for
Rappahannock County.
At a Court held for Rappahannock County on
Tuesday the 11th day of November 1845. The
Court doth certify that the Register of Yancey
Veney is Correctly made.
                    Teste W.J. Menefee Clerk
                    A Copy Teste W.J. Menefee
Rockingham County To wit
The Foregoing Register was presented to me
Erasmus Coffman Clerk of said County and
Entered according to Law & a Copy Delivered
him the 21st day of August 1849.
[In the margin] New Copy of the foregoing
register was delivered to Yancey Veney the
18th January 185_ by order of Court Made at
January 1853 L.W.G.

    Robert Taylor, No. 377, p. 143:
Rockingham County to Wit
Registered in my office as No. 377 on the 21st
day of August 1849 Robert Taylor A black man
about 32 years of Age, 5 feet 11 Inches high,
has a small scar on the left hand between the
forefinger and Thumb, and was Emancipated as

appears by the Will of William Taylor dec'd of Record in my Office. The foregoing Register was by the County Court of Rockingham compared with the Said Robert Taylor and found duly made. A Copy thereof was ordered to be furnished him as the Law directs, done at August Court 1849.
[In the margin] Cop'd & delv'd to self Sept 26th 1849 J.G.C.

Sally McMahon, No. 378, p. 143:
Rockingham County To Wit
Registered in my Office as No. 378 on the 22nd day of August 1849 Sally McMahon a yellow woman about 48 years of age, has a small scar in the centre of the forehead, no other visable marks, is Five feet Five inches high and is free as appears by the affidavits of Robert M. Kyle and P. Effinger filed in my office. The foregoing Register was by the Court of Rockingham compared with the said Sally McMahon and found duly made, a copy thereof was ordered to be furnished her as the Law Directs, done at August Court 1849.
[In the margin] Cop'd & delv'd to self Sept 27th 1849 E.C.

Jane Minor, No. 379, p. 144:
Rockingham County To Wit
Registered in my Office as No. 379 on the 22nd day of August 1849, Jane Minor a Mulattoe girl about 17 years of age (who has a male child aged about 2 years) is 5 feet 3 1/2 inches high, and was free born as appears by the affidavit of Robert M. Kyle filed in my office. The foregoing Register was by the County Court of Rockingham compared with the said Jane Minor and found duly made--a copy thereof was ordered to be furnished her as the Law directs, Done at August Court 1849.
[In the margin] Cop'd & delv'd to self 27th Sept 1849 E.C.

162

George Harrison, No. 380, p. 144:
Rockingham County To Wit
Registered in my Office as No. 380 on the 22nd
day August 1849, George Harrison a mulattoe
boy about 15 years of age has a small scar on
the second joint of the forefinger of the
right hand also a small scar on the first and
second joints of the forefinger of the left
hand and is 5 feet 4 3/4 inches high, and was
free born as appears by the affidavit of
Robert M. Kyle filed in my office. The
foregoing Register was by the County Court of
Rockingham compared with the said George
Harrison and found duly made. A Copy thereof
was ordered to be furnished him as the Law
directs--Done at August Court 1849.
[In the margin] Cop'd & Del'd to self Sept
27th 1849 E.C.

Frances Curtis, No. 381, p. 144:
Rockingham County To Wit
Registered in my Office as No. 381 Frances
Curtis a black Girl about 20 years of age, is
5 feet 1 1/4 inches high, and is free born as
appears by the affidavit of ... John Camic
filed in my office. The foregoing Register
was by the County Court of Rockingham compared
with the said Frances Curtis and found duly
made. A Copy thereof was ordered to be
furnished her as the Law directs done at
August Court 1849.
[In the margin] Cop'd & del'd to self August
22nd 1849 J.G.C.

Mildred Ann Veney, No. 382, p. 145:
Rockingham County To Wit
Registered in my Office as No. 382 on the 17th
day of September 1849 Mildred Ann Veney a
black Girl about 21 years of age, Five feet 1
1/4 inches high, has a small scar on the right
cheekbone, also one above & on the Elbow of
the right arm, and is free born as appears by
the affidavit of Algernon S. Gray filed in my

163

office. The foregoing Register was by the County Court of Rockingham compared with the said Mildred Ann Veney, and found duly made, a copy thereof was ordered to be furnished her as the law directs--Done at September Court 1849.
[In the margin] Cop'd & delivered to self Oct. 15, 1849 J.G.C. Renewed at Aug't Ct 1857 & delv'd L.W.G.

William Strother Buling, No. 383, p. 145:
Rockingham County To Wit
Registered in my Office as No. 383 on the 17th day of September 1849 William Strother Buling, a black man about 34 Years of Age, 5 feet 7 inches high, has a ... scar on the forehead above the right eye and is free as appears by a deed of Emancipation from Hane Buling to said William Strother Buling which is of record in my office. The foregoing Register was by the County Court of Rockingham compared with the said William Strother Buling and found duly made a copy thereof was ordered to be furnished him as the Law directs--Done at September Court 1849.
[In the margin] Cop'd & delivered to self March 18, 1850 J.G.C.

Patsey Tausley, No. 384, p. 145:
Rockingham County To Wit
Registered in my Office as No. 384 on the 15th day of October 1849 Patsey Tausley a black woman about 50 Years of age 5 feet 5 3/4 inches high and has no visible marks & scars and was emancipated as appears by the Last Will and Testament of Henry S. Pirkey dec'd--upon Record in my Office. The foregoing Register was by the County Court of Rockingham compared with the said Patsey Tausley and found duly made--a Copy thereof was ordered to be furnished her as the Law directs, Done at October Court 1849.
[In the margin] Copied & delivered to self

November 15th 1851 E.C.

Elias Johnson, No. 385, p. 146:
Rockingham County To Wit
Registered in my Office as No. 385, the 15th
day of October 1849, Elias Johnson a black man
about 35 years of age has a Scar on the Side
of the right Eye, and is 5 feet 8 3/4 inches
high--and was emancipated as appears by the
Last Will & Testament of Henry S. Pirkey
Dec'd--Upon Record in my Office. The
foregoing Register was by the County Court of
Rockingham compared with the said Elias
Johnson and found duly made a Copy thereof was
ordered to be furnished him as the Law
directs, done at October Court 1849.
[In the margin] Copied & Delivered to self the
13th day of November 1849 L.W.G.

Nancey Smith, No. 386, p. 146:
Rockingham County To Wit
Registered in my Office as No. 386 on the 19th
day of November 1849 Nancey Smith a black
Woman about 24 years of age, Five feet Two
inches high, and has no marks or scars--And
was free born as appears by the affidavit of
Judge Daniel Smith filed in my Office. The
foregoing Register was by the County Court of
Rockingham compared with the said Nancey Smith
and found duly made--A copy thereof was
ordered to be furnished her as the Law
directs, done at November Court 1849.

Adison Morris, No. 387, p. 146:
Rockingham County To Wit
Registered in my Office as No. 387 on the 19th
day of November 1849 Adison Morris A black man
about 22 years of age--5 feet 8 inches high,
has a small scar on the left hand between the
forefinger and Thumb, and is free born as
appears by the affidavit of Jane Pollock filed
in my office. The foregoing Register was by
the County Court of Rockingham compared with

165

the said Adison Morris and found duly made, a copy thereof was ordered to be furnished him as the Law directs, done at November Court 1849.
[In the margin] Copied & Delivered to self the 9th of Dec. 1852 L.W.G.

Ransom Williamson, No. 388, pp. 146-147:
Rockingham County To Wit
Registered in my Office as No. 388 on the 29th [or 28th] day of January 1850 Ransom Williamson, A Black Man Twenty five years of age, Five feet 11 inches high, has 2 small scars on the back of his neck, and has a scar on each side of the left arm Midway between the Shoulder and elbow caused by running a pitch fork through the arm, and was free born as appears by the affidavit of Jonathan Shaver filed in my office. The foregoing register was by the county court of Rockingham compared with the said Ransom Williamson and found duly made, A copy thereof was ordered to be furnished him as the law directs--done at February court 1850.

Lagrand Sampson, No. 389, p. 147:
Rockingham County To Wit
Registered in my office as No. 389 on the 13th day of February 1850 Lagrand Sampson a Bright Mulatto Man about 33 years of age Five Feet Nine Inches high has a small Scar on the back of the right hand between the Thumb and fore finger some small scars on the fore finger of the left hand and a small scar on the little finger of the left hand and also a large scar on the out side of the right leg above the Ankle Joint and was free Born as appears by his former Register of Freedom from the County of Orange filed in my office. The foregoing Register was by the County Court of Rockingham Compared with the said Lagrand Sampson and found duly made a Copy thereof was ordered to be furnished him as the Law directs done at

166

February Court 1850.
[In the margin] No. 389 Copied and delivered to Self May 30th 1850 E.C.

Walker Johnson, No. 390, p. 147:
Rockingham County To Wit
Registered in my Office as No. 390 on the 18th day of February 1850 Walker Johnson a mulatto Boy about 21 years of age--5 feet 5 1/2 Inches high--has a small scar upon the forehead above the left eye--and was free born as appears by the affidavit of Peter Thomas filed in my office. The foregoing register was by the county court compared with the said Walker Johnson and found duly made--a copy thereof was ordered to be furnished him as the law directs done at February Court 1850.
[In the margin] Delivered to self April 2nd 1850 J.G.C.

Marcellus Gibson, No. 391, p. 147:
Rockingham County to Wit
Registered in my Office as No. 391 on the 14th day of March 1850 Marcellus Gibson a Mulatto [deleted: Yellow] boy about Twenty One years of age Five Feet Eleven Inches high & has a small scar on the upper lip under the right nostril & was free born as appears by the affidavit of Polly Long filed in my office. The foregoing register was by the County Court of Rockingham compared with the said Marcellus Gibson & found duly made a Copy thereof was ordered to be furnished him as the Law directs done at March Court 1850.
[In the margin] Examined & delivered to self July 20 1852 L.W.G. Renewed by order of Ct June 1859 & transf'd to New Book.

Abbey Epperson, No. 192 [Note: the numbers abruptly change.], p. 148:
Rockingham County to Wit
Registered in my Office as No. 192 on the 18th day of March 1850 Abbey Epperson a dark

167

mulatto woman about Twenty years of age Five
feet 2 1/4 inches high, and was free born as
appears by the certificate of Judge Daniel
Smith filed in my office. The foregoing
Register was by the County Court of Rockingham
compared with the said Abbey Epperson and
found duly made, a Copy thereof was ordered to
be furnished her as the law directs, done at
March Court 1850.
[In the margin] Cop'd and delivered to self
March 22nd 1850 J.G.C.

Elizabeth Poindexter, No. 193, p. 148:
Rockingham County to Wit
Registered in my Office as No. 193 on the 17th
day of June 1850 Elizabeth Poindexter a
Mulatto Woman about 31 years of age, has a
small scar on the left wrist, Five feet four &
1/2 inches high, and was free born as appears
by the affidavit of Henry Sheets filed in my
Office. The foregoing Register was by the
County Court of Rockingham compared with the
said Elizabeth Poindexter, and found duly
made, A Copy thereof was ordered to be
furnished her as the Law directs, done at June
Court 1850.
[In the margin] Cop'd and delivered to self
June 17th 1850 J.G.C.

Henry Bailey, No. 194, p. 148:
Rockingham County to Wit
Registered in my Office as No. 194 on the 15th
day of July 1850 Henry Bailey a Black boy
about 21 years of age, has a small scar on the
upper lip below the left nostril, a small scar
upon the Middle Joint of the forefinger of the
left hand a small scar on the third Joint of
the thumb of the left hand, Also a scar upon
the first large joint of the finger of the
right hand, Five feet Seven & 3/4 Inches high
and was free born as appears by the affidavit
of Daniel Flook filed in my office. The
foregoing Register was by the County Court of

Rockingham compared with the said Henry
Bailey, and found duly made, a Copy thereof
was ordered to be furnished him as the law
directs, done at July Court 1850.
[In the margin] Cop'd and delivered to self
the 15th day of March 1854 L.W.G.

<u>Gabriel Bicks</u>, No. 195, p. 149:
Rockingham County to Wit
Registered in my Office as No. 195 on the 1st
day of July 1850 Gabriel Bicks a dark mulatto
man about Fifty three years old has a
perpendicular scar upon the right side of the
upper lip and the little finger of the left
hand contracted so that he cannot open it,
caused by a burn--no other marks--Five feet
ten inches high, And was emancipated by the
last Will & Testament of St. Clair Kirtly
dec'd. as appears by a copy of said will
furnished to him by the Clerk of the Superior
Court in accordance with a decree of said
Court in the case of Bicks against Kirtley
[sic] & others. The foregoing Register was by
the County Court of Rockingham compared with
the said Gabriel Bicks, and found duly made a
copy thereof was ordered to be furnished him
as the law directs, done at July Court 1850.
[In the margin] Cop'd and delivered to self
November 20 1850 J.G.C.

<u>Clarissa Baugher</u>, No. 196, p. 149:
Rockingham County to Wit
Registered in my Office as No. 196 on the 19th
day of August 1850 Clarissa Baugher a dark
Mulatto Woman about 27 years old 5 feet 2 3/4
Inches high, has no visible marks or scars and
was emancipated by the last will and Testament
of Nicholas Baugher dec'd, which will is upon
Record in the clerks office of the County
Court of Rockingham County. The said Clarissa
has a female child, a bright Mulatto named
Margaret Ellen about seven years old who was
also emancipated by said will. The foregoing

Register was by the County Court of Rockingham
compared with the said Clarissa Baugher and
found duly made--A Copy thereof was ordered to
be furnished her as the law directs, done at
August Court 1850.
[In the margin] Cop'd and Examined & delivered
to self May 27th 1851 J.G.C.

    Washington, No. 197, p. 150:
Rockingham County to Wit
Registered in my Office as No. 197 on the 16th
day of September 1850 Washington a black man
about 21 years old 5 feet 7 1/2 Inches high,
has a Small Scar upon the 1st Joint of the
forefinger of the left hand, and a Scar upon
the 2nd Joint of the large finger of the left
hand, and was emancipated by the last Will and
Testament of James Gibson, dec'd of Record in
the Clerks Office of Culpepper County, Va. as
appears by a copy of said Will furnished to
me. The foregoing Register was by the County
Court compared with the said Washington and
found duly made a copy thereof was ordered to
be furnished him as the law directs, done at
September Court 1850.
[In the margin] Copyed & Delivered to Self on
the 11th of September 1850.

    Susan Thompson, No. 198, p. 150:
Rockingham County to Wit
Registered in my Office as No. 198 on the 21st
day of October 1850 Susan Thompson a dark
mulatto Woman about Twenty two years of age,
Five feet two inches high, has no visible
marks or scars--and was free born as appears
by the affidavit of Abraham Smith filed in my
office. The foregoing Register was by the
county court of Rockingham compared with the
said Susan Thompson and found duly made--a
Copy thereof was ordered to be furnished her
as the law directs--done at October Court
1850.
[In the margin] Cop'd and Examined. Renewed

Aug't Ct 1856 & delivered by L.W.G.

Francis Peters, No. 199, p. 150:
Rockingham County to Wit
Registered in my Office as No. 199 on the 5th
day of November 1850 Francis Peters a dark
mulatto woman about 28 years of [age] Five
feet 3 inches high, has a small mole near the
corner of her right eye, the right eye very
weak (naturally so) and was free born as
appears by the affidavit of John Miller filed
in my office. The foregoing register was by
the county court of Rockingham compared with
the said Francis Peters and found duly made a
copy thereof was ordered to be furnished her
as the law directs, done at November Court.
[In the margin] Cop'd and examined.

Charles Williamson, No. 200, p. 151:
Rockingham County to wit
Registered in my Office [as] No. 200 on the
18th day of November 1850 Charles Williamson a
black man about thirty two years of age five
feet eight and 1/4 inches high has a scar on
the back of the left hand, a small scar on the
brow of the left eye, also a scar above the
wrist of the right arm, And was born of free
parents as appears by the affidavit of Joseph
Coffman filed in my office. The foregoing
register was by the county court of Rockingham
compared with the said Charles Williamson and
found duly made a copy thereof was ordered to
be furnished him as the law directs, Done at
November Court 1850.
[In the margin] Cop'd and Examined.

George Byrd, No. 201, p. 151:
Rockingham County to Wit
Registered in my Office as No. 201 on the 26th
day of January 1851 George Byrd a light
complexioned boy about 21 years old last
August, has a slight scratch or scar on the
left Cheek, no other visible marks Five feet

171

three inches high, And was born of free parents as appears by the affidavit of John Conrad filed in my office. The foregoing register was compared with the said George Byrd and found duly made, a Copy thereof was ordered to be furnished him as the law directs, done at January Court 1851.
[In the margin] Copied delv'd May 20th 1854 W.D.T. Renewed at Ap'l Ct 1856 with add'n of 26 yrs & delv'd Sept 3 1860.

<u>Wilson Mickens</u>, No. 202, p. 151:
Rockingham County to Wit
Registered in my Office as No. 202 on the 15th day of February 1851 Wilson Mickens a black man about 23 years old, has a small scar above the right eye, a scar on the inside of the wrist of the ... left hand, a large scar on the thigh of the right leg, caused by a burn, 5 feet 11 inches high, and was born of free parents in the county of Rockingham, as appears by the affidavit of Joseph Mauzy filed in my office. The foregoing register was by the County Court of Rockingham compared with the said Wilson Mickens and found duly made, a copy thereof was ordered to be furnished his [sic] as the law directs, Done at Feb'y Court 1851.
[In the margin] Copied & delv'd Dec 28th 1854 W.D. Trout.

<u>Nelson Mickens</u>, No. 203, p. 152:
Rockingham County to Wit
Registered in my Office as No. 203 on the 15th day of February 1851 Nelson Mickens a black man about 35 years of age, has a small piece cut out of the lower side of the left ear, a scar on the wrist of the left hand, a large scar on the big toe of the left foot, a large scar on the instep of the right foot 5 feet 7 1/4 inches high, and was born of free parents in the county of Rockingham as appears by the affidavit of Joseph Mauzy ... filed in my

office. The foregoing Register was by the
county court of Rockingham compared with the
said Nelson Mickens and found duly made--a
copy thereof was ordered to be furnished him
as the law directs--done at Feb'y Court 1851.
[In the margin] Copied Delv'd Dec 18th 1854
Teste W.D. Trout.

Harrison Mickens, No. 204, p. 152:
Rockingham County to Wit
Registered in my Office as No. 204 on the 15th
day of February 1851 Harrison Mickens a black
man about 31 years of age, has a large scar on
the second joint of the left thumb, a small
scar on the corner of the right eye, a very
large scar on the calf of the right leg--5
feet 9 inches high, and was born of free
parents in the county of Rockingham as appears
by the affidavit of Joseph Mauzy filed in my
office. The foregoing Register was by the
county court of Rockingham compared with the
said Harrison Mickens and found duly made--a
copy thereof was ordered to be furnished him
as the law directs--done at Febr'y Court 1851.
[In the margin] Copied Delv'd Dec 28 1854 W.D.
Trout.

Frances Mickens, No. 205, p. 152:
Rockingham County to Wit
Registered in my Office as No. 205 on the 15th
day of February 1851 Frances Mickens a black
woman about 24 years of age has a small round
scar on the back of the left hand, 5 feet 1
1/4 inches high--and was born of free parents
in the county of Rockingham as appears by the
affidavit of Joseph Mauzy filed in my office.
The foregoing Register was by the county court
of Rockingham [compared] with the said Frances
Mickens and found duly made a copy thereof was
ordered to be furnished her as the law
directs, done at Febr'y Court 1851.
[In the margin] Copied & delivered to self
Ap'l 22 185_ J.G.C.

173

<u>Mary Mickens</u>, No. 206, p. 153:
Rockingham County to Wit
Registered in my Office as No. 206 on the 15th
day of February 1851 Mary Mickens a black
Girl--about 19 years of age has no marks or
scars 5 feet 5 1/4 inches high--and was born
of free parents in the county of Rockingham as
appears by the affidavit of Joseph Mauzy filed
in my office.   The foregoing Register was by
the county court of Rockingham compared with
the said Mary Mickens and found duly made a
copy thereof was ordered to be furnished her
as the law directs--done at Febr'y Court 1851.
[In the margin] Copied.

<u>Jesse Lewis</u>, No. 208 [<u>sic</u>, 207 omitted],
p. 153:
Rockingham County to Wit
Registered in my Office as No. 208 on the 17th
day of February 1851 Jesse Lewis a black boy
about 23 years of age next August has four
Scars on the left side of the Neck and Cheek
almost in a strait line a scar on the upper
edge of the left corner of the forehead, left
eye defective 5 feet 6 inches high, and was
born of free parents in the county of
Rockingham as appears by the affidavit of Adam
Showalter filed in my office.   The foregoing
register was by the county court of Rockingham
compared with the said Jesse Lewis and found
duly made, done Febr'y at Court 1851.
[In the margin] Copied and delivered to Self
the 31st day of March 1851 E.C.

<u>Martin Johnson</u>, No. 209, p. 153:
Rockingham County to Wit
Registered in my Office as No. 209 on the 17th
day of February 1851 Martin Johnson a light
complexioned man about 33 years of age he has
a small scar below the left eye, 5 feet 10
inches high--and was born of free parents in
the county of Rockingham as appears by the
Affidavit of John Austin filed in my office.

The foregoing Register was by the county court of Rockingham compared with the said Martin Johnson and found duly made done Febr'y at Court 1851.
[In the margin] Copied.

Mary Ann Johnson, No. 210, p. 154:
Rockingham County to Wit
Registered in my Office as No. 210 on the 17th day of February 1851 Mary Ann Johnson a bright Mulatto woman about 23 years of age 5 feet 4 inches high, she has a slight scar on the back of the right hand apparently caused by a burn, a small scar on the right cheek supposed to be the pit of a chicken pock. She has a small child about four months old, and was born of free parents in the county of Rockingham as appears by the affidavit of John Austin filed in my Office. The foregoing Register was by the county court of Rockingham compared with the said Mary Ann Johnson and found duly made, done Febr'y at Court 1851.
[In the margin] Copied.

Mathew Becks, No. 211, p. 154:
Rockingham County to Wit
Registered in my Office as Number 211 on the 18th February 1851, Mathew Becks, a dark Mulatto man about forty six years of age, his head is bald, little finger of the left hand is crooked, at the first joint, a scar on the left side caused by being stabbed, has lost his front teeth, a small scar on the end of the third finger of the left hand, Five feet 10 inches high, and was emancipated by the Last Will and Testament of St. Clair Kirtley dec'd as appears by a copy of said Will furnished me by the clerk of the superier court in accordance with a decree of the said court in the case of Becks against Kirtley & others. The foregoing Register was by the County Court of Rockingham compared with the said Mathew Becks and found duly made--a copy

thereof was ordered to be furnished him as the Law directs, done Febr'y at Court 1851.
[In the margin] Copied & delivered to self Ap'l 22nd 1851 J.G.C.

Elias Byrd, No. 212, p. 155:
Rockingham County to Wit
Registered in my Office as Number 212 on the 19th day of February 1851--Elias Byrd a dark mulatto man about 54 years [of] age, he has slight scars above the right and left eyebrows, a large scar on the back of the right hand, five feet 7 1/2 inches high, and was born free as appears by the affidavit of Nathaniel Hord filed in my office. The above Register of the said Elias Byrd is a renewal of a former Register directed to be made by an Order of the County Court of Rockingham on the 18th day of February 1851. The foregoing Register was by the County Court of Rockingham compared with the said Elias Byrd and found duly made, a copy thereof was ordered to be furnished him as the law directs, done at February Court 1851.
[In the margin] Copied & delivered to self Ap'l 22nd 1851 E.C. [See No. 39, p. 16.]

William Alexander, No. 213, p. 155:
Rockingham County To Wit
Registered in my Office as Number 213 on the 19th March 1851--William Alexander, a very bright Mulatto Man between 35 & 36 years of age 5 feet 4 1/2 inches high, with features very much like a white man & having but little resemblance to a Negro. A scar on the wrist of the left hand near where the thumb joins the wrist, a small scar on the brow of the right eye, a scar on the upper lip occasioned by a burn [and one] on the upper and outer part of the left wrist, dimple in the chin, has an intelligent & sprightly countenance--and was born of free parents in the county of Rockingham as appears by the

176

affidavit of Nancy Tanksly filed in my Office.
The foregoing Register was by the County Court
of Rockingham compared with the said William
Alexander and found duly made a copy thereof
was ordered to be furnished him as the Law
directs Done at April Court 1851.
[In the margin] Examined & delivered to self
Ap'l 21 1851 J.G.C.

Washington Williams, No. 214, p. 155:
Rockingham County To Wit
Registered in my Office as Number 214 on the
19th March 1851, Washington Williams, a bright
Mulatto man about 25 years of age, slender in
form, & has an intelligent countenance, a scar
on the brow of the right eye, a very small
scar on the under part of the left wrist, and
was born of free parents in the county of
Rockingham as appears by the affidavit of
Nancy Tanksly filed in my office--5 feet 9
inches high. The foregoing Register was by
the county court of Rockingham compared with
the said Washington Williams and found duly
made a copy thereof was ordered to be
furnished him as the law directs--done at May
Court 1851.
[In the margin] Copied & delivered to self May
19th 1851 J.G.C.

Martha Ellen Alexander, No. 215, p. 156:
Rockingham County to Wit
Registered in my Office as No. 215 on the 19th
March 1851--Martha Ellen Alexander a bright
Mulatto woman, 5 feet 1 inch high about 19
years old, sprightly and intelligent
countenance, has a small scar on the right
side of the forehead, has a warty formation on
the little finger of each hand, a long scar on
the back of the right hand apparently
occasioned by a scratch, and was born free in
the county of Rockingham, as appears by the
affidavit of Betsy Hans filed in my Office.
The foregoing Register was by the county court

of Rockingham compared with the said Martha Ellen and found duly made--a copy thereof was ordered to be furnished her as the law directs--Done at April Court 1851.
[In the margin] Exam'd and delivered to self April 21st 1851 J.G.C. Renewed by order May Ct 1863 & cop'd & delv'd June 4th/63.

George Collins, No. 216, p. 156:
Rockingham County to Wit
Registered in my Office as Number 216 on the 22nd day of March 1851 George Collins a very bright Mulatto man about twenty two years of age, with features very much like a whiteman & having little resemblance to a Negro, has a scar on the left thumb, two slight scars on the back of the left hand, and was free born in the county of Rockingham as appears by the affidavit of Betsy Hain filed in my office. The foregoing Register was by the court of Rockingham compared with the said George Collins and found duly made A copy thereof was ordered to be furnished him as the law directs, Done at ____ Court 1851.

Moses Holeman, No. 217, p. 156:
Rockingham County to Wit
Registered in my Office as Number 217 on the 16th day of April 1851--Moses Holeman a very black man--of slender form, 5 feet 9 1/2 inches high--about 25 years of age, he has no visible marks or scars--and was free born as appears by the affidavit of John Smith filed in my office. The foregoing Register was by the county court of Rockingham compared with the said Moses Holeman and found duly made--a copy thereof was ordered to be furnished him as the law directs--Done at Ap'l Court 1851.
[In the margin] Copied.

Mary Elizabeth Detrick, No. 218, p. 157:
Rockingham County to Wit
Registered in my Office as number 218 on the

19th day of April 1851--Mary Elizabeth
Detrick, a black woman Twenty five year[s] old
in November next 5 feet 1/2 inch high, has no
visible marks or scars--(she has two small
children both Girls one called Mary Ann, about
one year old--the other called Martha
Jane--who will be two years old in July next)
and was born free in the county of Rockingham
as appears by the affidavit of Andrew Lago
filed in my Office. The foregoing Register
was by the county court of Rockingham compared
with the said Mary Elizabeth Detrick and found
duly made, A copy thereof was ordered to be
furnished her as the Law directs--Done at
April Court 1851.
[In the margin] Copied.

James Detrick, No. 219, p. 157:
Rockingham County to Wit
Registered in my Office as Number 219 on the
19th day of April 1851 James Detrick--a black
boy about Twenty two years old in October
Next--5 feet 2 1/2 inches high, he has a
slight mark on the forehead above the right
eye--no other visible marks or scars, and was
born of free parents in the county of
Rockinghyam as appears by the Affidavit of
Andrew Lago filed in my Office. The foregoing
Register was by the county court of Rockingham
compared with the said James Detrick and found
duly made--A copy thereof was ordered to be
furnished him as the law directs--Done at
April Court 1851.
[In the margin] Copied & delivered to self
Sept 20th 1851 E.C.

John Detrick, No. 220, p. 157:
Rockingham County to Wit
Registered in my Office as number 220 on the
19th day of April 1851 John Detrick--a light
complexioned black boy--nineteen years old, 5
feet 7 3/4 inches high--he has two small scars
over the centre of his forehead, no other

visible marks or scars--And was born of free parents in the county of Rockingham as appears by affidavit of Andrew Lago filed in my Office. The foregoing Register was by the county court of Rockingham compared with the said John Detrick and found duly made, a copy thereof was ordered to be furnished him as the Law directs, Done at April Court 1851.
[In the margin] Copied & delivered to Self Sept 21st 1851 E.C.

Henry Wesley Detrick, No. 221, p. 158:
Rockingham County to Wit
Registered in my Office as Number 221 on the 19th day of April 1851, Henry Wesley Detrick--a black boy about 17 years old, 5 feet 4 1/2 inches high, he has a long scar on the wrist of the right hand, a scar on the side of the right hand, no other visible marks, and was born of free parents in the county of Rockingham as appears by the affidavit of Andrew Lago filed in my Office. The foregoing Register was by the county court of Rockingham compared with the said Henry Wesley Detrick and found duly made--A copy thereof was ordered to be furnished him as the Law directs--Done at April Court 1851.
[In the margin] Copied & delivered to self Sept 21st 1851 E.C.

Charles Detrick, No. 222, p. 158:
Rockingham County to Wit
Registered in my Office as number 222 on the 19th day of April 1851 Charles Detrick a blackman about 45 years of age, 5 feet 5 1/4 inches high, he has a scar on the little finger of the left hand, a scar above the left Eye, lame in the left leg--and was emancipated by the last will and Testament of Adam Detrick Dec'd of record in my office. The foregoing Register was by the county court of Rockingham compared with the said Charles Detrick and Found duly made, a copy thereof was ordered to

180

be furnished him as the law directs--Done at
April Court 1851.
[In the margin] Copied & delivered to Self
Ap'l 22nd 1851 E.C.

William Cook, No. 223, p. 158:
Rockingham County to Wit
Registered in my Office as number 223 on the
21st day of April 1851 William Cook--a bright
mulatto boy about 21 years of age 5 feet 3 1/4
inches high--he has no visible marks or scars
and was free born as appears by the affidavit
of Polly Holsinger filed in my office. The
foregoing Register was by the county court of
Rockingham compared with the said William Cook
and found duly made A Copy thereof was ordered
to be furnished him as the law directs--Done
at April Court 1851.
[In the margin] Copied.

Jacob Detrick, No. 224, p. 159:
Rockingham County to Wit
Registered in my Office as Number 224 on the
21st day of April 1851--Jacob Detrick a black
boy about 13 years old--he has a large scar
above the left Eye brow, no other visible
marks or scars--4 feet 9 inches high and was
free born as appears by the affidavit of
Andrew Lago filed in my Office. The foregoing
Register was by the County Court of Rockingham
compared with the Said Jacob Detrick and found
duly made a Copy thereof was ordered to be
furnished him as the law directs--Done at
April Court 1851.
[In the margin] Copied & delivered to Self
Sept 21st 1851 E.C.

Margaret Poindexter, No. 225, p. 159:
Rockingham County to Wit
Registered in my Office as Number 225 on the
21st day of April 1851--Margaret Poindexter a
very bright mulatto woman--about 34 years of
age--5 feet 5 1/4 inches high--sprightly and

intelligent countenance, she has a scar
between the eyes, a small scar on the left
side of the forehead where the hair commences
to grow, no other visible marks or scars, and
was born free as appears by the affidavit of
Daniel Flook filed in my Office. The
foregoing Register was by the county court of
Rockingham compared with the said Margaret
Poindexter and found duly made, a copy thereof
was ordered to be furnished her as the Law
directs, Done at April Court 1851.
[In the margin] Examin'd and delivered to self
April 21 1851 J.G.C.

Levi Lewis, No. 226, p. 159:
Rockingham County to Wit
Registered in my Office as Number 226 on the
21st day of April 1851--Levi Lewis--a black
man between 30 and 31 years of age--5 feet 4
inches high--has a scar across his nose--a
scar on his forehead--a scar on the right side
of his right eye--a scar on the left eye brow,
and was free born as appears by the affidavit
of James Hopkins filed in my Office. The
foregoing Register was by the court of
Rockingham county compared with the said Levi
Lewis--and found duly made--a copy thereof was
ordered to be furnished him as the law
directs--Done at April Court 1851.
[In the margin] Copied.

Phoebe Smith, No. 227, p. 160:
Rockingham County to Wit
Registered in my Office as Number 227 on the
22nd day of April 1851--Phoebe Smith--a dark
mulatto woman about 37 years of age 5 feet
high--a scar near the second joint of the
forefinger of the right hand--no other visible
marks or scars--and was Emancipated by the
last Will and Testament of Dianna
Smith--deceased, which will is of record in my
Office. The foregoing Register was by the
county court of Rockingham compared with the

182

said Phoebe Smith and found duly made a copy
thereof was ordered to be furnished her as the
Law directs, Done at Sept. Court 1851.
[In the margin] Copied & delivered to E.H.
Smith Nove. 3rd 1851 E.C.

Eveline Lewis, No. 228, p. 160:
Rockingham County to Wit
Registered in my Office as Number 228 on the
21st day of April 1851--Eveline Lewis a Negro
[deleted: black] woman about 26 years of
age--has a small scar on the left side of the
forehead near the hair 5 feet 3 1/2 inches
high--and was free born in the county of
Rockingham as appears by the affidavit of
Abraham Breneman filed in my Office. The
foregoing Register was by the county court of
Rockingham compared with the said Eveline
Lewis and found duly made--a copy thereof was
ordered to be furnished him [sic] as the law
directs--Done at July Court 1851.
[In the margin] Copied & delivered June 29th
1852 J.G.C.

Thornton Smith, No. 229, p. 160:
Rockingham County to Wit
Registered in my Office as Number 229 on the
5th day of May 1851--Thornton Smith--a light
complexioned Negro boy about 25 years of age,
5 feet 4 inches high--he has four scars on the
right side of the Neck and throat--a scar on
the left cheekbone--a long scar on the inside
of the left hand--and was emancipated by the
last will and Testament of Dianna Smith
deceased--(which will is of record in my
office.) The foregoing Register was by the
Court of Rockingham county compared with the
said Thornton Smith and found duly made a copy
thereof was ordered to be furnished him as the
Law directs--Done at Sept. Court 1851.
[In the margin] Copied & delivered to E.H.
Smith Nov. 3rd 1851 E.C.

Sally Bryant, No. 230, p. 161:
Rockingham County to Wit
Registered in my Office as number 230--on the
17th day of May 1851--Sally Bryant--a negro
woman about 35 years of age--5 feet 2 1/2
inches high--a small round scar on the inside
of the left wrist about 2 inches from the
hand--no other marks--and was born of free
parents in the county of Shenandoah County,
from the personal knowledge of the Clerk of
Rockingham County. The foregoing Register was
by the County Court of Rockingham compared
with the [said] Sally Bryant and found duly
made a copy thereof was ordered to be
furnished her as the Law directs--Done at May
Court 1851.
[In the margin] Copied.

Frances Mary Holeman, No. 231, p. 161:
Rockingham County to Wit
Registered in my Office as Number 231 on the
17th day of May 1851 Frances Mary Holeman a
black woman 5 feet 6 inches high--about 26
years of age, has no visible marks or scars on
the face or hands--was free born as appears by
the affidavit of John Smith filed in my
office. The foregoing Register was by the
County Court of Rockingham compared with the
said Frances Mary Holeman and found duly made
a copy thereof was ordered to be furnished her
as the Law directs Done at May Court 1851.
[In the margin] Copied.

Elizabeth Strother, No. 232, p. 161:
Rockingham County to Wit
Registered in my Office as Number 232 on the
17th day of May 1851 Elizabeth Strother a
bright mulatto woman about 18 years of age--5
feet 2 1/2 inches high--has a small scar near
the middle joint of the fore finger of the
left hand--a whitish mark or blemish on the
lower part of the Iris of the right eye--and
free born as appears by the affidavit of John

Smith filed in my Office. The foregoing
Register was by the county court of Rockingham
compared with the said Elizabeth Strother and
found duly made--a copy thereof was ordered to
be furnished her as the Law directs--Done at
May Court 1851.
[In the margin] Copied.

Eda Ann Williams, No. 233, p. 162:
Rockingham County to Wit
Registered in my Office as Number 233 on the
19th day of May 1851--Eda Ann Williams a
bright Mulatto woman about 23 years of age
Five feet five inches high--has a small scar
on the left wrist occasioned by a burn no
other visible marks--and was born [deleted:
of] free [deleted: parents] as appears by the
affidavit of Nancy Tanksley filed in my
office. The foregoing Register was by the
county court of Rockingham compared with the
said Eda Ann Williams and found duly made a
copy thereof was ordered to be furnished her
as the Law directs--Done at May Court 1851.
[In the margin] Copied Examined and delivered
to self May 19 1851 J.G.C.

Margaret Lewis, No. 234, p. 162:
Rockingham County to Wit
Registered in my Office as Number 234 on the
19th day of May 1851 Margaret Lewis a black
woman about 26 years of age--Five feet, 1 1/2
inches high--has a small scar on the brow of
the left eye a scar on the third joint of the
forefinger of the left hand--small lumps on
the back of each hand near where the hand
Joins the wrist--And was born free in the
county of Rockingham as appears by the
Affidavit of Henry A. Chrisman filed in my
Office. The foregoing Register was by the
county court of Rockingham compared with the
said Margaret Lewis and found duly made--Done
at May Court 1851.
[In the margin] Copied & Delivered to self the

185

30th of June 1852 L.W.G.

    <u>Thomas Robertson</u>, No. 235, p. 162:
Rockingham County to Wit
Registered in my Office as Number 235 on the
19th day of May 1851--Thomas Robertson a black
man about 27 years old, Five feet 3 3/4 inches
high--has a small scar on the side of the nose
near the corner of the right eye--a scar on
the breast--no other visible marks or
scars--and was born free in the county of
Louisa as appears by evidence filed in my
office. The foregoing Register was by the
county court of Rockingham compared with the
said Thomas Robertson and found duly made a
copy thereof was ordered to be furnished him
as the law directs--Done at May Court 1851.
[In the margin] Copied & Delivered to self the
31st day of May 1851 L.W.G. Renewed at Sept
Ct 1855 & deliv'd.

    <u>Madison Moore</u>, No. 236, p. 163:
Rockingham County to Wit
Registered in my Office as Number 236 on the
19th day of May 1851 Madison Moore a black man
about 38 years of age--Six feet high--he has a
scar on the upper lip near the right corner of
the mouth--a scar near the corner of the left
eye--a scar above the left eye--a scar on the
thin joint of the forefinger of the left hand,
a scar on the first joint of the large finger
of the left hand--and is free from the
personal knowledge of the clerk of Rockingham
county. The foregoing Register was by the
county court of Rockingham compared with the
said Madison Moore and found duly made a copy
thereof was ordered to be furnished--Done at
May Court 1851.
[In the margin] Copied.

    <u>Mary Elizabeth Lewis</u>, No. 237, p. 163:
Rockingham County to Wit
Registered in my Office as Number 237 on the

19th day of May 1851 Mary Elizabeth Lewis, a
bright mulatto woman about 19 years of age,
she has a small scar on the back of the left
hand near the wrist joint--no other visible
marks or scars--Five feet one inch high, and
was free born as appears of record in my
Office. The foregoing Register was by the
County Court of Rockingham compared with the
said Mary Elizabeth Lewis and found duly made
a copy thereof was ordered to be furnished her
as the law directs--Done at May Court 1851.
[In the margin] Copied & delivered to self
June 7th 1851 E.C.

Grandison Gordon, No. 238, p. 164:
Rockingham County to Wit
Registered in my Office as Number 238 on the
14th day of June 1851 Grandison Gordon a dark
mulatto man about 37 years of age bald headed,
5 feet 7 inches high, has a small black mole
on the edge of the upper lip on the right
side, & was Emancipated since the 1st day of
May 1806 by the will of John Hoover dec'd, now
of record in this Office, and no permission
has been granted the said Grandison Gordon by
the court of this county to remain in this
State. The foregoing Register was by the
county court of Rockingham compared with the
said Grandison Gordon and found duly made a
copy thereof was ordered to be furnished her
[sic] as the law directs Done at Augt Court
1851.
[In the margin] Copied & delivered to self
Sept 8th 1851 E. Coffman.

Milly Gordon, No. 239, p. 165:
Rockingham County to Wit
Registered in my Office as Number 239 on the
14th day of June 1851 Milly Gordon, dark
mulatto woman about 30 years of age, dumpy in
figure & inclined to be corpulent, 4 feet 11
inches high, no visible marks or scars, was
emancipated by the Will of John Hoover dec'd,

187

now of record in this Office, and no permission has been granted the said Milly Gordon by the court of this county to remain in this state. The foregoing Register was by the County Court of Rockingham compared with the said Milly Gordon and found duly made a copy thereof was ordered to be furnished her as the law directs, Done at ____ Court.

Abraham Louderberry, No. 240, p. 165:
Rockingham County to Wit
Registered in my Office as No. 240 on the 17th day of June 1851 Abraham Louderberry, a negro man about 5 feet 6 inches high aged about 24 years has a small scar above the right eyebrow, a scar upon the back of the left wrist, a scar upon the middle finger of the left hand near the knuckle joint, as [sic] was free born as appears by the affidavit of Wm. K. Gailey filed in my Office. The foregoing Register was by the County Court compared with the said Abraham Louderberry and found duly made a copy thereof was ordered to be furnished him as the law directs--Done at July Court.
[In the margin] Copied & delivered to self November 11th 1851 J.G.C.

Henry Amos, No. 241, p. 165:
Rockingham County To Wit
Registered in my Office as Number 241 on the 17th day of June 1851--Henry Amos a negro man about twenty years of age 5 feet 5 inches high, has a scar between the eyes, left eye is rather smaller than the right, a scar on the back part of the head, and was free born as appeared to this Court on the testimony of Wm. G. Stevens. The foregoing Register was by the County Court of Rockingham compared with the said Henry Amos and found duly made a copy thereof was ordered to be furnished him as the law directs, Done at June Court 1851.
[In the margin] Examined & delivered to self

188

June 17th 1851 J.G.C.

Gessner Bird, No. 242, p. 166:
Rockingham County To Wit
Registered in my Office the 19th day of June
1851 as No. 242 Gessner Bird a dark mulatto
boy about 18 years of age, 5 feet 6 inches
high--has a scar on the outside of the left
wrist, a scar on the third joint of the
forefinger of the left hand, a scar on the
inside of the third finger of the right hand,
no other marks or scars visible as [sic] was
free born in the County of Rockingham as
appears by the affidavit of Andrew J. VanPelt
filed in my office. The foregoing Register
was by the County Court of Rockingham compared
with the said Gessner and being found duly
made a copy thereof was ordered to be
furnished him as directed by Law--Done at
November Court 1851.
[In the margin] Copied & delivered to Gessner
Bird Nov 17th 1851 J.G.C.

Caroline Lewis, No. 243, p. 166:
Rockingham County, to Wit
Registered in my Office the 21st day of July
1851 as No. 243 Caroline Lewis a black woman
about 28 years of age, 5 feet 2 1/2 inches
high has a scar on the middle joint of the
large finger of the left hand, no other
visible marks or scars and was free born in
the county of Rockingham as appears by the
affidavit of Andrew Bear filed in my Office.
The foregoing Register was by the County Court
of Rockingham compared with the said Caroline
Lewis, and found duly made a copy thereof was
ordered to be furnished her as the law
directs, Done at July Court 1851.
[In the margin] Copied & delivered to self
July 21 1851 J.G.C.

Caroline Gordon, No. 244, p. 166:
Rockingham County to Wit

Registered in my Office as No. 244 on the 21st
day of July 1851--Caroline Gordon a bright
complexioned negro woman about 34 years of
age, 5 feet 3 inches high, has no visible
marks or scars on the hands or face, and was
emancipated since 1806 by the last will &
testament of John Hoover dec'd of record in my
office, and no permission has been granted her
by the county court to remain in this county.
The foregoing Register was by the County Court
of Rockingham compared with the said Caroline
Gordon and found duly made A Copy thereof was
ordered to be furnished her as the law
directs, Done at July Court 1851.
[In the margin] Copied & delivered to self
1851 J.G.C.

Christina Moyers, No. 245, p. 167:
Rockingham County to Wit
Registered in my Office as No. 245 on the 21st
day of July 1851 Christina Moyers, a bright
mulatto woman about 50 years of age, 5 feet 5
1/2 inches high, she has no visible marks or
scars on the hands or face, and was free born
in the county of Shenandoah as appears by the
affidavit of Elizabeth Pirkeypile filed in my
Office. The foregoing Register was by the
county Court of Rockingham compared with the
said Christina Moyers and found duly made, A
copy thereof was ordered to be furnished her
as the law directs, Done at July Court 1851.
[In the margin] Copied.

Peggy Moyers, No. 246, p. 167:
Rockingham County, to Wit
Registered in my Office as Number 246 on the
21st day of July 1851 Peggy Moyers, a very
bright mulatto woman about 28 years of age, 5
feet 5 3/4 inches high, has no visible marks
or scars on the face or hands and was free
born in the county of Rockingham as appears by
the affidavit of Elizabeth Pirkeypile filed in
my Office. The foregoing register was by the

County Court of Rockingham compared with the said Peggy Moyers, and found duly made a copy thereof was ordered to be furnished her as the law directs, Done at July Court 1851.
[In the margin] Copied & delivered to Peggy Moyers July 22 1851 J.G.C.

Mary Jane Moyers, No. 247, p. 167:
Rockingham County, to Wit
Registered in my Office as No. 247 on the 21st day of July 1851, Mary Jane Moyers, a black woman [deleted: Girl] about 25 years of age, 5 feet 3 inches high, a Slight Scar on the back of the right hand, no other visible marks or scars, and was freeborn in the County of Rockingham as appears by the affidavit of Elizabeth Pirkeypile filed in my office. The foregoing Register was by the county court of Rockingham compared with the said Mary Jane Moyers and found duly made, a copy thereof was ordered to be furnished her as the law directs--Done at July Court 1851.
[In the margin] Copied.

Sarah Ann Moyers, No. 248, p. 167:
Rockingham County, to Wit
Registered in my Office as No. 248 on the 21st day of July 1851--Sarah Ann Moyers, a dark mulatto woman about 22 years of age, 5 feet 3 inches high, has no visible marks or scars on the hands or face, and was freeborn in the county of Rockingham as appears by the affidavit of Elizabeth Pirkeypile filed in my office. The foregoing Register was by the county court of Rockingham compared with the said Sarah Ann Moyers, and found duly made a copy thereof was ordered to be furnished her as the law directs, Done at July Court 1851.
[In the margin] Copied.

Lucinda Moyers, No. 249, p. 168:
Rockingham County, to Wit
Registered in my Office as Number 249 on the

21st day of July 1851, Lucinda Moyers, a mulatto girl about 14 years of age, 5 feet 2 1/2 inches high, has a slight scar on the fore finger of the left hand, no other visible marks or scars, and was freeborn in the county of Rockingham as appears by the affidavit of Elizabeth Pirkeypile filed in my office. The foregoing register was by the county court of Rockingham compared with the said Lucinda Moyers and found duly made, a copy thereof was ordered to be furnished her as the law directs--done at July Court 1851.
[In the margin] Copied.

Samuel Veney, No. 250, p. 168:
Rockingham County, to Wit
Registered in my Office as No. 250 on the 21st day of July 1851, Samuel Veney a very blackman about 41 years of age, 5 feet 5 inches high, a scar on the upper part of the forehead, a small scar on the right side of the right hand, no other marks or scars--and was free born in the County of Rockingham as appears by evidence produced to the county court of Rockingham. The foregoing Register was by the county court of Rockingham compared with the said Samuel Veney & found duly made a copy thereof was ordered to be furnished him as the Law directs--Done at July Court 1851.
[In the margin] Copied & delivered to self Febr'y 7th 1852 J.G.C.

Dianna Hackley, No. 251, p. 168:
Rockingham County, to Wit
Registered in my Office as No. 251 on the 21st day of July 1851 Dianna Hackley a blackwoman about 24 years of age, 5 feet 3 1/2 inches high, has a large scar on the left side of the nose, a scar on the under side of the third finger of the right hand, and was freeborn in the county of Rockingham as appears by the affidavit of William Harrison filed in my office. The foregoing register was by the

county court of Rockingham compared with the said Dianna Hackley and found duly made, a copy thereof was ordered to be furnished her as the law directs--Done at July Court 1851. [In the margin] Copied.

Amanda Catharine Barnet, No. 252, p. 168: Rockingham County to Wit
Registered in my Office as No. 252 on the 21st day of July 1851 Amanda Catharine Barnet a Negro [deleted: black] woman about 23 years of age, 5 feet 2 1/2 inches high, has a scar on the left side of the neck, a scar on the under side of the left thumb and was freeborn in the county of Rockingham as appears by the affidavit of Henry Miller filed in my office. The foregoing register was by the county court of Rockingham compared with the said Amanda Catharine Barnet and found duly made, a copy thereof was ordered to be furnished her as the law directs--Done at July Court 1851. [In the margin] Copied.

Mary Jane Barnet, No. 253, p. 169: Rockingham County, to Wit
Registered in my Office as No. 253 on the 21st day of July 1851 Mary Jane Barnet a Negro [deleted: black] girl about 18 years of age, 5 feet high, has a large scar on the inside of the left wrist, no other visible marks or scars on the hands or face and was freeborn in the county of Rockingham as appears by the affidavit of Henry Miller filed in my office. The foregoing Register was by the county court of Rockingham compared with the said Mary Jane Barnet and found duly made, a copy thereof was ordered to be furnished her as the law directs--Done at July Court 1851. [In the margin] Copied.

Sarah Koontz, No. 254, p. 169: Rockingham County, to Wit
Registered in my Office as No. 254 on the 21st

193

day July 1851--Sarah Koontz a light
complexioned negro woman about 39 years of
age, has a slight scar on the left side of the
upper lip, no other visible marks or scars, 5
feet 3 1/2 inches high, and was emancipated
since May 1806 by the last will and testament
of John Koontz dec'd, of record in my Office,
& no permission has been granted her by the
county court to remain in this county. The
foregoing register was by the county court of
Rockingham compared with the said Sarah Koontz
and found duly made--a copy thereof was
ordered to be furnished her as the law
directs--Done at July Court 1851.
[In the margin] Copied & delivered to Peter
Koontz March 18th 1852 J.G.C.

Rhoda Peck, No. 255, p. 169:
Rockingham County, to Wit
Registered in my office as No. 255 on the 21st
day of July 1951 Rhoda Peck a light
complexioned negro girl about 19 years of age,
5 feet 2 1/4 inches high, has a Scar on the
left side of the face near the temple, no
other visible marks or scars--and was freeborn
in the county of Rockingham as appears by the
affidavit of Jackson Horn filed in my Office.
The foregoing Register was by the county court
of Rockingham compared with the said Rhoda
Peck and found duly made a copy thereof was
ordered to be furnished her as the law
directs. Done at July Court 1851.
[In the margin] Copied & delivered to R.C.
Thompson by her request August 18th 1851
J.G.C.

Elizabeth Barnet, No. 256, p. 169:
Rockingham County, to Wit
Registered in my Office as No. 256 on the 21st
day of July 1851 Elizabeth Barnet a negro
[deleted: black] girl about 16 years of age 4
feet 11 inches high, has no visible marks or
scars on the hands or face, and was freeborn

194

in the county of Rockingham as appears by the affidavit of Henry Miller filed in my Office. The foregoing register was by the county court of Rockingham compared with the said Elizabeth Barnet and found duly made--a copy thereof was ordered to be furnished her as the law directs--done at July Court 1851.
[In the margin] Copied.

Charles Hackley, No. 257, p. 170:
Rockingham County, to Wit
Registered in my office as No. 257 on the 21st day of July 1851, Charles Hackley a very black man about 31 years of age, 6 feet 1 inch high, the little finger of the left hand considerably contracted & stiff occasioned by a burn, a scar on the inside of the third finger of the left hand, the finger also contracted from effect of a burn And was freeborn in the county of Rockingham as appears by the affidavit of John Shoemaker. The foregoing register was by the county court of Rockingham compared with the said Charles Hackley and found duly made, a copy thereof was ordered to be furnished her as the law directs--Done at July Court 1851.
[In the margin] Copied.

John Hackley, No. 258, p. 170:
Rockingham County, to Wit
Registered in my Office as number 258 on the 21st day of July 1851, John Hackley a very black man about 26 years of age, 5 feet 8 1/2 inches high has a scar at the extremity of the right eye brow near the corner of the eye on the outside, and was freeborn in the county of Rockingham as appears by the affidavit of John Shoemaker filed in my office. The foregoing register was by the county court of Rockingham compared with the said John Hackley and found duly made, a copy thereof was ordered to be furnished him as the law directs--done at July Court 1851.

Betsy Hackley, No. 259, p. 170:
Rockingham County, to Wit
Registered in my Office as No. 259 on the 21st
day of July 1851 Betsy Hackley a very black
woman about 36 years of age 5 feet 3 inches
high has no visible marks or scars on the
hands or face and was freeborn in the county
of Rockingham as appears by the affidavit of
John Shoemaker filed in my office. The
foregoing register was by the county court of
Rockingham compared with the said Betsy
Hackley and found duly made a copy thereof was
ordered to be furnished her as the law
directs. Done at July Court 1851.
[In the margin] Copied.

John Moyers, No. 260, p. 170:
Rockingham County, to Wit
Registered in my office as number 260 on the
21st day of July 1851 John Moyers, a light
complexioned Negro boy about 20 years of age,
5 feet 9 1/2 inches high has a slight scar on
the right side of the face near the eye, a
scar on the forefinger of the left hand a scar
on the little finger of the right hand, and
was free born in the county of Rockingham as
appears by the affidavit of Elizabeth
Pirkeypile filed in my office. The foregoing
register was by the county court compared with
the s'd John Moyers & found duly made, a copy
thereof was ordered to be furnished him as the
Law directs, done at July Court 1851.
[In the margin] Copied & Deliverd to self the
16th of Augt 1851 L.W.G. Augt Ct 1855 It was
found to the satisfaction of the Court that
Jno. Moyers has lost the copy of his register
it was ordered that another copy be delivered.

Susannah Moyers, No. 261, p. 171:
Rockingham County, to Wit
Registered in my Office as No. 261 on the 18th

day of August 1851--Susannah Moyers--a bright
Mulatto woman about 31 years of age--5 feet 6
1/4 inches high--has no visible marks or scars
on the hands or face and was free born in the
county of Rockingham as appears by the
affidavit of Elizabeth Pirkeypile filed in my
office. The foregoing register was compared
by the county court with the said Susannah
Moyers and found duly made a copy thereof was
ordered to be furnished her as the law
directs--Done at August Court 1851.
[In the margin] Copied and delivered to self
August 18th 1851 J.G.C.

Louisa Garrison, No. 262, p. 171:
Rockingham County to Wit
Registered in my Office as No. 262 on the 18th
day of August 1851--Louisa Garrison a Negro
[deleted: light complexioned] woman about 21
years of age--5 feet 1 inch high, has a scar
on the left hand near the wrist, a slight scar
on the right wrist and free born in the County
of Rockingham as appears by the affidavit [of]
Samuel Moyers filed in my Office. The
foregoing register was by the County Court
compared with the said Louisa Garrison and
found duly made--a copy thereof was ordered to
be furnished her as the law directs--done at
August Court 1851.

Barbara Ann Strother, No. 263, p. 171:
Rockingham County, to Wit
Registered in my Office as No. 263 on the 18th
day of August 1851 Barbara Ann Strother a
light complexioned negro woman about 23 years
of age--5 feet 2 inches high, has no visible
marks or scars on the hands or face--and free
born in the county of Rockingham as appears by
the evidence filed in my office. The
foregoing Register was by the county court
compared with the said Barbara Ann Strother
and found duly made--a copy thereof was
ordered to be furnished her as the law

directs, Done at August Court 1851.

Reuben Madden, No. 264, p. 172:
Rockingham County, to Wit
Registered in my Office as No. 264 on the 18th day of August 1851--Reuben Madden a light complexioned negro boy about 23 years of age--5 feet 3 inches high--has a scar on the right side of the face below the eye a scar on the left eye brow, a slight scar on the left temple, and free born in the county of Rockingham as appears by testimony produced to the court. The foregoing Register was by the county court of Rockingham compared with the said Reuben Madden and found duly made a Copy thereof was ordered to be furnished her [sic] as the law directs--Done at August Court 1851. [In the margin] Transfered to New Book.

Henry Madden, No. 265, p. 172:
Rockingham County to Wit
Registered in my Office as No. 265 on the 18th day of August 1851--Henry Madden a Negro boy about 21 years of age 5 feet 6 inches high--a scar on the right temple--no other visible marks or scars on the hands and face--and free born in the county of Rockingham as appears by testimony produced to the court. The foregoing Register was by the county court of Rockingham compared with the said Henry Madden and found duly made--a Copy thereof was ordered to be furnished him as the law directs--Done at August Court 1851.

Andrew Eiler, No. 266, p. 172:
Rockingham County to Wit
Registered in my Office as number 266 on the 9th day of September 1851 Andrew Eiler a very black man, about 33 years of age, 5 feet 10 1/2 inches high, has lost the thumb of the left hand & one of the centre teeth of the upper Jaw, and was Emancipated since May 1806 by the will of Margaret Eiler dec'd, now of

198

record in my office. The said Andrew has not
obtained permission from the court of this
county to remain in this commonwealth. The
foregoing Register was by the county court of
Rockingham compared with the said Andrew Eiler
and found duly made a copy thereof was ordered
to be furnished him as the law directs--Done
at September Court 1851.
[In the margin] Examined and delivered to self
Sept 29 1851 J.G.C.

<u>John Smith</u>, No. 267, p. 173:
Rockingham County to Wit
Registered in my Office as Number 267 on the
15th day of September 1851 John Smith a Negro
boy about 21 years of age, 5 feet 5 inches
high, marked with a dark stain below the
corner of the right eye, a scar on the middle
of the wrist of the right arm, a small scar on
the back of the left hand, and was emancipated
since May 1806 by the will of Diana Smith
dec'd, Now of Record in my office. The
foregoing Register was by the county court of
Rockingham compared with the said John Smith
and found duly made a copy thereof was ordered
to be furnished him as the law directs--done
at Sept Court 1851.
[In the margin] Copied & delivered to E.H.
Smith Nov 3 1851 E.C.

<u>John Thompson</u>, No. 268, p. 173:
Rockingham County to Wit
Registered in my Office as Number 268 on the
15th day John Thompson, a light mulatto boy
about 20 years of age 5 feet 7 inches high,
has a small scar on the outside of the left
wrist, has a slight and indistinct scar or
mark above the corner of the left eye brow
near the temple no other visible marks or
scars, and was free born in the county of
Rockingham as appears by the affidavit of
Abr'am Smith filed in my office. The
foregoing Register was by the county court of

Rockingham compared with the said John
Thompson and found duly made, a copy thereof
was ordered to be furnished him as the law
directs, Done at ____ Court 1851.

James Holeman, No. 269, p. 173:
Rockingham County, to Wit
Registered in my Office as Number 269 on the
15th day of September 1851, James Holeman a
Mulatto man, about 37 years of age 6 feet
high, he has a large Scar on the left side of
the neck and face, a Scar on the third joint
of the little finger of the right hand, and
was free born as appears by evidence filed in
my office. The foregoing Register was by the
county court of Rockingham compared with the
said James Holeman and found duly made a copy
thereof was ordered to be furnished him as the
law directs--done at September Court 1851.
[In the margin] Copied & delivered to James
Holeman Nov 17th 1851 J.G.C.

John Jones, No. 270, p. 174:
Rockingham County to Wit
Registered in my Office as number 270 on the
19th day of November 1851--John Jones a
mulatto man about 25 years of age--5 feet four
and 1/2 inches high--has a scar near the
centre of his forehead, a slight scar or
scratch on the right wrist, no other visible
marks, and free born as appears from evidence
filed in my office. The foregoing Register
was by the county court of Rockingham compared
with the said John Jones and found duly made a
copy thereof was ordered to be furnished him
as the law directs--Done at November Court
1851.

George Rinker, No. 271, p. 174:
Rockingham County, to Wit
Registered in my Office as Number 271 on the
15th day of December 1851 George Rinker a
black man about 38 years of age 5 feet 6 1/4

inches high, has a large Scar on the little
finger of the left hand no other scars or
marks visible--was emancipated by the will of
John Brock of record in my office since May
1806 & has never obtained permission from the
court to remain in this commonwealth. The
foregoing Register was by the county court of
Rockingham compared with the said George
Rinker and found duly made--a copy thereof was
ordered to be furnished him as the law
directs--done at December Court 1851.
[In the margin] Copied & delivered to self
Febr'y 7th 1852 J.G.C.

   John Thompson, No. 272, p. 174:
Rockingham County to Wit
Registered in my Office as Number 272 [see
entry no. 268] on the 15th day of December
1851 John Thompson a mulatto boy about 20
years of age, 5 feet 7 inches high--has a
small scar on the outside of the left wrist, a
small scar on the second joint of the right
thumb--and free born in the county of
Rockingham as appears by the affidavit of
Abraham Smith filed in my office. The
foregoing Register was by the county court of
Rockingham compared with the said John
Thompson and found duly made--a copy thereof
was ordered to be furnished him as the law
directs--done at December Court 1851.
[In the margin] Copied & Delivered to self the
20th of September 1856 L.W.G.

   George Gordon, No. 273, p. 175:
Rockingham County To Wit
ReRegistered in my Office on the 18th of
August 1851 as number 273 in pursuance of an
order of the county court made at August Court
1851--George Gordon a dark mulatto man about
41 years of age 5 feet 10 inches high has two
scars on the back of the right hand, has two
scars the left arm or wrist, a large scar
across the brow of the left eye, and a small

201

scar above the same eye and a small scar near
the right corner of the mouth, and was
emancipated by the will of Philip Koontz dec'd
which is of record in my office. The
foregoing register was by the court compared
with the said George Gordon and found duly
made a copy thereof is ordered to be furnished
the said George Gordon as the law
directs--Done at August [deleted: December]
Court 1851.
[In the margin] Copied & delivered to self
26th Dec'r 1851 E.C.

Lucinda Morris, No. 274, p. 175:
Rockingham County to Wit
Registered in my Office as number 274 on the
... 15th day of March 1852 Lucinda Morris a
light complexioned Negro woman about 40 years
of age, 5 feet 1 1/2 inches high, has a slight
Scar on the inside of the right wrist, (she
has a small male child called Edward Nathaniel
about 2 months old) and free born as appears
by the affidavit of William Eiler of record in
my office. The foregoing Register was by the
county court of Rockingham compared with the
said Lucinda Morris & found duly made, a copy
thereof is ordered to be furnished her as the
law directs--Done at March Court 1852.
[In the margin] Copied & delivered to self Dec
13th 1852 B.F.M.

Frances Morris, No. 275, p. 175:
Rockingham County to Wit
Registered in my Office as Number 275 on the
15th day of March 1852 Frances Morris a bright
Mulatto Girl about 23 years of age, 5 feet 2
inches high, has a large scar on the front
part of the neck, (she has a small male child
called James William Franklin about 2 months
old) and free born in the county of Rockingham
as appears by affidavit of William Eiler filed
in my Office. The foregoing Register was by
the county court of Rockingham compared with

202

the said Frances Morris and found duly made, a
copy thereof was ordered to be furnished her
as the law directs--Done at March Court 1852.
[In the margin] Copied & delivered to self Dec
13th 1852 B.F.M.

Mary Jane Morris, No. 276, p. 176:
Rockingham County, to Wit
Registered in my Office as number 276 on the
15th day of March 1852, Mary Jane Morris a
Negro Girl about 21 years of age, 5 feet 3
inches high, has no visible marks or scars,
and free born in the county of Rockingham as
appears by the Affidavit of Wm. Eiler filed in
my Office. The foregoing Register was by the
county court of Rockingham compared with the
said Mary Jane Morris and found duly made a
copy thereof was ordered to be furnished her
as the law directs--Done at March Court 1852.
[In the margin] Copied & delivered to self Dec
13th 1852 B.F.M.

John Morris, No. 277, p. 176:
Rockingham County, to Wit
Registered in my Office as Number 277 on the
15th day of March 1852 John Morris a light
complexioned negro boy about 20 years of age,
5 feet 7 1/2 inches high, has no visible marks
or scars, and freeborn in the county of
Rockingham ... as appears by the Affidavit of
Wm. Eiler filed in my Office. The foregoing
Register was by the county court of Rockingham
compared with the said John Morris and found
duly made--a copy thereof was ordered to be
furnished him as the law directs--Done at
March Ct 1852.
[In the margin] Copied & delivered to self Dec
13th 1852 B.F.M.

Layton Morris, No. 278, p. 176:
Rockingham County, to Wit
Registered in my Office as Number 278 Layton
Morris a Negro boy about 14 years of age 4

feet 11 1/2 inches high, has no visible marks or scars, and free born in the county of Rockingham as appears by the Affidavit of Wm. Eiler filed in my Office. The foregoing Register was by the county court of Rockingham county compared with the said Layton Morris and found duly made, A Copy thereof was ordered to be furnished him as the law directs--Done at March Court 1852.
[In the margin] Copied & delivered to self Dec 13th B.F.M.

Julia Ann Morris, No. 279, p. 177:
Rockingham County, to Wit
Registered in my Office as number 279 on the 15th day of March 1852 Julia Ann Morris a mulatto girl about 12 years old, 4 feet 8 inches high, has a scar on the right side of the neck--no other visible marks or scars--and free born in the county of Rockingham as appears by the Affidavit of Wm. Eiler filed in my Office. The foregoing Register was by the county court of Rockingham compared with the said Julia Ann Morris and found duly made--a copy thereof was ordered to be furnished her as the law directs--Done at March Court 1852.
[In the margin] Copied & delivered to self Dec 13th 1852 B.F.M.

Catharine Moon, No. 280, p. 177:
Rockingham County To Wit
Reregistered in my Office on the 21st day of June 1852 as Number 280 in pursuance of a special order of the county court of Rockingham made at June Term 1852--Catharine Moon a negro [deleted: Black or dark Mulatto] woman about Thirty two years of age Five feet four inches high, has a scar on the little finger of the left hand & a scar on the upper lip (she has a female child called Mary Ellen about 9 months old) and was emancipated by the will of Thomas Moon dec'd since May 1806 now of record in my office & no permission has

been granted her to remain in this Commonwealth by the county court. The foregoing register was by the County Court of Rockingham compared with the said Catharine Moon and being found duly made a copy thereof was ordered to be furnished her as the Law direct. Done at June Court 1852.
[In the margin] Copied & delivered to self 30th Nov 1852.

Isaiah Welsh, No. 281, p. 177:
Rockingham County To Wit
Registered in my office on the 31st day of September 1852 as Number 281 in pursuance of a Special order of the County Court of Rockingham made September Term 1852, Isaiah Welsh a dark Mulatto Man about 34 years of age Five Feet Seven inches high and has a Small Scar on left Cheek and a Scar on the inside of the left hand on Thumb and was free born as appears by a certificate of the county court of Orange Filed in my Office. The foregoing Register was by the Court Compared with the said Isaiah Welch [sic] and found duly made a Copy thereof is ordered to be furnished him according to Law, done at September Court 1852.
[In the margin] Copied & delivered to ...

George Peters, No. 282, p. 178:
Rockingham County To Wit
Registered in my office on the 20th day of Oct 1852 as Number 282 George Peters a mulatto man about 22 1/2 years of age 5 feet 7 inches high has a Scar above his left eye, also one on his left fore-finger, one on his left Thumb and wrist, and also a Scar on his right hand near the little finger, and free born in the county of Rockingham as appears by the affidavit of Joseph C. Braithwait filed in my office. The Foregoing Register was by the County Court of Rockingham compared with the said George Peters and found duly made, A Copy thereof was

205

ordered to be furnished him as the Law
directs. Done at November Court 1852.
[In the margin] Copied & delivered to self the
5th day of April 1855 L.W.G.

John Amos, No. 283, p. 178:
Rockingham County To Wit
Registered in my office on the 17th day of
January 1853 as Number 283 John Amos a very
black man, 21 years and 3 1/2 months of age,
about 5 feet 4 1/4 inches high, a Scar on his
right leg just below the Knee and free born in
the county of Rockingham as appears by the
affidavit of Jacob Miller and Conrad H. Kite
filed in my office. The foregoing Register
was by the county court of Rockingham compared
with the said John Amos and found duly made, A
Copy thereof was ordered to be furnished him
as the Law directs. Done at January Court
1852 [sic].
[In the margin] Copied and delivered to self
January 18th 1853 B.F.M.

Isaac Thompson, No. 284, p. 178:
Rockingham County To Wit
Registered in my Office on the 17th day of
February 1853, as Number 284 Isaac Thompson a
dark Mulatto Man about 23 years of age 5 feet
11 inches high, has quite a Small Scar on the
little finger of the left hand, and a Small
Scar on the left wrist, and also a Small Scar
on the right Cheek, And free born in the
County of Rockingham as appears by the
Affidavit of Levi Shaver filed in my Office.
The foregoing Register was by the County Court
of Rockingham compared with the Said Isaac
Thompson and found duly made, A Copy Thereof
was ordered to be furnished him as the Law
directs. Done at February Court 1853.
[In the margin] Copied and delivered to self
Febr'y 21st 1853 B.F.M.

William Hally, No. 285, p. 179:

Rockingham County To Wit
Registered in my office on the 19th day of
February 1853 as Number 285 William Hally a
Mulatto Man about 23 years of age Five feet
Eleven inches high, No scar or Marks except a
Small Scar on the left leg just below the
Knee, and free born in the County of
Rockingham as appears by the affidavit of
Clement Irvine filed in my office. The
foregoing Register was by the County Court of
Rockingham compared with the said William
Hally, and found duly made, A Copy Thereof was
ordered to be furnished him as the Law
directs. Done at February Court 1853.
[In the margin] Copied and delivered to self
Febr'y 21st 1853 B.F.M.

William Peters, No. 286, p. 179:
Rockingham County To Wit
Registered in my Office on the 24th day of
February 1853, as Number 286, William Peters a
very black Man about 33 years of age Five feet
Eight inches high A Scar just above the left
eye, also Two Small Scars on the left arm just
below the elbow and free born in the County of
Rockingham as appears by evidence filed in my
Office. The foregoing Register was by the
County Court of Rockingham compared with the
said William Peters, and found duly made, A
Copy Thereof was ordered to be furnished him
as the Law directs. Done at February Court
1853.
[In the margin] Copied and delivered to Self
Febr'y 26th 1853 B.F.M.

Harvey Peck, No. 287, p. 179:
Rockingham County To Wit
Registered in my office on the 19th day of
September 1853 as Number 287 Harvey Peck a
dark mulatto man about 21 years of age Five
feet 5 1/4 inches high no visible marks or
Scars and free born in the County of
Rockingham as appears by the affidavit of A.S.

Rutherford filed in my Office. The foregoing
Register was by the County Court of Rockingham
compared with the said Harvey Peck and found
duly made, A Copy thereof was ordered to be
furnished him as the Law directs. Done at
September Court 1853.
[In the margin] Copied and delivered to self
Sept 19th 1853 B.F.M.

David Greenlee Johnson, No. 288, p. 180:
Rockingham County To Wit
Registered in my office on the 17th day of
October 1853 as Number 288 David Greenlee
Johnson a dark mulatto man about 31 years of
age Five feet 6 1/2 inches high a Small Scar
on the thumb of the right hand (no other
Visible marks or Scars) and free born in the
County of Rockingham as appears by the
affidavit of Herod Homan filed in my Office.
The foregoing Register was by the county court
of Rockingham compared with the Said David
Greenlee Johnson And found duly made, A copy
thereof was ordered to be furnished him
according to Law. Done at October Court 1853.

George Poindexter, No. 289, p. 180:
Rockingham County To Wit
Registered in my office on the 16th day of May
1854 as Number 289 George Poindexter a Black
man 34 years of age Five Feet Eight Inches
high and has a scar under the left Eye Brow no
other visible mark or scars was free Born as
appears by the affidavit of Samuel Sheets
filed in my office. The foregoing register
was by the County Court compared with the said
George Poindexter and found duly made a copy
thereof was ordered to be furnished him
according to Law done at May Court 1854.
[In the margin] Copy & Delivered to self the
16th of May 1854 L.W.G.

Lavina, Frances, Margaret, and Charlotte,
No. 290, p. 180:

Rockingham county To wit
Registered in my office on the 16th day of May
1854 as number 290 Lavina and her three
children viz. Frances--Margaret and
Charlotte--The said Lavina is a dark mulatto
aged 27 years 5 feet three inches high Frances
a dark Mulatto age 7 years four feet 1/2 an
inch high, Margaret of dark color 4 years old
three feet 2 1/4 inches high and Charlotte a
dark mulatto one year old two feet 6 1/2
inches high all of whom were emancipated by
John Wise by deed bearing date the 9th day of
May 1854 and duly recorded in my office. The
foregoing register was by the county court
compared with the said negroes and found duly
made a copy thereof was ordered to be
furnished according to law done at May Court
1854.
[In the margin] Exa & Delivered to Lavina the
16th of May 1854 W.D.T.

Clara Scott, No. 291, p. 181:
Rockingham County To wit
Registered in my office on the 19th day of
June 1854 as number 291--Clara Scott a
daughter of Milly Parrot, who was emancipated
by Jacob Parrot dec'd, said Clara is five feet
one and one half inch high in her 46th year,
color black a large scar on the right arm
below the elbow resulting from a burn and a
scar on the back of the left hand. The
foregoing register was by the county court of
Rockingham compared with the said Clara Scott
and found duly made, a copy thereof was
ordered to be furnished her according to law.
Done at June Court 1854.

Fannie Strother, No. 292, p. 181:
Rockingham County To wit
Registered in my office on the 19th day of
June 1854 as number 292 Fannie Strother
daughter of Milly Parrot (who was emancipated
by Jacob Parrot dec'd--the said Fannie is five

209

feet two inches high in her 43rd year, color black, an upper tooth out in front, no scars perceivable. The foregoing register was by the county court of Rockingham compared with the said Fannie Strother and found duly made, a copy thereof was ordered to be furnished her according to law. Done at June Court 1854.

John Pirkey, No. 293, p. 181:
Registered in my office on the 19th day of June 1854 as No. 293--John Pirkey son of Clara Scott, and grand-son of Milly Parrot who was emancipated by Jacob Parrot dec'd--the said John is six feet two inches high, twenty four years old, dark color, a scar on the left hand above the thumb on the wrist. The foregoing register was by the county court of Rockingham compared with the said John Pirkey and found duly made, a copy thereof was ordered to be furnished him according to law. Done at June Court 1854.

Aaron, No. 294, p. 181:
Rockingham County To Wit
Registered in my office on the 19th day of June 1854 as No. 294 Aaron a black man, aged 29 years next fall, five feet eight inches high, with a scar about an inch & a half long over the left eye, and was emancipated by John H. Austin. The foregoing register was by the court compared with the said Aaron & found duly made, a Copy thereof was ordered to be furnished him according to law. Done at June Court 1854.
[In the margin] Aug 22 Copy delv.

George Lewis, No. 295, p. 182:
Rockingham County To Wit
Registered in my office on the 18th day of July 1854 as No. 295, George Lewis of Black color five feet 10 3/4 inches high aged about 25 years, no marks or scars visible, born free in the county of Rockingham. The foregoing

Register was by the County Court of Rockingham compared with the said George Lewis and being duly made a copy thereof was ordered to be furnished to him. Done at June Court 1854.

Robert L. Sampson, Albert Frances, Douglas Frances, and Margaret Ann Harrison, Nos. 296, 297, 298, 299, p. 182:
Rockingham County to wit
The following free negroes are registered in my office in pursuance to an order of the County Court of Rockingham:
Robert L. Sampson of mulatto complexion born May 17th 1843 four feet 6 1/2 inches high, curly hair, has three moles on the left side of his face.
[In the margin] No. 296 Delivered to the Mother of boy Augt 23rd 1854.
Albert Frances of bright mulatto complexion, born June 18th 1846, has a scar on the right eye brow, and a small mole on the left side of his nose, also a small one on his left cheek, said boy is four feet one inch high and born free in the county of Rockingham.
[In the margin] No. 297 Delivered to his mother Augt 23rd 1854.
Douglas Frances white skin, born April 9th 1851 no marks or scars perceivable, Straight hair said boy is three feet high.
[In the margin] No. 298 Delivered to his mother Augt 23rd 1854.
Margaret Ann Harrison aged fifteen years, five feet 4 3/4 inches high of dark mulatto complexion, has a large scar on her right elbow, hair nearly Straight and black, the last named four negroes were born free in the County of Rockingham. Done at August Court 1854.
[In the margin] No. 299 Delivered Augt 23rd 1854.

Madison Mayho, No. 300, p. 182:
Registered in this office in pursuance to an

order of the Court of Rockingham entered on the 23rd day of Nov'r 1854 Madison Mayho, a free negroe of light black complexion, aged about 34 years of age, 5 feet 8 1/2 inches high, with a scar on the third finger of the left hand said to have been cut with a sickle, was born free in the County of Shenandoah. Done at Nov Court 1854.
[In the margin] No. 300.

Jason Peters, No. 301, p. 183:
Rockingham County To wit [Intended to apply to the entire page.]
Registered in this office in pursuance to an order of the Court of said County on the 21st day of Febr'y 1855 Jason Peters of Dark mulatto complexion aged about 22 years five ... [feet] 6 1/2 inches high has a scar between the eyes, also a scar on the wrist of the right hand, also a scar on the [k]nuckels of the same hand, also a scar on the Small finger of the same hand and also a scar near the groins caused by the bite of a dog. No. Three hundred and one.
[In the margin] No. 301.

Margaret Cochran, No. 302, p. 183: [The entry is missing.]

Benjamin Homes, No. 303, p. 183:
Registered in this office in pursuance to an order of the County Ct of Rockingham entered on the 20th day of August 1855 Benjamin Homes (son of Lucy Homes) aged about Thirty seven years, five feet nine and a half inches high of light complexion & bushy hair, a free man of color, as appears from the certificate (under seal) of the Clerk of Green County Va.
[In the margin] No. 303 Renew'd & transf'd to New Book Sept 1860.

William Campbill, No. 304, p. 183:
Registered in this office in pursuance to an

212

order of the Court of Rockingham entered on the 23rd day of August 1855 William Campbill (son of Robert Campbill) aged Twenty two years on the 29th day of August 1855, has a scar on the Knuckle of the forefinger of the right hand, also a scar on his forehead near the right temple, and was born free as appears by a certificate (under seal) filed in my office of the Clerk of the Hustings Court of Staunton.
[In the margin] No. 304 Copy delv'd Sept 1855.

John Richardson, No. 305, p. 183:
Registered in this office in pursuance to an order of the Court of Rockingham entered at the August term 1855 John Richardson a bright mulatto man five feet seven 3/4 inches high 27 years of age on the 25th day of Dec. 1854 a scar on the ... front finger of the left hand occasioned by a Cut, thick lips, flat nose, large eyes, and bushy hair & was born free.
[In the margin] No. 305.

Henry Norris, No. 306, p. 184:
Rockingham se. [Probably short for et sequens, "and the following." Intended to apply to the entire page.]
Registered in my office pursuant to an order of the Court of said County entered on the 17th day of Sept 1855 Henry Norris a free Negro, dark mulatto, gray hair Six feet one inch high about 65 years of age, the little finger of the left hand crooked and was born free. Done at Sept Court 1855. Given under my hand this 24 Sept 1855 L.W. Gambill C.R.C.
[In the margin] No. 306.

Daniel Lewis, No. 307, p. 184:
Registered in this office in pursuance to an order of the County Court of Rockingham entered on the 17th day of Sept 1855 Daniel Lewis a free negro, very Dark mulatto, 5 feet 9 inches high, about 17 years of age, a small

213

scar on the right cheek & was emancipated by
the last will and testament of Catharine
Perkey dec'd (no leave to remain in Comwth).
Given under my hand this 24th Sept 1855 L.W.
Gambill.
[In the margin] No. 307.

<u>Morrison Jones</u>, No. 308, p. 184:
Registered in this office in pursuance to an
order of the Court of Rockingham County
entered on the 17th day of September 1855
Morrison Jones a free negro, six feet one inch
high, Thirty years old, Stout made & has a
scar over the left eye & was born free in the
County of Shenandoah.   Given under my hand
this 24th day of Sept 1855 L.W. Gambill C.R.C.
[In the margin] No. 308 Delv'd Apl 28th 1857
fee & tax p'd L.W.G.

<u>Joseph Moore, Caroline Moore, Mary C.</u>
<u>Moore, Lucinda Moore, George W. Moore, Calvin</u>
<u>Moore, and Harriet H. Moore</u>, No. 309, p. 184:
Registered in this office in pursuance to an
order of the Court of Rockingham entered on
the 17th day of Sept 1855 Joseph Moore of dark
color Thirty three years old on the 25 day of
Dec. last, has no scars perceivable & was born
free, also the following children of Joseph
Moore and his wife Caroline Moore who is a
free negro viz. Mary C. Moore 9 years & 11
months old, Lucinda Moore 8 years 2 mo. & 20
days, George W. Moore aged 6 years 4 mo. & 14
days, Calvin Moore aged 3 years 4 mo. & 2 days
& Harriet H. Moore aged 17 mo. & 2 days all of
whom were born free.   Given under my hand this
24th Sept 1855 L.W. Gambill.
[In the margin] No. 309 Copy delv'd to Jos.
Moore Octo 2nd 1855 W.D. Trout D.C.

<u>John Morgan Tams</u>, No. 310, p. 184:
Registered in this office pursuant to an order
of the County Ct of Rockingham entered on the
18th day of Sept 1855 John Morgan Tams a

mulatto boy twenty three years old last
Christmast, 5 feet 9 inches high, dark copper
color & was born free.   Given under my hand
this 24th Sept 1855 L.W. Gambill.
[In the margin] No. 310 Copy & delivered March
23rd 1858 W.D.T. 1864 Jan'y new copy made &
delv'd.

John Peck, No. 311, p. 185:
Rockingham County se. [Intended to apply to
the entire page.]
Registered in this office in pursuance to an
order of the County Court of Rockingham
entered on the 19th day of November 1855 John
Peck a dark mulatto aged Twenty one in June
last has a scar on the back of the right hand
& was born free.   Given under my hand this 7th
day of Dec 1855 L.W. Gambill C.R.C.
[In the margin] No. 311 Copied & Delv'd to
self the 31st of January 1856 L.W.G.

Polly Collins, No. 312, p. 185:
Registered in this office in pursuance to an
order of the County Court of Rockingham County
entered on the 20th day of November 1855 Polly
Collins wife of Sandy Byrd, a bright mulatto
aged about Twenty five years, five feet Two
inches high, no marks visible and was born
free.   Given under my hand this 7th day of
December 1855.   L.W. Gambill C.R.C.
[In the margin] No. 312.

James Arthur Nelson, No. 313, p. 185:
Registered in this office in pursuance to an
order of the County Court of Rockingham County
entered on the 21st day of November 1855 James
Arthur Nelson a bright mulatto aged Twenty
three years, five feet nine inches high, has a
scar over the left eye a slight scar above the
second joint of the index finger of the left
hand and a scar nearly the whole length of the
third finger of the right hand, and was born
free.   Given under my hand this 7th day of

December 1855. L.W. Gambill C.R.C.
[In the margin] No. 313.

<u>Martha Peters</u>, No. 314, p. 185:
Registered in this office in pursuance to an
order of the County Court of Rockingham
entered on the 22nd day of November 1855
Martha Peters a black Girl eighteen years old
five feet one inch high a scar on the right
cheek a small scar below the right eye brow,
also a scar under the right eye and a scar in
the palm of the left hand and was born free.
Given under my hand this 7th day of December
1855 L.W. Gambill C.R.
[In the margin] No. 314.

<u>Alexander Johnson</u>, No. 315, p. 185:
Registered in this office in pursuance to an
order of the County Court of Rockingham
entered on the 18th day of February 1856
Alexander Johnson a free Negro A Black Man
Five feet Three Inches high between Twenty One
& Twenty Two years of age and has a scar or
pit on the end of the Nose. Given under my
hand this 19th day of February 1856 L.W.
Gambill C.R.C.
[In the margin] Copied & Delivered to self the
19th February 1856 L.W.G.

<u>Preston Spangler</u>, No. 316, p. 186:
Rockingham County se. [Intended to apply to
the entire page.]
Registered in this office in pursuance to an
order of the County Court of Rockingham
entered on the 15th day of Sept. 1856 Preston
Spangler a free negro of dark complexion about
21 years of age, 5 feet 11 inches high, has a
scar near the corner of the right eye, a scar
on the left side of the forehead and also a
scar on the big toe of the right foot, and was
born free in the County of Rockingham. Given
under my hand this 16 of Sept 1856.
[In the margin] No. 316.

<u>Levi Lewis</u>, No. 317, p. 186:
Registered in my office in pursuance to an
order of the County Court of Rockingham
entered on the 17th day of November 1856 Levi
Lewis a free negro of light black color but
not a mulatto, eighteen years old next July,
five feet seven inches high, no marks or scars
visible, and was born free in the County of
Rockingham. Given under my hand this 18th day
of Nov 1856 L.W. Gambill C.R.C.
[In the margin] No. 317 Delv'd Nov 18th 1856 &
fee & tax p'd L.W.G.

<u>John Poindexter</u>, No. 273 [Note: the
numbers abruptly change.], p. 186:
ReRegistered in my office in pursuance of an
order of the County Court of Rockingham at the
August Court 1856 as No. 273 John Poindexter a
dark mulatto aged about 39 years, marked with
a scar near the end of the tongue, a scar
above the right eye and also a scar on the
back of the right wrist & was born free.
Given under my hand this 20th Nov 1856 L.W.
Gambill C.R.C.
[In the margain] No. 273 Delv'd Nov 20th 1856
& fee & tax paid L.W.G.

<u>Joe Epperson</u>, No. 274, p. 186:
Registered in this office in pursuance to an
order of the County Court of Rockingham
entered on the 17th day of November 1855 Joe
Epperson a free negro of black color five feet
ten inches high, has a large scar on the left
hand and one on the right hand about three
inches long--age Twenty five years on the 25th
day of January 1857. Given under my hand this
29th of December 1856 L.W. Gambill C.R.C.
[In the margin] No. 274 Delv'd Oct 26th 1858
L.W.G.

<u>James Jackson</u>, No. 275, p. 186:
Registered in this office in pursuance to an
order of the County Court of Rockingham

entered on the 20th day of May 1856 James
Jackson a free negro of mulatto complexion
five feet six and a half inches high, has a
small scar on the nose, also a scar on the
[k]nuckle of the fore finger of the right
hand, and was born free in the County of
Louisa. Given under my hand this 2nd of Jan'y
1857 Wm. D. Trout D.C.
[In the margin] No. 275 Delv'd Jan'y 2nd 1857
W.D.T. fee & tax p'd L.W.G.

John Perkey, No. 276, p. 187:
Rockingham County se. [Intended to apply to
the entire page.]
Registered in this office in pursuance to an
order of the County Court of Rockingham
entered on the 16th day of June 1856 John
Perkey a very black Negro aged about Twenty
two years five feet five inches high & has a
scar on the left cheek bone & was emancipated
by the will of Catharine Perkey. Given under
my hand this 5th day of March 1857 L.W.
Gambill.
[In the margin] No. 276 Delv'd to Self March
5th 1857 W.D.T.

John Thompson, No. 277, p. 187:
Registered in this office in pursuance to an
order of the County Court of Rockingham
entered on the 16th of March 1857 John
Thompson a free negro born in the County of
Shenandoah five feet five inches high, aged 21
years last October & of copper color, a scar
from a cut on the left side of his face.
[In the margin] No. 277.

Hannah Perkey, Susan Perkey, Polly Lewis,
and Ann Maria Lewis, Nos. 278, 279, 280, 281,
p. 187:
Registered in this office in pursuance to an
order of the County Court of Rockingham
entered on the 20th day of August 1856 Hannah
Perkey a black woman eighty years old, five

feet four inches high, has a slight scar on the right wrist and a deep scar on the left breast.
[In the margin] No. 278 Delv'd Apl 28th 1857 fee & tax p'd L.W.G.
Susan Perkey a black woman about fifty seven years old five feet three inches high, has a slight scar on the left thumb and a slight scar on the right thumb.
[In the margin] No. 279 Delv'd Apl 28th 1857 L.W.G.
Polly Lewis a dark mulatto woman five feet four and a half inches high, between fifty two and fifty three years old no marks or scars visible.
[In the margin] No. 280 Delv'd Apl 28th 1857 L.W.G.
Ann Maria Lewis a dark mulatto girl between fifteen and sixteen years of age four feet ten inches high, the little finger of both hands stiff, no other marks or scars visible.
[In the margin] No. 281 Delv'd Apl 28th 1857 L.W.G.
All said negroes [nos. 278-281] were emancipated by the last will and testament of Catharine Perkey deceased no leave was granted them to remain in the Commonwealth. Given under my hand this 9th day of April 1857 L.W. Gambill.

<u>George Mickins and Charley Mickins</u>, Nos. 282 and 283, p. 187:
Registered in this office in pursuance to an order of the County Court of Rockingham entered on the 20th of August 1856 George Mickins a free negro aged six and a half years a bright mulatto with a burn on the left temple, was born free in the County of Rockingham.
[In the margin] No. 282 Delv'd Apl 28th 1857 L.W.G.
Charley Mickins one year old black color, no marks visible, was born free in the County of

Rockingham. Given under my hand this 9th day of April 1857 L.W. Gambill.
[In the margin] No. 283 Delv'd Apl 28th 1857 L.W.G.

Harriet Peters, No. 284, p. 188:
Registered in this office in pursuance to an order [of] the County Court of Rockingham entered on the 21st day of April 1857 Harriet Peters a bright mulatto woman aged 37 years five feet high has a scar above the left eye and was born free in the County of Rockingham. Given under my hand this 1st day of Augt 1857 L.W. Gambill.
[In the margin] No. 284 Copy delv'd Augt 1st 1857.

George Wanson, No. 285, p. 188:
Registered in the Clerk's office of the County Court of Rockingham on the 18th day of August 1857 in pursuance to an order of said Court entered on that day George Wanson a free negro, of dark mulatto complexion about thirty two years of age, five feet six inches high no marks or scars about him, and was born free in the County of Shenandoah, Virginia. Given under my hand this 1st day of October 1857.
[In the margin] No. 285.

Isaac Lowderberry, No. 286, p. 188:
Registered on the 18th day of November 1856 [sic] in pursuance to an order of the Court of Rockingham entered on that day. Isaac Lowderberry a free negro of black color aged 38 years, has a scar above the right eye and one above the left eye, and was born free in the County of Rockingham. Given under my hand this 24th day of December 1857 L.W. Gambill.
[In the margin] No. 286 Copied & Delv'd to self the 24th of Dec 1857 L.W.G.

Charles, No. 287, p. 188:
Registered on the 16th day of February 1858 in

pursuance to an order of the County Court of
Rockingham entered on that day Charles a negro
of black complexion aged fifty years &
considerably gray, and is five feet seven
inches high no marks or scars visible, and was
the s'd 16th of Febr'y 1858 emancipated by
Jno. H. Austin. Given under my hand this 22nd
day of Febr'y 1858 L.W. Gambill C.R.C.
[In the margin] No. 287 Delv'd 22nd of Febr'y
1858. Transferred to New Book No. 2.

Stanfield Jackson, No. 318 [Note: the
numbers abruptly change.], p. 189:
Registered in this office in pursuance to an
order of the County Court of Rockingham
entered on the 17th day of Nov. 1858 Stanfield
Jackson a mulatto aged (now) about 27 years--5
feet 8 1/2 inches high, has a scar above the
left eye, and also a scar on the left arm
occasioned by a burn just below the elbow, and
was born free in the County of Rockingham.
Given under my hand this 25th day of October
1859 L.W. Gambill C.R.C.
[In the margin] No. 318.

[At this point, the register ends. The
numerous remaining pages in the volume are
blank.]

APPENDIX

Both the wills and the deeds of Rockingham County sustained damage during the Civil War (1864). The wills which survived the burning are contained within Will Book A at the Rockingham County Court House. The following list of names and dates is drawn from that source. The first 376 pages of the volume are numbered sequentially, then there is a break. Seventy-three pages are seemingly missing. The numbering resumes with page 449. In fact, no pages are actually missing. Additional pages were simply added to the end of the book as necessity dictated, as additional wills were periodically "re-discovered" after the burning.

The first date after the name indicates when the will was written; the second when the will was probated. Entries/names which are underlined represent additions and/or major corrections since the publication by John W. Wayland of his Rockingham County will abstracts in 1930.[1]

Barbara Alder, 24 May 1848; June 1848, p. 142.
Joseph Altaffer, 25 October 18__; May 1852, p. 220.
Christopher Amon, 24 ____ 1830; July 1842, p. 112.
Mary Anderson, 10 May 1847; May 18__, p. 137.
Ananias Armentrout, 1 August 1850; December 1850, p. 185.

---

[1]John W. Wayland, <u>Virginia Valley Records</u> (Dayton, VA: Ruebush-Elkins Company, 1930; Rpt. Baltimore, MD: Genealogical Publishing Co., Inc., 1978), pp. 391-439.

Henry Armentrout, 9 July 1806; September 18___,
     p. 54.
Henry Armentrout, Sr., 17 April 1847; April
     1848, p. 133.
John Backer [Baker], 20 December 1827; May
     1830, p. 285.
Michael Baker, 10 January 1801; December 1803,
     p. 4.
Alesabeth Bare, 16 November 1842; December
     1842, p. 119.
Charles T. Barns, 23 September 1851; November
     1851, p. 202.[2]
Rebeca T. Barret, no date; February 1861, p.
     262.
Nicholas Baugher, 11 April 1848; February
     1849, p. 155.
Margaret Bazzle, 5 October 1852; ____ 18___, p.
     226.
Andrew Bear, 28 April 1832; March 1842, p.
     106.
Henry Bear, 17 January 1851; June and August
     1852, p. 224.
John K. Bear, 29 December 1857; no date, p.
     215.
Jane Belin, 16 March 1852; April 1852, p. 218.
Kenly Berry, 18 July 1842; October 1842, p.
     114.
Joseph Bierly, 28 September 1850; November
     1850, p. 183.
Sarah Bierly, 5 November 1839; ____ 18___, p.
     153.
Joseph Bilhimer, 20 August 1851; September
     18___, p. 199.
Joseph Billhimer, Sr., 27 June 1842; December
     1842, p. 118.
Henry Billhymer, 15 April 1861; August 1861,

---

[2]The name of his wife, Elizabeth Barnes,
appears in the index at the Court House.
There is, however, no will. What does appear
in Will Book A is a deed of renunciation,
dated March 1852 (p. 215).

p. 260.

William Black, 14 March 1857; April 1861, p. 232.

John Bloser, 1 April 1852; April 1852, p. 218.

Betsy Boswell, 14 November 1843; August 18__, p. 199.

Esther Bowman, 16 January 1837; June 1841, p. 93.

George W. Bowman, Sr., 5 April 1850; May 1850, p. 173.

Samuel Bowman, Sr., 22 June 1861; January 1862, p. 273.

George Branner, __ March 1861; ____ 186_, p. 230.

Christian Breneman, no date; ____ 18__, p. 281.

John Brenner, __ January 1859; April 18__, p. 233.

Peter Bright, 13 January 1803; March 18__, p. 22.

Elizabeth Brock, 3 February 1860; January 1862, p. 270.

Frances [Fannie] E.C. Brock, 8 May 1852; October 1852, p. 226.

John Brower, 24 October 1842; November 1842, p. 116.

John Brown, 22 February 1848; October 1850, p. 178.

Isaac Burk, 30 September 1856; ____ 18__, p. 455.[3]

Peter Burkholder, 15 May 1839; ____ 18__, p. 465.

Isaac Burner, 1 February 1862; ____ 18__, p. 269.

Julius Burtram, no date; ____ 18__, p. 111.

Andrew Byrd, 17 June 1823; August 1823, p. 92.

John H. Campbell, 30 ____ 1850; June 1850, p. 175.

Elizabeth Carpenter, 22 September 1818;

---

[3]The will was re-recorded on 19 March 1866.

September 1818, p. 288.
John Carpenter, 13 July 1841; January 1842, p. 98.
John Carr, 23 October 1861; December 1861, p. 268.
Frederick Click, 7 May 1821; July [?] 1821, p. 71.
John Click, 14 March 1851; ____ 18__, p. 205.
Lucy Coe, 19 January 1839; February 1843, p. 121.
Christian Coffman, 20 June 1848; ____ 18__, p. 144.
David Coffman, 30 March 1815; ____ 18__, p. 290.
Samuel Coffman, __ February 1857; January 1860, p. 245.
Barbara Conrad, 16 November 1847; May 1848, p. 138.
Caroline E. Conrad, 2 March 1853; 8 May 1854, p. 463.
Susan Conrad, 24 August 1861; November 1861, p. 251.
John Cook, 3 November 1859; July 18__, p. 238.
Martin Coontz, 12 March 1805; June 1805, p. 27.
Catharine Cratzer, 17 December 1855; ____ 18__, p. 240.
Catharine Dashner, 6 January 18_6; August 1821, p. 73.
Robert Davis, 11 September 18__; November 1804, p. 21.
Nancy Deaver, 20 October 1853; May 1861, p. 246.
Philip Deeds, 9 December 1846; November 1851, p. 202.
Robert Dekey, 7 January 1804; March [?] 18__, p. 9.
Benjamin Denton, no date; ____ 18__, p. 277.
Christian Depoy, __ January 1860; February 18__, p. 239.
Mary Depoy, 7 June 1853; February 18__, p. 239.
Adam Detrick, 7 September 1847; July 1849, p.

159.

Sarah Dever, 15 December 1848; April 1849, p. 152.

Hugh Devier, 12 September 1812; May 1815, p. 291.

Balser Dingledine, 28 January 1862; ____ 18__, p. 272.

James Duff, __ ____ 1843; July 1843, p. 128.

Catharine Dundore, 19 March 1850; August 1850, p. 177.

Andrew Ebert, 22 May 1804; July 1804, p. 15.

Margaret Eiler, 24 March 1850; June 18__, p. 196.

Jacob C. Ervin, 29 June 1842; April 1848, p. 132.

John Ervin, 16 February 1811; June 1822, p. 88.

George Evers, 4 April 1846; November 1849, p. 162.

Jacob Eversole, 8 April 1804; April 1804, p. 32.

Elizabeth Flook, 30 April 1857; June 1861, p. 228.

Henry Flook, 12 August 1841; November 1841, p. 96.

Jacob Flory, 14 February 1842; April 1842, p. 108.

William Fowler, 8 April 1796; May 1823, p. 90.

Calup Francis, 7 June 1856; ____ 18__, p. 245.

Catharine Fulk, 17 June 1851; March 1852, p. 214.

George Fulk, 12 April 1850; April 18__, p. 194.

John Fuls, 18 July 18__; June 1806, p. 47 and bottom of p. 49.

Elizabeth Fulton, 21 June 1805; March 1806, p. 40.

James Gaines, 28 February 1852; May 1852, p. 221.

Henry J. Gambill, 7 November 1847; ____ 18__, p. 129.

Christian Garber, 18 June 1849; August 1850, p. 176.

Daniel Garber, 17 February 1842; December
    1849, p. 164.
Solomon Garber, 20 August 1848; November 18__,
    p. 149.
Lucy Gilmer, 25 September 1838; January 1850,
    p. 166.
Mary Gilmer, 1 October 1805; November 1805, p.
    28.
Daniel Good, __ ____ 1849; February 1850, p.
    169.
Elizabeth Good, 28 November 1844; November
    1848, p. 150.
Peter Good, 26 December 1821; ____ 18__, p.
    77.
Robert Gray, 17 March 1859; December 18__, p.
    234.
Abraham Grove, 17 March 1855; June 1855, p.
    277.
Peter Grub, 9 January 1849; February 1849, p.
    151.
Frederick Haines, 9 January 1811; 22 April
    1812, p. 61.
George Halterman, 2 September 1858; December
    1861, p. 266.
Henry Hamer, Sr., 22 August 1831; April 1841,
    p. 92.
Thomas Hannah, 6 December 1808; August 1811,
    p. 295.
Emanuel Hansberger, 25 July 1844; November
    1849, p. 163.
Jacob Harnsberger, 25 March 1852; October
    1861, p. 263.
Nancy Harnsberger, 27 February 1847; August
    1848, p. 145.
David Harrison, 27 February 1846; ____ 18__,
    p. 190.
George W. Harrison, __ ____ 1821; November
    18__, p. 75.
Hannah Harrison, 12 September 1803; December
    1803, p. 6.
Jesse Harrison, 18 January 1836; February 1826
    [sic 1836], p. 449.
John Harrison, 17 April 1806; September 1806,

227

p. 52.

Peachey Harrison, 26 February 1848; May 1848, p. 134.

Reuben Harrison, 2 May 1802; April 1807, p. 300.

Thomas Harrison, 4 June 1799; April 1800, p. 296.

George Hauk [Hauke], 20 March 1822; May 1822, p. 85.

Uriah Head, 3 September 1849; November 1849, p. 162.

John Heaston, 5 September 1861; November 1861, p. 256.

David Heatwole [Heatwoole], Sr., __ ____ 1842; April 1843, p. 124.

Catharine Hedrick, 29 March 1833; July 1833, p. 302.

Marcus Heiserman, 30 June 1839; May 1842, p. 305.

John Helfrey, 11 August 1804; December 1805, p. 30.

Samuel Henry, 1 July 1846; ____ 18__, p. 221.

Benjamin Henton, 16 April 1804; March 180_, p. 36.

Margaret Henton, 28 April 1860; May 18__, p. 236.

Elizabeth Herring, __ ____ 18__; February 1821, p. 69.

Philip Hess, 13 ____ 18__; August 1850, p. 177.

Margaret Hinton, 11 July 1859; 21 July 1863, p. 275.

John R. Homan, 22 May 1861; January 1862, p. 270.

Robert Hooks, __ July 18__; September 1804, p. 19.

John Hoover, 7 July 1829; ____ 18__, p. 283.[4]

James Hord, 6 March 1806; April 1806, p. 43.

Christopher Howard, 20 March 1806; April 1806,

---

[4]The will was re-recorded 10 September 1935.

p. 41.[5]

Anthony Huffman, 26 June 1861; _____ 18__, p. 257.

Barnett [Barned] Huffman, 16 April 1846; December 1851, p. 210.

Frederick Hummel, 12 March 1850; July 1860, p. 237.

Sarah Hurley, 3 November 1851; March 1852, p. 215.[6]

Archibald Huston, 28 March 1774; 16 August 1774, p. 459.[7]

Harriet S. Irvine, 10 February 18__; March 1852, p. 214.

Gabriel Jones, 1 December 1804; November 1806, p. 60.

Henry Keezel, 20 April 1859; March 1861, p. 250.

Pheby Keezel [Keazol], __ _____ 1821 [?]; August 1821, p. 74.

Catharine Ann Keller, 22 February 1849; August 1849, p. 161.

Philip Keller, 4 May 1849; June 1849, p. 158.

Nicholas Kern, 3 August 1812; February 1815, p. 307.

Catharine Kiblinger, 6 February 1822; March 1822, p. 78.

St. Clair Kirtley, 5 February 1836; 27 July 1846, p. 310.

St. Clair D. Kirtley, 23 July 1849; February 1852, p. 212.

---

[5]The name was transcribed as Christopher Honer by Wayland.

[6]The will begins in the following manner: "I Sarah Hurley a free woman of Colour ...." Although the will is fragmentary, it clearly indicates that her husband, Banaster, was a slave.

[7]He rightly cites his place of residence as Augusta County.

John Kite, Sr., 18 August 18__; ____ 18__, p.
    74.
William Kite, 22 September 1798; July 1806, p.
    50.
Philip Knopp, Sr., 15 February 1845; March
    1850, p. 170.
John Kool, 8 June 1852; August 1852, p. 225.
Philip Kool, 11 March 1805; April 1805, p. 24.
John Koontz, 22 March 1852; May 1852, p. 219.
Peter P. Koontz, 12 June 1861; August 1861, p.
    259.
Robert M. Kyle, 4 June 1850; ____ 18__, p.
    451.[8]
Catherine Lair, 9 July 1799; January 1804, p.
    8.
Jeremiah Lamb, __ ____ 18__; March 1843, p.
    122.
James Laird, Sr., 1 March 1789; December 1803,
    p. 7.
Michael Layman, 22 May 18__; December 18__, p.
    4.
Benjamin Lewis, no date; ____ 18__, p. 90.
Delia M. Lewis, 5 August 1857; February 1861,
    p. 262.
Thomas Lewis, 21 July 1845; ____ 18__, p. 136.
Abraham Lincoln, 14 May 1851; July 1851, p.
    197.
Jacob Lincoln, 7 February 1822; ____ 18__, p.
    81.
Preston Lincoln, 26 April 1848; June 18__, p.
    140.
Robert Liskey, 15 April 1858; February 1861,
    p. 265.
Dorman Lofland, 23 May 1849; August 1849, p.
    159.[9]

---

[8]The will was re-recorded 1 September
1865.

[9]This individual's name appears twice in
the index, as Dorman Lofland and as Dorman
Sofland. The former spelling is the more

Isaac Long, __ _____ 18__; December 1849, p. 164.

John Long, Sr., no date; _____ 18__, p. 453.

John Ludy [Leedy], 12 September 1849; May 1850, p. 172.

Robert Magill, 10 February 1836; _____ 18__, p. 315.

James Manning, 14 January 1849; February 1849, p. 150.

Michael March, __ _____ 18__; January 1815, p. 319.[10]

James Marshall, 18 January 1778; 24 August 1778, p. 317.

Hiram Martz, 7 October 1861; November 1861, p. 252.

Jacob Martz, 16 February 1850; April 1851, p. 191.

Peter Martz, 11 April 1814; June 1814, p. 320.

Sebastian Martz, 13 April 1815; May 1818, p. 322.

Stephen Matheny, 7 August 1848; May 1849, p. 153.

Daniel Mathews, 21 December 1841; February 1842, p. 100.

Mary C. Maupin, 2 February 1848; _____ 18__, p. 195.

Jane McAtee, 19 November 1847; _____ 18__, p. 148.

William McCausland, 5 October 1841; March 1843, p. 123.

Casper Mefferd, 28 November 1805; December 180_, p. 31.

Adam Michael, 3 January 1836; March 1836, p. 461.

Peter Michael, 6 September 1859; November

---

likely.

[10]The name Michael March does not actually appear in the Court House index; instead, the name of Martin Martz appears. Martz was one of the witnesses to the will of Michael March.

18___, p. 242.
Henry Miley, 20 October 1___; June 1___, p. 157.
Adam Miller, 3 February 18___; 19 May 1812, p. 67.
Agness Miller, 21 April 1840; May 1843, p. 125.
Catherine Miller, 9 June 1821; _____ 18___, p. 76.
Christian Miller, 1 February 1821; May 1822, p. 82.
Christian Miller, 28 June 1851; April 1852, p. 217.
Henry Miller, 26 January 1840; July 18___, p. 143.[11]
Joseph Miller, 16 July 1850; December 1851, p. 208.
Peter Miller, Sr., 10 February 1821; June 18___, p. 71.
Samuel Miller, Sr., 9 January 1858; _____ 18___, p. 464.
Conrad Miltenberger, no date; _____ 18___, p. 152.
Henry Moffett, 28 August 1836; November 1841, p. 96.
John Moore, 13 July 1833; September 1841, p. 95.
Reuben Moore, __ August 1803; November 1803, p. 1.
Thomas Moore, 9 August 1818; September 1818, p. 328.
Henry Moyers, 11 August 18___; February 18___, p. 151.
Samuel Myers, 26 May 1861; _____ 18___, p. 229.
Jacob Nave, 14 April 1852; _____ 18___, p. 223.
Mathias Nave, 6 January 1842; December 1842,

---

[11]Internal evidence within the will fragment indicates that Wayland's transcription of the name as Henry Will____ was incorrect. The index at the Court House follows Wayland and lists Henry Will____.

p. 119.

Henry Neff, 4 June 184_; August 1842, p. 112.[12]

Isaac Nieswander, no date; May 1821, pp. 331 (German)/332.

William Alfred H.P. Noland, 15 ____ 1851; ____ 18__, p. 194.

Rebecca Oarbaugh, 29 October 1849; February 1850, p. 169.

Jacob Parret, 17 May 1827; June 1829, p. 334.

Henry Palser, __ ____ 1845; March 18__, p. 131.

Catharine Pence, 30 June 1803; June [?] 1803, p. 25.

George Pence, 4 April 1850; May 1850, p. 338.

John Petefish, 10 June 1859; July 1859, p. 241.

John Peterfish 20 November 1802; March 1804, p. 9.

Ann Mary Pifer, 16 March 1806; April 1806, p. 43.

Christena Pirkey, 28 May 1842; June 1855, p. 278.

Henry S. Pirkey, 4 March 18__; ____ 18__, p. 154.

Jacob Pirkey, 11 May 1809; June 1809, p. 341.

Mary Ann Pirkey, 1 May 1849; June 1849, p. 156.

Roseanna Poindexter, 11 March 185_; April

---

[12]At this point in the list, the name of Jacob Nicholas might very well appear. While his name does not appear in the Court House index and there is no will attributed to him in Will Book A, there was a commission established to settle his estate and their activities are recorded on page 457. Apparently, Nicholas died in the early part of 1835.

18__, p. 193.[13]

Jared Powe, 31 January 1852; 13 May 1856, pp. 345, 349.[14]

James Quinn, 16 November 1821; ____ 18__, p. 83.

James Rankin, 4 August 1826; January 1827, p. 282.

Jacob Reed, 25 May 1848; August 1848, p. 147.

Isaac Reid, 4 November 1861; November 1861, p. 253.

Henry Rhodes, no date; ____ 18__, p. 281.

Thomas Rice, 21 November 1849; February 1850, p. 168.

William Rice, 30 June 1852; October 1852, p. 353.[15]

Philip Ritchie, 19 February 1841; October 18__, p. 115.

Anthony Rode, 27 January 1806; March 1806, p. 38.

Conrad Rodehafer, no date; May 1857, p. 357.

Mary Rodehafer, 24 August 1859; January 1861, p. 249.

David Rodes, no date; October 18__, p. 282.

Benjamin H. Rolston, 13 July 18__; August 18__, p. 232.

David Rolston, 21 April 1849; ____ 18__, p.

---

[13]The will begins in the following manner: "I Roseanna Poindexter (a woman of color) ...." She mentions five children, three sons (George Poindexter, St____, and John) and two daughters (Margaret and Eliza).

[14]This name appears twice in the Court House index. There are actually two copies of the will on file.

[15]The name of his wife, Elizabeth M. Rice, mistakenly appears in the Court House index (p. 355). She left no will. Rather, Will Book A contains her acknowledged deed of renunciation.

156.

George Ruebush, 30 June 1849; February 1851,
p. 187.

Jacob Runcle, 12 January 1850; October 18__,
p. 200.

Lewis Runkle, 10 December 1804; April 1805, p.
35.

Peter Runkle, __ ____ 1820; ____ 18__, p. 361.

Peter Runkle, __ ____ 1821; August 1821, p.
72.

Charles Rush, 4 April 1806; June 1806, p. 44.

Robert Rutherford, __ ____ 18__; 19 March
1811, p. 68.

Robert R. Samples, 28 October 1797; December
1797, p. 314.

Conrad Sanger, 7 December 1821; March 1822, p.
79.

Thomas Scott, 26 March 1822; May 1822, p. 367.

Henry Sellers, 30 August 1841; June 1843, p.
126.

John Sellers, Sr., 17 January 1804; March
1804, p. 12.

Sarah Jane Sesser, 7 May 1862; 21 July 1862,
p. 276.

Zachary Shackelford, 27 April 18__; May 1822,
p. 87.

George Shaver, __ ____ 18__; 16 October 1810,
p. 68.

Samuel Sheets, 10 November 1846; 21 November
1859, p. 236.

John Shepp, 2 July 1842; September 1842, p.
114.

Benjamin Sherfy, 27 March 18__; February 18__,
p. 100.

Daniel Shickel, 7 August 1852; ____ 18__, p.
247.

Jonothan Shipman, 30 January 1848; June 1848,
p. 141.

Barbara Shloesser, 19 October 1836; June 1842,
p. 110.

Christian Shoemaker, 16 March 1850; June 1861,
p. 227.

George Showalter, 12 April 1855; May 1855, p.

279.
Jacob Showalter, 10 April 1847; _____ 18__, p. 203.
Adam Shultz, 16 February 1842; May 18__, p. 138.
Elizabeth Sims, 29 January 1850; March 1850, p. 171.
David Sipe, 18 _____ 18__; July 18__, p. 196.
Margaret Sipe, 18 October 1832; March 1834, p. 456.
Peter Sipe, 24 March 1806; June 1806, p. 45.
Ann Smith, 10 December 1850; January 1851, p. 185.[16]
Daniel Smith, 10 March 1848; November 1850, p. 180.
Dorotha Smith, __ December 1822; March 1823, p. 91.
Edward H. Smith, 24 April 1852; June 1852, p. 222.
James Smith, 18 June 1827; October 1827, p. 364.
John Smith, 4 June 1834; February 1842, p. 101.
William Smith, 3 October 1806; November 1806, p. 58.
Henry Snell, 13 February 1860; March 18__, p. 242.[17]
Jacob Sonefrank, 15 September 1855; December 18__, p. 244.
Catharine Spader, 25 March 1841; November 1841, p. 201.
Martin Speck, 11 September 1846; October 1846, p. 369.
George Speers, 14 October 1796; November 1803, p. 2.

---

[16]The clerk indicated that the will was presented to the court in January 1850. He should have indicated 1851.

[17]The name of Dorman Sofland appears next in the official index. Supra note 9.

Andrew Spitzer, 10 September 1836; October 1836, p. 371.

John Stalb, 22 August 1849; November 1850, p. 184.

David Steele, 4 April 1860; February 1861, p. 261.

Charles Stockard, 23 November 1820; 8 January 1821, p. 70.

Abraham Stoner, 6 _____ 1850; February 1851, p. 186.

Hannah Strine, 12 June 1852; August 1852, p. 225.

Alexander Stuart, 6 June 1822; October 1823, p. 91.

Joseph Swank, 17 October 1860; November 1860, p. 229.

James Taylor, 3 June 1843; June 1843, p. 126.

William Taylor, 18 July 1848; August 18__, p. 146.

Michael Trout, 12 April 1819; _____ 18__, p. 78.

Jacob Trumbo, 16 December 1826; February 1842, p. 102.

Leonard Tutwiler, 25 June 1804; September 1804, p. 16.[18]

Anna Wampler, 17 October 1851; February 1852, p. 213.

Henry Wedeck, 6 February 1822; _____ 18__, p. 84.

Philip Weggy, 6 February 18__; 19 March 1812, p. 66.

John Wetzel, Sr., 29 August 1849; September 1855, p. 280.

Daniel Whisler, 11 December 1847; _____ 18__, p. 139.

---

[18]Alphabetically, according to the index at the Court House, the next name on this list should be that of James Waite, p. 461. There is, however, no will for Waite on that page. Rather, as indicated above, the will of Adam Michael appears there.

William Whitezell, 18 December 1860; January
    1851, p. 248.
David G. Whitmer, __ ____ 1860; January 1861,
    p. 249.
John Whitmore, 11 April 1846; May 1846, p.
    373.
Martin Whitmore, 31 October 1835; January
    1843, p. 120.
Polly Wilhelm, 20 October 1851; November 1851,
    p. 204.
William Pinkney Williams, 14 February 1852;
    ____ 18__, p. 213.
James Williamson, 16 January 1804; March 1804,
    p. 14.
Thomas Williamson, 14 June 1806; ____ 18__, p.
    56.
Adam Wise, Sr., 10 January 1852; ____ 18__, p.
    216.
Jacob Witmer, 18 September 1800; March 1803,
    p. 23.
Daniel Witts, 20 November 1850; December 1851,
    p. 208.
Jacob Woodley, 6 March 1802; September 1804,
    p. 19.
Charles L. Yancey, 23 November 1850; February
    1851, p. 188.
Chas. A. Young, 22 February 18_2; May 185_, p.
    220.
Peter Zetty, Sr., 10 December 1838; February
    18__, p. 104.
Daniel Zirkle, 13 January 1850; January 1850,
    p. 167.

INDEX

A number of entries in the Register give only what appears to be a first name. These apparent first names have been indexed along with the surnames without employing the usual ----, (first name).

AUSTIN, Jno. H. 221
  John 174 175 John
  H. 210
AYLES, James 13
BACHUS, John 120
BACK, Caty 42
BACKER, John 223
BAGGS, Caty 42
BAILEY, Henry 168
  William 153
BAKER, Elizabeth 49
  John 17 223 Michael
  223
BALL, William 9 42
Banaster 229
BARBOUR, William 2
BARE, Alesabeth 223
  Jacob 50
BARNES, Elizabeth 223
BARNET, Amanda Catha-
  rine 193 Elizabeth
  194 Mary Jane 193
BARNS, Charles T. 223
BARRELL, Peachey 5
BARRET, Rebeca T. 223
BARRETT, Peachy 6
BAUGHER, Clarissa 169
  Margaret Ellen 169
  Nicholas 169 223
BAXTER, Jos. 17
  Joseph 14 16 18-20
  22 24 25
BAZZLE, Margaret 223
BEAR, Andrew 189 223
  Henry 87 223 Jacob
  51 John K. 223
BEASLEY, Eliza 118
BECKS, Mathew 175
BEIRM, Frances B. 151
BELCHER, Lucinda 72
  Patsy 72 Rebecah 73
  Rebeccah 73

BELIN, Jane 223
BERRY, Dennis 40
  Kenly 223 Lucey 40
  Lucy 40
BICKS, Gabriel 169
BIERLY, Joseph 223
  Sarah 223
BILHIMER, Joseph 223
  Joseph Sr. 223
BILLHYMER, Henry 223
BIRD, Burket 14 Elias
  17 George T. 128
  Gessner 189 Lewis
  58 149 William 60
BLACK, Samuel 18
  William 224
BLOSER, John 224
Bob 17
BOHANON, Thos 122 136
BOLLING, W. 29
BOSTIN, John 21 22
BOSWELL, Betsey 52
  Betsy 224 James 2
  52 123 John 2
  Thornton 123
BOWMAN, Esther 224
  George W. Sr. 224
  Samuel Sr. 224
BOYD-RUSH, Dorothy A.
  xiii
BOYS, W. 56
BOZWELL, Evaline 125
BRAITHWAIT, Joseph C.
  205
BRANDAM, Ezekiel 17
BRANNER, George 224
BRENEMAN, Abraham 183
  Christian 224
BRENNER, John 224
BRIDGES, Matthew 37
BRIGGS, Loundon 102-
  104

241

243

244

HIGGANS, John 5 Peter 5 7 32
HIGGINS, Peter 57 58
HILL, Shadrick 8
HINTON, Margaret 228
HITE, Cordelia 40 James 53 John 62 Lear 62 W. 62 William 62
HOLEMAN, Frances Mary 184 James 131 200 John 117 Mary 147 Moses 178
HOLLAY, Dennis 15
HOLLY, Dennis 28 Jerry 147 Shederick 148
HOLMAN, James 104 John 70 Ledirey 129 Rebecca 71
HOLSINGER, Polly 181
HOMAN, Herod 208 John R. 228
HOMES, Benjamin 212 Lucy 212
HONER, Christopher 229
HOOD, Robin 45
HOOKS, Robert 228
HOOVER, John 84 187 190 228 Robert 84
HOPKINS, Archibald 69 136 Daniel 24 Easter 25 Esther 70 Hannah 31 James 25 135 143 182 Jonathan 29 Nancy 31 76 Phebe 27
HORD, James 228 Nathaniel 18 30 59 149 176 Thomas 59 149

HORN Jackson 194
HOWARD, Christopher 228
HUBBARD, Haney 16 Jacob 114 Milly 114
HUFFMAN, Andrew J. 151 Anthony 229 Barned 229 Barnett 229
HUGHES, Anthony 17 William 33 122
HUGHS, Daniel 63 William 149
HULVA, Henry 160
HUMMEL, Frederick 229
HUNTER, S.M. 158
HURLEY, Daniel 93 Sarah 229
HUSTON, Archibald 229 Geo. 17 George 12 18 Mary Ann 19
HUTCHISON, Dan'l 150
HYWARDEN, James 2
IRVIN, Elizabeth 101
IRVINE, Clement 207 Harriet S. 229 Isaac 55 J.D.W. 57 58 J.E.C. 59 Jack 24
JACKSON, Abraham 88 Daniel 133 James 217 Malinda 35 Molly 35 Richard 34 35 Stanfield 221
James 8 25
JAMISON, John 1-3 5 Jemima 41 Jessee 32 88 John 11
JOHNSON, Alexander 216 David Greenlee

245

248

www.ingramcontent.com/pod-product-compliance
Lightning Source LLC
Chambersburg PA
CBHW070805270326
41927CB00010B/2294